The Word
of God
is Living
and Active

Reflections on the
weekday readings for the
liturgical year 2019~2020

MARTIN HOGAN

INTRODUCTION

This is the fourth successive book of Weekday Reflections for the Liturgical Year. For each volume, I have tried to write a new reflection for each set of weekday readings. Invariably, with this fourth set of reflections there may be some element of repetition of the reflections that are in the previous three volumes. However, I have tried to keep such repetition to a minimum. The reflections are largely based on the gospel readings of the weekday, but in this fourth volume I have linked in the first reading more often.

It has always been my intention that these reflections would be of help to priests who like to share a short reflection on the weekday readings. I hope that they may also be a resource to all who like to base their daily prayer on the weekday readings of the liturgy. The weekday gospel readings for Ordinary Time begin with a more or less continuous reading of Mark's gospel. By the time we get to the tenth week in Ordinary Time, we move to a more or less continuous reading of Matthew's Gospel, from chapter 5 onwards. On Monday of the twenty-second week in Ordinary Time, we begin to read from the Gospel of Luke for thirteen weeks. In the season of Advent, the weekday gospel readings are taken largely from Matthew and Luke, which is also the case with the first three weeks of the season of Lent. For the fourth and fifth week of Lent and for all seven weeks of the season of Easter, the weekday gospel readings are all taken from

John. Accordingly, we manage to read a significant portion of all four gospels during the weekdays of the liturgical year.

According to the letter to the Hebrews, 'the word of God is living and active, sharper than any two-edged sword, piercing until it divides soul from spirit, joints from marrow; it is able to judge the thoughts and intentions of the heart' (4:12). This sentence comes at the end of the author's lengthy reflection on Psalm 95:7-11 during which he emphasised that the 'today' of the psalm corresponded to the 'today' of those whom he was addressing with this letter or written sermon. The author was showing that the word of God was always contemporary. It wasn't a dead letter that belonged to a past that was gone, but a living and active word that spoke to the 'today' of each generation. As the author states, 'the good news came to us just as to them' (4:2). When the author wrote to the 'Hebrews', possibly Jewish Christian house churches in the city of Rome, there was no New Testament. For us as Christians today, the 'word of God' embraces both the Jewish Scriptures and what came to be called the New Testament. This 'word of God' is as living and active for us today as the Jewish Scriptures were for the author of the letter to the Hebrews towards the end of the first century.

Every day in its liturgy, the Church puts before us the living and active word of God. It is the living Lord we encounter in the weekday readings for the liturgical year. He continues to speak to the 'today' of our time and place and to my own personal 'today'. As we approach to listen to the Lord's living word, a good beginning would be to make the prayer of the young Samuel our own today. 'Speak, Lord, your servant is listening' (1 Samuel 3:9–10).

2 December, Monday, First Week of Advent

Matthew 8:5–11

The first reading of the first weekday of Advent depicts a great journey which is to be travelled by people of many nations. According to Isaiah, all the nations will journey to Jerusalem, the city of God's presence, saying to each other, 'Come let us go up to the mountain of the Lord, to the Temple of the God of Jacob'. They want to undertake this journey so as to hear and submit to the Lord's word, 'since the Law will go out from Zion, and the oracle of the Lord from Jerusalem'. Jesus' words at the end of today's gospel reading also speak of a journey involving people of many nations. 'Many will come from east and west to take their places with Abraham and Isaac and Jacob at the feast in the kingdom of heaven'. If Isaiah envisages people of many nations coming to Jerusalem to be fed by God's word, Jesus sees them as coming to the great feast in the kingdom of heaven. The centurion who comes to Jesus in his need is representative of that great throng who will come to the great banquet in the heavenly kingdom. In coming to Jesus, he is coming to the one who came to feed God's people. We are invited to join this great throng of people by identifying with this centurion. He shows us how to make this great journey. He was a humble man who knew he was not worthy to have Jesus in his home. He was a man of great faith in the power of Jesus' word. 'Just give the word and my servant will be cured'. We are all invited to have something of this pagan's humility and great trust in the Lord's word. Advent is a season when we are called to make our own journey to the Lord; it is a time to open ourselves afresh to the life-giving power of the Lord's word.

3 December, Tuesday, First Week of Advent

Luke 10:21–24

Every so often in the Gospels we are given an insight into the prayer of Jesus. It is as if we are being allowed to eavesdrop on the most intimate relationship in Jesus' life, his relationship with God, his Father. Today's gospel reading gives us such an insight into Jesus' prayer. It is a joyful prayer of praise inspired by the Holy Spirit. 'Filled with joy by the Holy Spirit, he said "I bless you Father, Lord of heaven and earth".' The prayer of praise is the most selfless form of prayer there is. It is a movement towards God without any reference to ourselves. Jesus praises God for who God is and for what God is doing. What is God doing, according to this prayer of Jesus? He is revealing something really important to those whom Jesus calls 'mere children'. God the Father is revealing to them the intimate relationship of love between himself and Jesus which leads to mutual knowledge. 'No one knows who the Son is except the Father, and who the Father is except the Son.' Who are these 'children' who are receiving this revelation? The reference is probably to those who have the openness of the child to God's message spoken through Jesus, in other words, the disciples. It is to the disciples that Jesus goes on to say, 'Happy the eyes that see what you see'. The disciples, who are receptive to what God is showing them, are contrasted with 'the learned and the clever', those who are so sure of what they know that they are closed to what God is trying to reveal to them about the relationship between himself and Jesus. 'Happy the eyes … '. There is a beatitude here that can potentially embrace us all, provided we have the same childlike openness of the disciple to what God wants to reveal to us through his Son and the Spirit.

4 December, Wednesday, First Week of Advent
Matthew 15:29–37
Elevated ground features in both of today's readings. In the first, the prophet speaks of a mountain where the Lord will be the host at a great banquet. This will be a banquet of rich food and fine wines, where all mourning, sadness and shame will have been removed, and

where even death itself will have been destroyed. Here is a vision which lifts us beyond the world as we know it towards another world where all is as God wants it to be. In the gospel reading, Jesus goes up into the hills and large crowds go up the hills after him. There in the hills of Galilee, Jesus gives speech to the dumb, mobility to the lame, sight to the blind. He goes on to feed the hungry with very limited resources. He feeds them so well that all eat as much as they wanted, and, even then, there are seven full baskets left over. The vision of Isaiah in the first reading becomes something of a reality in the gospel reading. Both readings speak to us of a God who wants us to have life and to have it to the full. It was Saint Irenaeus who said that the glory of God is the human person fully alive. In the gospel reading, the Lord needed others to bring the sick to him; he needed the disciples to help him feed the crowd. He continues to need us if his life-giving work is to get done. Advent calls on all of us to be instruments of the Lord's life-giving and healing presence in the world. In Advent we not only pray, 'Come Lord Jesus', but we also offer ourselves as channels for the Lord's coming into our world.

5 December, Thursday, First Week of Advent

Matthew 7:21, 24–27

When people were building houses in Palestine in the time of Jesus during the dry season as the weather was fine and warm, it was tempting to build them in a way that did not take into account the wilder weather to come during the winter, when heavy rain and strong winds could affect that part of the Near East. It was easier to build on sand than on rock but it was also shortsighted. What serves in good weather does not always serve in bad weather. Building on rock ensures that the house will stand regardless of the weather. The gospel reading suggests that we have to build our lives in such a way that we will stand firm, not just when all is well, but also when life gets difficult, when the storms come our way and threaten to engulf us. We are to build for the worst of times and not only for the best of times. Jesus declares in the gospel reading that if we do not just listen to his words but also try to act on them, we will be building our lives on rock. If we embrace his word and allow our own lives to be shaped by it, then we will be building our lives in such a way that we will stand firm when the trials and tribulations of life assail us. We need a firm foundation, we need resources to fall back on when our vulnerability is exposed by life's storms. Jesus tells us that he is our primary resource. He will be our firm foundation, if we keep on trying to take the path that he sets before us by his teaching and his way of life.

6 December, Friday, First Week of Advent

Matthew 9:27–31

It is striking how many times Jesus asks people a question in the Gospels. It can sometimes be helpful to read those questions as addressed to me personally. We find one such question in today's gospel reading. Two blind men follow Jesus, asking him to take pity on them; they are still there when Jesus reaches the house he was heading towards. He turns and asks them, 'Do you believe I can do this?' He didn't simply heal them immediately without a word, which he could have done. He wanted to engage with them personally in some way, and he wanted them to engage with him personally. His question was drawing out their faith in his ability to heal them. In response to Jesus' question, 'Do you believe?', the two blind men said, 'We do', 'We believe you can do this'. The faith of these men created the opening for Jesus' healing power to become effective in their lives. The Lord wants to engage with each one of us personally and he wants us to engage with him personally. He calls us into a personal relationship with himself. Saint Paul was someone who really experienced a deeply personal relationship with the Lord. He once said, 'I live by faith in the Son of

God who loved me and gave himself for me'. We can each say with Saint Paul, 'I believe that you love me and gave yourself for me'. The Lord asks each of us, 'Do you believe this?' He waits for each of us to answer, like the blind men in the gospel reading, 'I do'.

7 December, Saturday, First Week of Advent

Matthew 9:3–10.1, 6–8

As we draw closer to Christmas, many of us are thinking about buying gifts for people. It is a season of gift-giving. We give gifts to and we receive gifts from others. A gift doesn't have to be expensive to convey appreciation and regard. A lot of thought can go into a relatively inexpensive gift. There is something appropriate about giving and receiving gifts at this time of the year because Christmas is the feast of God's gift to us of his Son. Saint John puts it very simply in his Gospel. 'God loved the world so much that he gave his only Son'. At Christmas, we celebrate and give thanks for the most precious gift that God could have given us, the gift of his Son. At the end of today's gospel reading, Jesus declares to his disciples, 'You received without charge'. Jesus was God's free gift to us. Paul, in his letter to the Romans, speaks of 'the grace of God and the free gift of the one man, Jesus Christ'. Paul is reminding us that we have been greatly graced by God through this gift of his Son. God did not give us his Son because we are deserving of him or because we have done something to earn him. Jesus is God's free gift to us. The only appropriate response to such an extraordinary gift is gratitude. The feast of Christmas inspires us to be thankful to God for the many ways he has graced and blessed us through the gift of his Son. Having been graced in this way, we are called to live out of this grace. As Jesus says at the gospel reading, 'give without charge'; 'give to each other as you have received from God'. Having received the Lord freely, we are to give him to each other, by expressing in our lives his gracious and compassionate love.

9 December, Monday, Solemnity of the Immaculate Conception
Luke 1:26–38

The annunciation of the angel Gabriel to Mary has inspired artists down the centuries, painters, stained-glass artists, sculptors. Somehow they sensed the significance of this event in God's dealings with humanity. This was the moment when God needed Mary's consent to become the mother of his Son. A great deal would depend on how Mary responded to this choice that God was making of her. At that moment, the whole human race desperately needed her to say 'yes' to God's choice and God's call. The gospel reading speaks of Mary as being 'deeply disturbed' by this visitation from God and full of questions, and, yet, in the end she lived up to humanity's expectations, surrendering wholeheartedly to God's choice of her. She said 'yes' to God, on behalf of all of us.

Today we are celebrating Mary's complete responsiveness to God's call. To say that Mary was immaculately conceived is to say that there was no sin in her life from the first moment of her existence. Her life was one constant 'yes' to God's choice and call from her conception to her final breath. She allowed herself to be touched by God's grace in a very complete way. She was 'full of grace', full of God. She was a woman of God, and this made her a woman for others. According to the scene that follows today's gospel reading, she gave herself in love to Elizabeth, her older cousin, for several months. As a woman of God for others, we see in her the human person we were designed to be. In our second reading, Paul declares that God 'chose us in Christ to be holy and spotless, and to live through love in his presence'.

The story of Adam and Eve tells a very different story from the one Luke tells in the gospel reading. Adam had said 'no' to God's call, eating of the tree that was out of bounds. The break in his relationship with God led him to hide from God, and God had to cry out after him, 'Where are you?' In hiding from God, he also hid from himself.

Refusing to take responsibility for his actions, he blamed his wife Eve: 'It was the woman', and she in turn blamed the serpent. The story of Adam and Eve is the story of us all. We are all prone to going our own way, turning away from God's call, hiding from God, and, as a result, losing touch with our true selves and damaging our relationship with others. Yet, when that happens, the Lord continues to call after us in love, 'Where are you?' Mary's adult son declared that he had come to seek out and save the lost, which is all of us.

Today's feast reminds us that we have someone we can look towards in our efforts to respond to the Lord's call to us. Mary, the mother of Jesus, is also our mother. She knows the power of sin and what it can do to human lives; she saw what it did to her Son. She surrounds us with her intercessory prayer so that we can become the human persons God desires us to be. That is why we can ask her with confidence to pray for us sinners now and at the hour of our death.

10 December, Tuesday, Second Week of Advent

Matthew 18:12–14

The attitude of the shepherd in the parable that Jesus speaks in today's gospel reading reflects his own attitude and the attitude of God. In a flock of a hundred, the shepherd notices that one is missing. His focus immediately turns fully to the one sheep who has become separated from the flock and is therefore at great risk. The ninety-nine are safe, the one is at risk; all his attention is on the one who is lost. If he succeeds in finding this one lost sheep, it gives him more joy than the realisation that the ninety-nine are perfectly safe. The joy of the shepherd on finding the one lost sheep is a sign of how much value this one sheep has in his eyes. The Lord is deeply concerned for those who are at risk, those who are vulnerable to harm being done to them. He has a passion for the lost and it gives him great joy when they are brought to a place of safety and well-being. We can all find ourselves 'lost' in one form or another at different times in our lives. We go down some path that does not serve us well, or some set of circumstances, over which we may have little control, casts us adrift. When that happens, the Lord seeks us out, very often in and through some good shepherd or other. The Lord needs shepherds like the one he portrays in the gospel reading to give expression to his searching love. Sometimes, the Lord may be calling us to be that shepherd to someone. At other times in our lives, we can be the ones in need of such a shepherd.

11 December, Wednesday, Second Week of Advent
Matthew 11:28–30

Those of a certain age will be aware that with advancing years we don't always have the energy we once had, and this can be a source of frustration for us. Today's first reading from Isaiah acknowledges that even 'young men may grow tired and weary', and that even 'youths may stumble'. There is such a thing as a weariness of the spirit, which can affect people at any age. Some young people can seem listless, whereas some older people can be full of vitality. Isaiah declares in that reading that the Lord is the one who alone can address and deal with this kind of weariness of spirit. 'He gives strength to the wearied, he strengthens the powerless.' The Lord does not grow tired or weary. He is the Lord of life who remains vibrant at all times. By turning towards him in our weakness and weariness we can imbibe some of his perennial strength and vitality. In the words of Isaiah, 'those who hope in the Lord renew their strength'. This is the promise that Jesus makes in the gospel reading. 'Come to me, all you who labour and are overburdened, and I will give you rest.' There is much in life that can deaden our spirit, at any age. It is the Lord, and our relationship with him, that can keep us young and vital even in old age. The Lord comes to us as strength in our weakness, as vitality in our weariness, as hope in our despondency. What is asked of us is that we welcome his coming and be attentive to his energising presence to us.

12 December, Thursday, Second Week of Advent

Matthew 11:11–15

The people of Israel believed that the prophet Elijah would return one day to announce the imminent coming of the long-awaited Messiah or anointed one of God. In today's gospel reading, Jesus identifies John the Baptist with Elijah. 'He is the Elijah who was to return.' By implication, Jesus is claiming to be God's anointed one for whom the people of Israel have been waiting. John the Baptist, therefore, has a really significant role to play. As Jesus says in the gospel reading, 'a greater than John the Baptist has never been seen'. Yet John did not really live to see Jesus proclaim the coming of God's kingdom. He was executed by Herod Antipas early in the public ministry of Jesus. John knew nothing of the death and resurrection of Jesus and the coming of the Holy Spirit. That is why Jesus goes on to say, 'The least in the kingdom of heaven is greater than he is'. We are all greater than John the Baptist, not because we are better than him, or holier than he was, but because we have been more greatly graced. In and through the written Gospels, we have witnessed the full public ministry of Jesus, his death and resurrection. We have all benefited from the sending of the Holy Spirit. On one occasion, Jesus said to his disciples, 'Blessed are the eyes that see what you see'. That beatitude embraces us all, but not John the Baptist to the same extent. We spend our lives growing in appreciation of all we have received through the life, death and resurrection of Jesus. Our whole lives are to be a grateful response to God who has blessed us so abundantly in Christ, a response that graces the lives of others as we have been graced.

13 December, Friday, Second Week of Advent

Matthew 11:16–19

As we approach the feast of Christmas, children will be getting all kinds of Christmas presents, some of which will be quite sophisticated and high-tech. Yet I often think that what children enjoy most are the games that they make up themselves. Children in Jesus' day were no different. In today's gospel reading, Jesus comments on some of the games children play in the market square. They act out being part of a group of flute players, playing joyful music, such as would be heard at a wedding, hoping other children would dance to their joyful tunes, or they act out being the mourners at a funeral, singing dirges, hoping other children would weep loudly in response. It's the make-believe world of children. Sometimes, some of the other children wouldn't cooperate; they wouldn't dance to the flute players or mourn with the dirge singers. Their body language said, 'We don't want to play any game'. When Jesus noticed this, it reminded him of something else. So much of life reminded Jesus of how people were relating to him and to God. It occurred to him that the flute players were like himself and the dirge singers were like John the Baptist, and the children who refused to join either game were like some of Jesus' own contemporaries who rejected both himself and John the Baptist, for different reasons. Jesus identifies with the children who play joyful songs on the flute, because his ministry was a celebration of God's merciful and compassionate love. We are all invited to catch something of the celebratory presence of Jesus among us today, and to live out of the joyful energy that his presence gives us.

14 December, Saturday, Second Week of Advent

Matthew 17:10–13

Today's gospel reading from Matthew follows on immediately after the story of the transfiguration of Jesus, in which the disciples saw

Moses and Elijah speaking with the transfigured Jesus on the mountain. As they come down the mountain, the disciples ask Jesus a question about Elijah, whom they have just seen with Jesus. According to the Jewish Scriptures, Elijah was to return to prepare the way for the Messiah. If Jesus is the Messiah, where is Elijah, they wonder? In response, Jesus identifies John the Baptist with Elijah; John is the prophet who was to come to prepare the way for God's anointed one. By this time in Jesus' ministry John the Baptist had been executed by Herod Antipas, and Jesus now announces that he will experience the very same fate. Having witnessed Jesus in all his glory as Son of God on the mountain, it must have been difficult for the disciples to hear Jesus speak about himself as the Son of Man who must suffer as John did. As we approach the feast of Christmas we are being reminded that the baby in the crib became the crucified Son of Man, and that the wood of the manger points ahead to the wood of the cross. Mary's child was God's loving gift to humanity. 'God so loved the world that he gave his only Son'. The adult Jesus would, in turn, give himself completely to humanity, out of love. 'No one has greater love than this, to lay down one's life for one's friends.' The same divine love that we celebrate at Christmas is celebrated again on Good Friday and Easter Sunday. Both feasts, Christmas and Easter, call on us to share with each other the love that we have so abundantly received from God through his Son.

16 December, Monday, Third Week of Advent

Matthew 21:23–27

Authority can easily become a contentious issue. Who has authority? Who has the right to exercise it? How should authority be exercised? In our time 'authority' has become a somewhat negative word. Authority figures get a bad press, sometimes with very good reason. The issue of authority is central to today's gospel reading. Jesus had just performed a somewhat provocative act in the Temple in Jerusalem, driving out those who were buying and selling, overturning the tables of the moneychangers and the seats of those who sold doves. Those who considered themselves to have authority in the Temple understandably demanded to know who gave Jesus the authority to do what he had just done. We know the answer to that question. Jesus was acting on the authority of God. Jesus considered the Temple to be the house of his Father; that gave him all the authority he needed to do what he did. Today's gospel reminds us that when it comes to our faith, the ultimate authority is Jesus. We constantly have to submit our lives to God's Son. All human authority, including human religious authority, is secondary compared to the authority of Jesus. He alone is Lord of our lives. The Lord's authority is one that shows itself not in dominating others but in serving them. At the Last Supper, Jesus declared himself to be the Lord and Master of his disciples, yet he washed their feet, rendering them what would have been considered a demeaning service. He was showing them and us how authority in his name is to be exercised.

17 December, Tuesday, Third Week of Advent
Matthew 1:1–17

Today we begin the octave of Christmas. The Alleluia verse for these days is a special verse related to the coming of the Saviour. They are lovely prayers in their own right, and would make a perfect prayer programme for these eight days. The Alleluia verse or antiphon for today is, 'Wisdom of the Most High, ordering all things with strength and gentleness, come and teach us the way of truth'. The gospel readings for these eight days are all taken from the opening chapters of the Gospels of Matthew and Luke, the story of the birth and infancy of Jesus. Today's gospel reading is probably the strangest of all. Why do we read this long list of names on 17 December? It is the genealogy of

Jesus according to Matthew. This evangelist gives his version of the generations that led up to the birth of Jesus. In this way, he reminds us that this special child, who has the unique name 'God-with-us', has a human ancestry. He has a family tree, a Jewish family tree. Jesus, the Son of God, is also the son of Abraham. Some of his Jewish ancestors mentioned in this list left a lot to be desired. Yet God worked through them all to bring Jesus, God's Son, to the human race in the fullness of time. The evangelist may be reminding us that God can always bring good out of what falls short of his desire for us. That is true of our own personal lives, as well. Even the darker experiences of our lives can serve God's purpose for us, if we keep entrusting ourselves in love to God through it all. As Saint Paul says in his letter to the Romans, 'all things work together for good, for those who love God'. 'The Wisdom of the Most High' orders 'all things', including those aspects of our lives we may be tempted to dismiss as of no value.

18 December, Wednesday, Third Week of Advent
Matthew 1:18–24

When we hear the term 'annunciation', we tend to think of the annunciation of the birth of Jesus by the angel Gabriel to Mary, which is to be found in Luke's Gospel. There is another story of the annunciation of the birth of Jesus in Matthew's Gospel. Once again, an angel of the Lord announces the birth of Jesus, but, in Matthew's version, the announcement is made to Joseph, not to Mary. Indeed, whereas it is Mary who is prominent in the various stories relating to the birth of Jesus in Luke's Gospel, in Matthew's Gospel it is Joseph who is more prominent in the stories relating to the birth of Jesus. It is just one example of how the particular perspective of any one of the four gospels complements and enriches the perspectives of the others. In our gospel reading, the angel announces the birth of Jesus to Joseph after he discovers that Mary is pregnant. Joseph was betrothed to Mary but they hadn't come to live together as husband and wife. What was Joseph to think? His solution was to divorce her quietly, being sensitive to her situation, while being realistic about what had happened. The annunciation to Joseph was with a view to enlightening him as to what had really happened: 'She has conceived what is in her by the Holy Spirit'. Joseph was floundering until that moment. He speaks to our own experience as people of faith. We too can flounder when it comes to knowing what the best and decent thing to do is, what the Lord is asking of us. Our initial decision, well intentioned as it may be, is not always the best one. Like Joseph, we sometimes need the Lord's guidance to take the path that is best for all. We can be sure of receiving his guidance, if we ask for it in prayer.

19 December, Thursday, Third Week of Advent
Luke 1:5–25

Today's gospel reading is one of many examples in the Scriptures of the encounter between the divine and the human. The angel Gabriel, who stands in God's presence, brings an extraordinary message of good news to a priest advanced in years while he was exercising his priestly office in the Temple in Jerusalem. The good news was that Zechariah's wife, Elizabeth, would soon give birth to an exceptional child who would be filled with the Holy Spirit while still in his mother's womb. This child would go on to become the prophet whose role was to prepare people for the long-awaited coming of the Lord. This was such extraordinary news that Zechariah refused to believe it. 'How can I be sure of this?' he asked. He soon found himself dumb before this mystery that had broken into his life. We can all be slow to hear good news, especially good news that seems to defy human logic and reasoning. Our analytical minds can sometimes serve to keep the Lord at a distance. As believers we are encouraged to question, to seek understanding of the one in whom we believe, yet the essence of faith is a kind of childlike surrender to the surprising and undeserved gift of God's favour. Having given ourselves over to the good news of God's gracious initiative towards us, there is then much room for pondering these wonderful things in our heart, after the example of Mary.

20 December, Friday, Third Week of Advent

Luke 1:26–38

Luke describes a variety of responses on the part of Mary to the visit of Gabriel. Initially we are told that Mary was 'deeply disturbed' by Gabriel's opening greeting, 'Rejoice, so highly favoured! The Lord is with you'. Following on Gabriel's further word that Mary is to conceive and bear a son, Luke tells us that Mary was questioning. 'How can this come about?' In response to Gabriel's explanation that her child would be conceived through the power of the Holy Spirit, Mary is portrayed as surrendering fully to God's purpose for her life. 'I am the handmaid of the Lord, let what you have said be done to me.' According to Luke, Mary moved from a sense of being disturbed through a moment of questioning to a complete surrender of herself to God's call. That journey that Luke describes Mary as taking resonates with our own experience as people of faith. When the Lord comes knocking on the door of our lives, when he prompts us to take on some role, we may not respond initially. Our unease, our questions, can hold us back. However, we can come around to responding to what the Lord is asking of us. Luke's portrayal of the meeting between Gabriel and Mary suggests that the Lord is patient with us as we struggle to understand and to respond to his call. What matters is that we continue to engage with him in an open and heartfelt way, as Mary did. In engaging with the Lord who engages with us, we too, like Mary, can come to the point where we respond to his will for our lives.

21 December, Saturday, Third Week of Advent

Luke 1:39–45

In today's gospel reading, Elizabeth greets Mary as 'the mother of my Lord'. It is a lovely title for Mary, one we do not hear very often. We can each say of Mary that she is 'the mother of my Lord'. To speak of Mary as 'the mother of my Lord' is not far removed from referring to her as 'the mother of God'. Both of these titles, 'God' and 'Lord', apply equally to Jesus and express his divinity. Yet to speak of Jesus as 'my Lord' highlights the personal dimension of our relationship with him. It echoes the way Thomas, the disciple, addressed the risen Jesus towards the end of John's Gospel as 'my Lord and my God'. It was a very personal confession after a period of great doubt. Jesus is Lord and God, but for each one of us he is 'my Lord and my God'. If I address Jesus as 'my Lord' I am acknowledging my desire to allow Jesus to be Lord of my life, my unique and unrepeatable life. We venerate the child Jesus in the crib as someone who is now 'my Lord'. Like Elizabeth, we honour Mary as the mother of 'my Lord'. We honour her because it was through her that the Lord came to us. It is because of her that we can each come to know Jesus as 'my Lord and my God'.

23 December, Monday, Fourth Week of Advent

Luke 1:57–66

The naming of a child can often be a source of tension in a family. Different people will have different ideas about a good name for the child. At the end of the day, of course, it is the choice of the parents. In today's gospel reading relatives and neighbours expected Zechariah and Elizabeth to follow convention by calling their newborn child Zechariah, after his father. However, Zechariah and Elizabeth knew that this was not the name that God wanted the child to have. At this particular moment in history, God was not following convention, but was about to do something new. Zechariah and Elizabeth's child would be different from other children. The relatives and neighbours were right to ask the question, 'What will this child turn out to be?' He would turn out to be the man who would prepare people for the coming of someone much greater than himself, someone whose name would be Jesus, Emmanuel, God-with-us. At this moment of history God was indeed working in a new way; God was in the process of making a new covenant with all of humanity. It is this new and wonderful moment in God's dealings with humanity that we celebrate at Christmas, and it should never cease to fill us with excitement and gratitude. It is said in the gospel reading that the people treasured the circumstances of John's birth in their hearts. We have something even more wonderful to treasure in our hearts as we come to celebrate the birth of Jesus.

24 December, Tuesday, Fourth Week of Advent

Luke 1:67–79

Today's gospel reading has become one of the great prayers of the Christian community. The prayer of Zechariah, the father of John the Baptist, is part of the official morning prayer of the Church that is prayed in monasteries, convents, parishes and homes. The prayer opens with a reference to God visiting his people and it closes with a reference to the rising Sun coming to visit us from on high, which is a clear reference to the coming of Jesus into the world. When we hear the word 'visitation' we tend to think of Mary's visit to Elizabeth, but Zechariah's prayer suggests that the more fundamental visitation was God's visit to humanity through Jesus. God has visited his people in and through the person of his Son, Jesus. There is a powerful depiction of this visitation of God through Jesus in that prayer. This visitation reveals the tender mercy of God. Jesus' coming is spoken of as the rising Sun from on high bringing light to those who live in darkness and in the shadow of death. The sun is the source of light and life. In an even more fundamental sense, Jesus is the source of light and life. In revealing God's tender mercy, Jesus brings the light of God's merciful love into the darkness of our lives and he also offers us a sharing in God's own life, thereby scattering the shadow that death casts over us. The true meaning of Christmas is to be found here. In celebrating the birth of Jesus, we are celebrating the coming of God's light and life, a light that no darkness can overcome and a life that is stronger than all forms of death. Christmas is the feast of Jesus, the light of life. It is a truly hopeful feast because it proclaims that we need no longer remain in darkness or in the shadow of death.

26 December, Thursday, Saint Stephen
Matthew 10:17–22

Today's first reading suggests that Stephen was the first person to be put to death for professing his faith in Christ. His feast prompts us to remember all those who are suffering for their faith in the Lord today. Church in Chains is an independent Irish charity that encourages Irish Christians to pray and act in support of persecuted Christians worldwide. In its latest edition of its global guide to where Christians are persecuted throughout the world, it lists fifteen countries where the persecution of Christians is severe. Persecution of Christians often occurs alongside the persecution of other religious minorities. In the first reading Stephen is presented as a model of how Christians are to respond to the experience of persecution. He showed courage, witnessing to the glorious Son of Man before his infuriated opponents, and he also showed forgiveness, calling on the risen Lord, 'Do not hold this sin against them'. Both of these qualities were expressions of the Holy Spirit in his life. It is said of him that the Spirit 'prompted what he said', and he is referred to as 'filled with the Holy Spirit'. It was the Spirit who enabled Stephen to respond to the experience of persecution as Jesus did, with a courageous and forgiving heart. In the gospel reading, Jesus tells his disciples starkly that the time will come when they will be hated by all on his account, but he also assures them that the Holy Spirit will be their resource at that time: 'The Spirit of your Father will be speaking in you'. The same Holy Spirit is given to us all, to empower us to be courageous in our witness to our faith and to be forgiving of those who hold our faith against us. Times of persecution for the Church, especially when responded to in the spirit of Stephen, can bear rich fruit for the life of the Church. One of those who approved of Stephen's killing was a young man called Saul of Tarsus. He went on to become the great apostle to the Gentiles. Perhaps Stephen's martyrdom was significant in Paul's transformation from persecutor of the Church to apostle of the risen Lord. We are being reminded that, even in dark times for the Church, the Lord can be working powerfully.

27 December, Friday, Saint John, Apostle and Evangelist
John 20:2–8

It is appropriate that we celebrate the feast of Saint John the evangelist so close to Christmas. The opening eighteen verses of his gospel provide us with the memorable line which sums up in a few words what we are celebrating at Christmas, 'the Word became flesh and dwelt among us'. John's Gospel, the last of the four gospels to be written, is based on the eye-witness testimony of one of the followers of Jesus, the one described in today's gospel reading as the disciple Jesus loved. This description could give the impression that Jesus loved this disciple more than all the other disciples. However, Jesus loved and loves all his disciples equally. He said to all of his disciples as a group, and he says to us, 'As the Father has loved me, so I have loved you'. We are all beloved disciples. What distinguishes this particular disciple from the others, according to John's Gospel, is that he received and responded to the love of Jesus more fully than all the others did. According to this gospel, he was the only male disciple who was present at the foot of the cross; he remained faithful when others had shown themselves to be unfaithful. His faithful love brought him to the empty tomb quicker than Peter; his faithful love gave him the insight to recognise the true meaning of the empty tomb before anyone else understood its meaning: 'He saw and believed'. He is the disciple who encourages all of us to give ourselves wholeheartedly in love to Jesus as he has given himself fully in love to us.

28 December, Saturday, Feast of the Holy Innocents
Matthew 2:13–18

The portrayal of King Herod in today's gospel reading is that of a ruler who is prepared to lash out even at innocent children to defend against what he perceives to be a threat to his power. There have been many such figures down through the course of history, even up to recent times, rulers who are prepared to sacrifice any number of innocent people to ensure that they stay in power. This form of kingship, the kingship of Herod, was the polar opposite of the kingship that Jesus came to proclaim, the kingship of God. Jesus' kingship was one that finds expression not in the oppressive use of power but in the humble service of others. The child Jesus who escaped from Herod's tyranny went on as an adult to say to his disciples, 'You know that the rulers of the Gentiles lord it over them and their great ones are tyrants over them. It will not be so among you; but whoever wishes to be great among you must be your servant'. None of us will ever act like Herod, but none of us can afford to be complacent either; we can all be prone to dominate in one way or another. The first reading for this feast declares, 'If we say we have no sin in us, we are deceiving ourselves and refusing to admit the truth'. We have to be alert to the ways we can fail to take that path of humble, self-emptying service of others which is the way of Jesus, the way of God.

30 December, Monday, Sixth Day in the Octave of Christmas
Luke 2:36–40

It is striking that widows tend to have a very positive profile in the Gospels. In one of the parables that Jesus spoke, a widow keeps coming to a corrupt judge for the justice she is entitled to, until she finally gets him to take her seriously. Jesus told this parable as an encouragement to us to keep praying always and not lose heart. On another occasion, as Jesus was in the Temple in Jerusalem, he saw a widow put two copper coins, all she had to live on, into the Temple treasury. Jesus draws his disciples' attention to her as a model of complete self-giving to God. In today's gospel reading we find a widow named Anna who never left the Temple, serving God night and day with fasting and prayer. Widows were vulnerable in the time of Jesus. They didn't have a husband to provide for them and if they didn't have children, they were especially vulnerable. It may have been their very vulnerable status which led them to entrust themselves to God. If they had no one to rely on, they could rely on God. Being somewhat alone in the world, there was a space in their lives which was filled with God. Anna was in constant prayerful communion with God. It was only fitting that she should happen to come by just at the time that Mary and Joseph brought their child into the Temple and Simeon was announcing who this child would become. Later on, the adult Jesus would say, 'Ask and it will be given to you; search and you will find'. Anna was someone who sought the Lord in prayer, and one day she found the one whom she sought. Having found him, she shared him with others. The gospel reading says she spoke about the child to all who were looking forward to the deliverance of Jerusalem. We have much to learn from this widow. She reminds us that the Lord comes to those who prayerfully seek him and she encourages us to share with others the Lord who has come to us.

31 December, Tuesday, Seventh Day in the Octave of Christmas
John 1:1–18

Today is the last day of the year, the end of the year. Yet today's gospel reading does not speak about an ending but a beginning. The opening words, which are the beginning of John's Gospel, are, 'In the beginning was the Word'. When was this 'beginning' that is being referred to here? It is difficult to locate it in time, because the reference is to that mysterious moment before creation began. The Word was with God, in the beginning, before God created the universe. The reading goes on to say that God then created everything through the Word. 'Through him all things came to be'. If all things came into being through the Word, then, in some way, all that exists is itself a word; it speaks to us of God. Those opening verses of John's Gospel are a wonderful statement about the fundamental goodness of all creation, the capacity of all creation to reveal something of God to us. Yet they are only preparatory to the even more wonderful statement that follows a few verses later: 'The Word became flesh and dwelt among us'. The person of Jesus is God's Word become flesh. If all creation can speak to us of God, Jesus is the supreme and full revelation of God. He alone, in the words of the gospel reading, is full of God's grace and truth, God's gracious love and faithfulness. Jesus is the pinnacle of God's good creation. Jesus speaks to us of God more powerfully than anything or anyone else in all creation. He is the fullest revelation of God's love for the world. God calls out to us through Jesus to receive from the fullness of his love that resides in Jesus. We can all say, in the words of the gospel reading, 'from his fullness, we have, all of us, received'. We spend our lives receiving from that fullness of God's love in Jesus. No matter where we are on our life journey, there is always more to be received. It is in receiving God's love present in Jesus that we are empowered to give that love to others. As we face into a new year, we are called to keep giving out of what we have received.

1 January, Wednesday, Mary, the Holy Mother of God
Luke 2:16–21

There is no reference to Mary, the mother of Jesus, in the letters of Paul. The nearest Paul comes to mentioning Mary is in today's second reading from the letter to the Galatians, where he declares that 'God sent his Son, born of a woman'. In that succinct statement Paul sums up the meaning of today's feast. God's Son was born of a woman. Mary is the mother of God's Son and because God's Son, Jesus, is God in human form, Mary is the Mother of God. To say that Mary is the Mother of God is to make a statement not only about Mary but about Jesus. Jesus, Mary's Son, is God with us. This is the message that was given to the shepherds by the angels, according to Luke's Gospel: 'to you is born this day in the city of David, a Saviour, who is Christ, the Lord'. The term 'Lord' was the name of God in the Jewish Scriptures. This child is Lord or God, God become flesh. In today's gospel reading, we are told that the shepherds repeated to Mary and Joseph this message that had been given to them by the angels. Just as the angels were God's messengers to the shepherds, the shepherds now become God's messengers to Mary and Joseph. Just as the angels proclaim the Gospel to the shepherds, they in turn proclaim the Gospel to Mary and Joseph. The Gospel that the shepherds proclaim in Bethlehem meets with a twofold response. The gospel reading says that all who heard what the shepherds said were astonished at their message, including Mary and Joseph. It is also said of Mary that she treasured the words spoken by the shepherds and pondered them in her heart. We are all invited to respond to the good news that God is with us through the child of Mary and Joseph in the same twofold way. We are to retain a sense of astonishment at this extraordinary good news that God has come among us in the frailty of human flesh, in the vulnerable child who became the vulnerable adult on Calvary. We are also to keep treasuring this Gospel, and keep pondering on it so as to probe its wonderful richness. On this first day of a new year, we commit ourselves anew to appreciating the Gospel that has been proclaimed to us, and to sharing this Gospel with others.

2 January, Thursday before Epiphany

John 1:19–28

For the remainder of this week, we will be reading from the first chapter of John's Gospel. In today's gospel reading, John the Baptist is asked, 'Who are you?' We can spend most of our lives trying to answer the question, 'Who am I?' It is not a question that lends itself to a quick and easy answer. There is a sense in which we never really come to know ourselves fully. A first step in knowing ourselves is knowing who we are not, so that we don't try to be someone we are not. John the Baptist comes across in today's gospel reading as knowing who he is not. He is not the Messiah, he is not Elijah, and he is not the prophet. John does not claim to be someone he is not. He not only knows who he is not, but he also knows who he is. He declares that he is a 'voice that cries in the wilderness', preparing people for the Lord's coming. Having answered this fundamental question, John the Baptist is asked a further question, 'Why are you baptising?' The answer to this second question is already contained in John's answer to the first question. He baptises to prepare people for the Lord's coming. He baptises as a way of exercising his role as the witness, the person who points to Jesus and leads others to him. In a very real sense, that is what we are all called to be. Even though we might have difficulty fully answering the question, 'Who are you?', as members of the believing community we can all give the answer, 'I am a witness'. That is our baptismal calling, to point towards the Lord and to lead others to him by our lives.

3 January, Friday before Epiphany

John 1:29–34

The words of John the Baptist, 'Look, there is the lamb of God that takes away the sin of the world', are familiar to us as the words spoken by the celebrant at Mass just before communion, when he holds up the host. Our response to those words at Mass, 'Lord I am not worthy that you should come under my roof, but only say the word … ', is a version of the words spoken by the centurion to Jesus when Jesus offered to go to his house to heal his servant. That story is found not in John's Gospel but in the Gospels of Matthew and Luke. The liturgy has brought together two sets of words from the Gospels that, originally, had no connection with each other. Those two sets of words are, in a way, quite contrasting. John the Baptist is pointing out Jesus to his own disciples and saying to them, 'Look, there is the Lamb of God, go to him'. The centurion is saying to Jesus, 'Don't come to me, because I am unworthy'. Both sets of words express a truth. We are all unworthy of the Lord's coming to us, and yet we are invited not only to receive the Lord when he comes, but to take the initiative to go to him. Our unworthiness is not an obstacle to the Lord's relating to us or to our relating to him. The first reading invites us to 'think of the love that the Father has lavished on us, by letting us be called God's children; and that is what we are'. Through baptism, we have come to share in Jesus' own relationship with God, calling God 'Father', as he does. This is the fruit of God's love that has been lavished on us. It is as God's beloved sons and daughters that we are invited to receive the Lord's coming to us and to go towards him ourselves.

4 January, Saturday before Epiphany

John 1:35–42

The opening words that Jesus speaks in each of the four Gospels differ from each other. In John's Gospel Jesus' opening words take the form of the question that we find in today's gospel reading, 'What do you want?' Jesus addresses this question to the two disciples of John the Baptist who had started to follow him. Jesus asks many questions in the course of the Gospels and all of them are often worth pondering. The beginning of a new year is an especially appropriate time to hear Jesus' question, 'What do you want?' as a question that is addressed to each of us personally. Jesus' second set of words in John's Gospel, again addressed to the disciples of John the Baptist, take the form of an invitation, 'Come and see'. The question and the invitation very much go together. As we become aware of what it is we really want, we sense a call to set out on a journey towards the Lord as the one who alone can fully satisfy those deep hungers and thirsts in our hearts. The beginning of a new year is a good moment for us to get in touch with our deepest desire to see the Lord, and then to move closer to him, to grow in our relationship with him, so that we come to see and know him as he sees and knows us. Today we might allow both the question and the invitation of Jesus to resonate within us as we set out into the year that beckons.

6 January, Monday, The Epiphany of the Lord

Matthew 2:1–12

In Italy children are very fortunate because they receive gifts not only on the feast of Christmas but also on the feast of the Epiphany. Whereas Santa Claus brings gifts on Christmas Day, an old woman on a broomstick, called La Befana, brings gifts on the night of 5 January. According to an ancient tradition, the wise men on their way to Bethlehem stopped at an old woman's cottage and asked her for directions to where the king of the Jews was to be born. She couldn't help them but she offered them hospitality. The next morning the magi asked her if she would like to join them on their journey. She said she was too busy. However, later on she had a change of mind and she went looking for the child herself. In spite of much searching, she never found him. Every year on the evening of 5 January she brings gifts to children, hoping that one of them will be the child Jesus. It is a story that captures well the deeper meaning of this feast. The wise men from the east, like La Befana, were searchers. They are the ancestors of all who seek after light and truth. Guided by the draw of the mysterious, an unusual star, they set out in search of God's truth. They speak to that searching spirit that resides in each one of us. We have a restlessness for more than this life alone has to offer and it keeps us searching after the One who alone can fully respond to our restless spirit.

We will rest in God fully only beyond this earthly life. Yet, already in this earthly life we can begin to experience something of that eternal rest. In the course of the Gospels, Jesus calls out to the restless, 'Come to me all you who labour and are overburdened and I will give you rest'. Jesus was speaking here of a present experience of rest and not just one for the eternal future. The Lord who calls out to us to 'Come' is also drawing us to himself, so that we can experience something of his own rest, peace and joy. The Lord drew the magi from the east towards himself by means of a humble star. He provides a star of Bethlehem for all of us in response to our search for him. God's love that draws us will find different ways of bursting forth like a light that pierces the darkness and demands our attention. Once the Lord draws us to himself, he sends us out to be the star of Bethlehem for others who are seeking. As we encounter the Lord for ourselves, we become carriers of his light to others.

The Lord does not hide himself from us; he does not play hide-and-seek with us. He seeks us out in his love and draws us to himself. The word 'epiphany' means a manifestation, a laying open. The Lord lays himself open to everyone. Epiphany is the feast of the Lord's transparency. In contrast, there was nothing transparent about King Herod. He asked the magi to let him know when they had found the child, so that he could come and worship him also. In reality, he wanted to kill the child. Herod is not simply a figure of the past. We can all find ourselves having to deal with forceful people who are hostile to our search for the Lord's light and truth, yet the story of the journey of the magi teaches us that the drawing power of the Lord's loving presence is stronger than all the obstacles we might encounter.

7 January, Tuesday after Epiphany
Matthew 4:12–17, 23–25

Towards the end of today's gospel reading, the evangelist Matthew conveys a sense of the wide-scale impact of the beginning of Jesus' public ministry. People began to follow him from Galilee and Judea, corresponding to much of modern-day Israel, and from the Decapolis and Transjordania, corresponding to much of modern-day Jordan. It is said that Jesus' fame also spread throughout the Roman province of Syria, which corresponds more or less to modern-day Syria. What was it about Jesus' ministry that caused such a stir over such a wide area? The gospel reading says that it was like a great light coming to shine on people who lived in darkness and in the shadow of death. What was this light? Jesus' opening words in our gospel reading give us an answer: 'Repent, for the kingdom of heaven is at hand'. It was the light of the kingdom of heaven, the light of God's loving and life-giving rule. This was a kingdom or rule, which, according to the gospel reading, meant healing for the broken in body, mind and spirit. This light of God's kingdom, this light of God's loving and life-giving rule, continues to shine on us today, on each one of us and on all of us as a community of faith. As we begin a new year, we are being reminded that we walk and live and have our being in this light, a light that no darkness can overcome. What Jesus asks of us in the face of this light is that we repent, in other words that we keep turning towards the light and away from darkness of any form. The light of God's love is always shining upon us through the person of Jesus, our risen Lord. Our calling is to keep turning towards that light in our need, and then to reflect this light to others.

8 January, Wednesday after Epiphany
Mark 6:34–44

There are times when it can be wise to avoid certain situations that come our way. We sense that we really have no contribution to make that would help matters. There are other times when we can be tempted to avoid what we need to face into. We find an example of that misplaced avoidance in today's gospel reading. The disciples looked out on the hungry crowd that Jesus had been teaching at some length and they turned to Jesus and said, 'Send them away, so that they can go to the farms and villages round about, to buy themselves something to eat'. However, rather than complying with his disciples' request, Jesus encouraged them to face into the challenge of providing for this hungry crowd in this lonely place. 'Give them something to eat yourselves.' When the disciples resisted Jesus' suggestion, he pressed them further, calling on them to go and see how many loaves could be found among the crowd. Jesus was aware that he could feed this crowd, but he needed the disciples' help. The disciples discovered that there were five loaves and two fish among the crowd. Jesus had more work for the disciples to do, calling on them to arrange the crowd in groups of hundreds and fifties. Then, through his prayerful communion with God, Jesus managed to feed everyone with the five loaves and two fish, but again with the help of the disciples. He handed the food to the disciples to distribute among the people, and, when the crowd had eaten their fill, the disciples collected the scraps that were left over. There was a lot of work for the disciples to do. Jesus could not have fed the crowd without the work of the disciples, but, to an even greater extent, the disciples could not have fed the crowd without the prayerful presence of Jesus. Perhaps there is an image here of how the Lord continues to work among us today. We are totally dependent on the Lord's prayerful presence if his work is to get done, but he relies on us as well to continue his work of serving God's people.

9 January, Thursday after Epiphany

Mark 6:45–52

The Gospels often portray Jesus at prayer. In today's gospel reading, Mark tells us that after being busy feeding the five thousand in the wilderness, Jesus went off into the hills to pray. The reading we have just heard suggests that, even though Jesus went off alone to pray, his prayer did not in fact remove him from people. Indeed, his prayer seems to have made him more sensitive to the struggles of others. As he was praying in the hills, Jesus became aware of his struggling disciples, battling against a headwind and worn out with rowing. The Lord left his prayer and came to his struggling disciples, and spoke words of great reassurance to them. 'Courage! It is I! Do not be afraid.' Mark suggests that, while at prayer, Jesus was not only in communion with God; he was also in communion with those who were struggling. That can be true of our own prayer too. In prayer, we open ourselves to the Lord's presence; we become attuned to the Lord who is present to us, but as we do so, we will often find ourselves thinking of others, feeling with and for others. This should not surprise us. The Lord whom we approach in prayer is full of love for others; as we draw near to him in prayer, we will be caught up into his concern for others. It is not surprising that much of our prayer tends to be intercessory prayer, prayer for others. Authentic prayer will deepen not only our communion with the Lord, but our communion with others as well, especially with those who, like the disciples in the gospel reading, are struggling with and battling the storms of life.

10 January, Friday after Epiphany
Luke 4:14–22

We sometimes ask people to do us a favour. In using the word 'favour' we understand that this is a request to which the other person does not have to respond. There is no requirement on someone's part to do us a favour. Our favouring someone, in that sense, is sheer gift. According to Luke's Gospel, when Jesus was born, the shepherds heard a multitude of the heavenly host praising God and saying, 'Glory to God in the highest and on earth peace among those whom God favours'. The birth of Jesus was the greatest possible sign of God's favour. Through the birth of this child, God was favouring all of humanity in the most complete way imaginable. According to today's gospel reading from Luke, when this child became an adult, he went to the synagogue of his home town, Nazareth, and proclaimed the 'Lord's year of favour'. Jesus understood that his whole ministry was a making present of God's favour for all, especially for those who had been made to feel out of favour with God and with others, such as the poor, the captives, the blind, the downtrodden and the lost. That 'year of the Lord's favour' was not a calendar year. It coincided with the whole of Jesus' public ministry and, also, his ministry as risen Lord in the Church, which continues until the end of time. We continue to be graced by God's favour through Jesus today. Our calling is to keep opening ourselves to God's favour, to allow ourselves to be deeply touched by it, and then to reveal something of God's favour to others, especially those most in need of it.

11 January, Saturday after Epiphany
Luke 5:12–16

Today's first reading from the first letter of Saint John makes a very striking statement, 'Anyone who has the Son has life'. It reflects Jesus' own declaration in John's Gospel that he has come that we may have life and have it to the full. If we receive his coming in faith, we will discover that our relationship with him is life-enhancing and life-giving. The gospel reading is the story of someone who received Jesus' coming and experienced Jesus as life-giving. A leper fell on his face before Jesus, imploring him, 'if you want to, you can cure me'. This profound act of faith in Jesus cured him of his leprosy. It gave him a new and fuller life; he would no longer be required to live apart from the community. He would no longer feel separated from God. The leper had great faith in Jesus' power to heal him. His only concern was whether Jesus actually wanted to heal him: 'if you want to'. He must have wondered if Jesus really wanted to involve himself with someone who was shunned by everyone else. Jesus did the one thing no healthy person would have done; he reached out his hand and touched the leper. There could be no doubt about Jesus' willingness to be in communion with this man, so as to cure him and bring him a fuller life. Jesus' willingness to be in communion with us in a way that is life-giving for us is never in doubt. He is never put off by whatever may be broken or out of joint in our lives. His life-giving coming and presence can be relied upon each day. What is needed from us is something of the leper's faith, a readiness to come before him in our need and entrust ourselves to him.

13 January, Monday, First Week in Ordinary Time
Mark 1:14–20

A lot of the news that we hear through the media is bad news. We can sometimes feel overwhelmed by it all. We might even be tempted at times not to listen to a radio station or read a newspaper. It is worth reminding ourselves in this context of bad news that Jesus was always in the business of proclaiming good news. According to today's gospel reading, the first words Jesus spoke at the beginning of his public ministry were good news: 'He proclaimed the good news from God'. What was that good news from God? Jesus expresses this good news very succinctly. 'The time has come, and the kingdom of God is close at hand.' The time that God's people had been waiting for over many centuries had finally arrived. God was present in a powerful way through the person of Jesus, God's Son. The kingdom of God, the reign of God's liberating love, was close at hand. It was as close as the person of Jesus himself. What Jesus called for in response to this good news was that people 'repent and believe the good news'. That good news continues to be proclaimed today. The reign of God's liberating love is at hand today, this day, through the risen Lord and Holy Spirit. The same call goes out to us today: 'Repent and believe the good news'. We are to turn towards Jesus, the bearer of this good news, and allow ourselves to be graced by this good news, this gospel. Then, like Peter, Andrew, James and John, in the gospel reading, we are to go forth as messengers of this good news to others. We are to proclaim, by our lives, the reality of the kingdom of God, the reign of God's liberating love.

14 January, Tuesday, First Week in Ordinary Time
Mark 1:21–28

According to the Book of Ecclesiastes in the Jewish Scriptures, 'there is nothing new under the sun'. 'What has been is what will be, and what has been done is what will be done'. The people of Capernaum, as portrayed in today's gospel reading, would not agree with that sentiment. When they heard Jesus teach and saw him heal a seriously disturbed man in the synagogue, they said in astonishment, 'Here is a teaching that is new, and with authority behind it'. There was a freshness, a newness, to the message of Jesus, the word of Jesus. There was also a new authority to this word; Jesus did not just speak of the presence of God's kingdom but he showed that this kingdom was present by his actions, such as his healing of the man in the synagogue. Here was a word that accomplished what it said. We have heard the teaching of Jesus so often that sometimes it can no longer feel new to us. We can think, 'I have heard this before', and we don't pay too much attention to it. Yet Jesus himself retains his newness today as risen Lord, and his word, his message, retains its originality, its freshness and, also, its power and authority. We need the capacity to hear his word afresh and to experience its power anew. Saint Augustine once addressed God as 'Beauty, ever ancient, ever new'. The word, the teaching, of Jesus is itself ever ancient, ever new. It can speak anew to us every day of our lives.

15 January, Wednesday, First Week in Ordinary Time
Mark 1:29–39

Both of today's readings remind us in different ways that we need others to lead us to the Lord. In the first reading, Samuel was being called by the Lord but he did not recognise that it was the Lord who was calling him. Eli, who was more experienced in the ways of the lord than Samuel, recognised that it was the Lord who was calling Samuel. He guided Samuel as to what he should say in response to the Lord's call that he was hearing. He was to say, 'Speak, Lord, your servant is listening'. Eli helped Samuel to meet the Lord; he mediated between the Lord and Samuel. We find something similar happening in the gospel reading. Simon Peter's mother-in-law was in bed with a fever. Other people in the house where she was lying told Jesus about her, and, as a result, Jesus came to her and healed her. These people made it possible for this ill woman to experience the healing presence of Jesus; they mediated between her and the Lord, as Eli had mediated between Samuel and the Lord. All of us have a similar calling; we are called to bring each other to the Lord, and the Lord to each other. The Lord continues to need people to mediate between him and others. Every day we will be given opportunities to help one another to recognise and respond to the Lord's coming.

16 January, Thursday, First Week in Ordinary Time
Mark 1:40–45

Today's first reading tells the story of a moment of great catastrophe for the people of Israel. They suffered a defeat at the hands of the Philistines. Even when they brought the Ark of the Covenant, the symbol of God's covenant with them, into their camp, they were defeated again. Their distress at God's seeming absence is expressed in their question, 'Why has the Lord allowed us to be defeated today?' Another form of that question, addressed directly to God, is found in the final verse of today's responsorial psalm, 'Why do you hide your face, and forget our oppression and misery?' The gospel reading is the story of a leper who approaches Jesus. Lepers were used to people hiding their faces from them; they probably would have presumed that God had also hidden his face from them. However, this leper finds a very different response from Jesus. Jesus does the unthinkable; he touches the leper. He turns his face towards the leper in the most personal way imaginable and restores him to health and to the community from which his disease separated him. There are two very different experiences of God in the two readings, the experience of God's absence at a very vulnerable time, and the experience of God's compassionate presence at a time of great distress and isolation. Both experiences are part of the journey of faith. There will be times when we will ask 'Why?' and there will be other times when we sense the healing touch of the Lord. The same was true for Jesus. On the cross he cried out 'Why?' but in the resurrection he experienced the Lord's healing and life-giving presence. If we remain faithful to the Lord in the dark times, we will come to experience the Lord's healing touch in our own lives.

17 January, Friday, First Week in Ordinary Time
Mark 2:1–12

We often speak of a faith that can move mountains. In today's gospel reading, the faith of a small group of people moved the roof of a house. A paralysed man and his four friends who carried him had such faith in Jesus' healing power that they would allow no obstacle to prevent them reaching Jesus, including the obstacle of a crowd that blocked the way to Jesus and the obstacle of the roof of the house where Jesus was teaching. When the paralytic made his unorthodox entry to the house, Jesus immediately recognised the depth of faith from which it sprang, not only the faith of the paralytic but the faith of his companions as well. As this gospel reading says, 'Seeing *their* faith, Jesus said to the paralytic … '. The faith of a number of people together is often stronger than the faith of just one person. The faith of a community can accomplish a great deal more than the faith of one isolated individual. There was a community of faith in action in today's gospel reading, which Jesus recognised, 'seeing their faith'. The Lord can work more powerfully through a community of faith than through one person's solitary faith. We each belong to a community of faith. We refer to that community of faith as the Church, and the parish is the local church. We are called to work together in faith, so that the Lord's ministry to the broken can continue today. We need each other's faith. The faith of any one of us builds up the faith of the community, and the faith of the community strengthens our own personal faith.

18 January, Saturday, First Week in Ordinary Time

Mark 2:13–17

Jesus uses a variety of images drawn from ordinary life to express who he is and what he is about. In the Gospels, he speaks of himself as a shepherd searching for his lost sheep, a bridegroom at a wedding banquet, a traveller who comes upon a wounded man by the wayside, as well as in many other ways. In today's gospel reading, he speaks of himself as a doctor whose primary interest is the sick, rather than the healthy. He spoke of himself in this way in response to the criticism of the religious experts of his day who took a dim view of Jesus frequenting the company of those who did not live according to God's law, such as tax collectors. They were scandalised by his custom of sharing table with such people, entering into communion with them. The gospel reading says that there were 'many' tax collectors and sinners among his followers. The more religious people of Jesus' day avoided those they regarded as sinners, for fear they would be contaminated by them. Jesus revealed a different side to God. He revealed God as wanting to enter into communion with us, regardless of how others see us or, even, how we see ourselves. Jesus did not wait for people to be virtuous to befriend them. The Lord does not turn away from us because we are not all we could be. He keeps entering into communion with us, in all our weakness, frailty and sinfulness, so that he can empower us to live more fully as God's sons and daughters. Like the doctor who deals with the sick to make them better, the Lord keeps dealing with us to help us to become more fully the persons God desires us to be.

20 January, Monday, Second Week in Ordinary Time

Mark 2:18–22

In today's gospel reading, Jesus uses a real celebratory image to speak of himself and his ministry. He is like the bridegroom at his wedding banquet, and his disciples are like those who attend the bridegroom. The presence of Jesus is a celebratory presence. That is as true today as it was during the public ministry of Jesus. As Jesus was with his first disciples then, so the risen Lord is with us now in the same celebratory way. There is no doubt that life can be full of sorrow and distress for people, for any one of us at some time or other. The presence of the risen Lord does not spare us from the trials and tribulations of life which can bring us deep sorrow and grief. Yet the Lord's presence in itself is never to be a cause of sadness or gloom. In another gospel, the Gospel of John, Jesus says to his disciples, 'I have said these things to you so that my joy may be in you, and that your joy may be complete'. Even in the midst of life's sorrows and losses, Jesus wants us to experience something of his joy. This joy is the fruit of the Holy Spirit, the Spirit of God's Love. It has its source in God's love for us, revealed in the life, death and resurrection of Jesus, and poured into our hearts through the Holy Spirit. Regardless of what comes our way in life to cause us distress, God's life-giving love for us is assured. Just as the love of God the Father brought Jesus through death into a new life, so it will always bring the light of life into our darkness.

21 January, Tuesday, Second Week in Ordinary Time
Mark 2:23–28

We are all familiar with sayings like, 'never judge a book by its cover', 'all that glitters is not gold'. Such sayings put into words a truth that people have picked up from long experience. We know that something can look good, but the reality may not measure up to the appearance. The opposite, of course, can also be the case. What looks unimpressive can turn out to be of great quality. People can be in possession of treasures for many years without realising it. What is true of objects is also true of people; appearances can be deceptive. That comes across very clearly in today's first reading. When Samuel caught sight of Jesse's first son, he said, 'Surely the Lord's anointed one stands there', but he was wrong. The son of Jesse whom the Lord had chosen was someone whom Jesse hadn't even considered it worth his while to bring to Samuel. As the reading expresses it, 'God does not see as we see, we look at appearances, but the Lord looks at the heart'. The Lord sees deeper than we do, and that is why his choices can seem so strange to us. It is because the Lord sees deeper than we do that we should leave judgement to the Lord as much as possible. We have to keep on suspending judgement, because our capacity for real insight into others is very limited. In the gospel reading, the Pharisees were judging Jesus' disciples because they were looking at appearances. Jesus, however, knew their hearts and did not hesitate to defend them before their critics. Because the Lord looks at the heart, it is important for us to get our hearts in the right place, to keep focusing our heart on the Lord and on his will for our lives.

22 January, Wednesday, Second Week in Ordinary Time
Mark 3:1–6

Mark's Gospel gives us the most human portrait of Jesus. Mark, more than the other evangelists, often attributes emotions to Jesus. In today's gospel reading he makes reference to Jesus' grief and anger. 'Grieved to find them so obstinate, he looked angrily round at them'. Jesus was grieved that the religious authorities were so opposed to his work of healing a man on the Sabbath. His grief, as is often the case with human grief, was mixed with anger. The evangelist is portraying Jesus as being in a highly emotionall state. We know from our own experience that strong emotions like grief and anger can easily control us and take us over. Jesus was able to channel these strong emotions in a life-giving way. The energies of these emotions in his life became energies for the furthering of God's kingdom. He went on to heal the man with the withered hand. We can sometimes make a very negative judgement about the strong emotions that we experience within us. Such feelings in themselves are not something negative; it is how we channel them that matters. Like Jesus, we are called to channel our strong emotions in ways that serve God's purpose for our lives and for the lives of others. Grace builds on nature and grace can transform all our emotional energies into sources of life and well-being for all who cross our path in life. The Spirit can direct all our emotional energies towards the doing of God's work.

23 January, Thursday, Second Week in Ordinary Time
Mark 3:7–12

According to today's gospel reading, 'all who were afflicted in any way were crowding forward to touch Jesus'. People wanted to get as close as possible to Jesus because they recognised God's life-giving power at work in his ministry. They recognised Jesus as the Life-Giver, as one who could heal their brokenness. In the first reading, Saul, the first king of Israel, takes on the opposite role to that of Jesus. Far from being a life-giver, he shows himself to be a death-dealer. He grew jealous of the young David's success on the battlefield, especially when people began to compare David's successes favourably to Saul's. His jealousy fuelled his anger, and his anger led him to resolve to kill David. It took Jonathan, Saul's son, to restrain Saul's murderous intent. We are told that Jonathan held David in great affection. Jonathan's affection for David was a truly life-giving power. Because of Jonathan's affection, David was preserved from Saul's murderous intent. In this way, Jonathan showed that he possessed something of the life-giving quality of Jesus as portrayed in the gospel reading. There are many Saul figures in our world who are driven by jealousy and anger to bring death to others. There are also Jesus figures to be found, like Jonathan, who bring life to those who are threatened by death. We are all called to share in Jesus' life-giving ministry. As in the case of Jonathan, that will often mean having the courage to stand up to the forces of death.

24 January, Friday, Second Week in Ordinary Time
Mark 3:13–19

The person of David features in our first reading from the first book of Samuel in these days. David is portrayed in the biblical literature as a somewhat complex character. He is capable of both great virtue and great vice. He had Uriah, one of his commanders, killed because he wanted to marry Uriah's wife, thereby breaking two of the Ten Commandments. It is the virtuous side of David that is reflected in today's first reading. Saul, the king of Israel, considered David his enemy, because he was jealous of David's popularity. Saul sought to do David harm. However, when David had the opportunity to do Saul harm, he refused to take it. He preserved the life of his enemy. In the words of Saul to David, 'You have repaid me with good, while I have repaid you with evil'. David showed love towards his enemy, anticipating the teaching of Jesus in the Sermon on the Mount. The character of David teaches us that, even when we fail in some serious way, we can still be capable of great good. In the gospel reading, Jesus appoints twelve of his disciples to be his companions and to be sent out in his name. Many of them would fail him in a very serious way. All of them would desert him, Peter would deny him publicly and Judas would betray him. Yet each of them was also capable of great good. Apart from Judas, they would all become proclaimers of the Easter gospel to others, founders of a community of believers. The Lord can continue to work powerfully through us, even though we may fail him. We need never allow our weaknesses and failings to blind us to the good that is in us, or to inhibit us from allowing the Lord to do his good work through us.

25 January, Saturday, Conversion of Saint Paul

Mark 16:15–18

There was clearly a violent streak to Paul before he became a follower of the Lord. He says of himself in today's first reading that he persecuted the followers of Jesus to the death, and sent women and men to prison in chains. When he left Jerusalem for Damascus, it was with the intention of bringing believers in Jesus back to Jerusalem as prisoners for punishment. After he encountered Christ on the road to Damascus, the violent streak in Paul seems to have disappeared. He was just as zealous as an apostle of the Lord as he had been as a Pharisee, yet now his zeal did not take a violent or destructive form. Indeed, he experienced the same suffering and persecution from the authorities as he himself had previously inflicted on others. He went from inflicting suffering on others in God's name to enduring suffering from others in the service of the Lord. On the road to Damascus Paul had a profound experience of God's love for him through Christ. He came to appreciate that this love of God, revealed through the life, death and resurrection of Jesus, embraced all of humanity, Jews and pagans. From now on, it was this love of God, revealed in Christ, that would shape his zeal. His destructive zeal became a loving zeal. He wrote in one of his letters, 'the love of Christ urges us on'. He is not speaking there about his love for Christ but about Christ's love for him. Christ's love for him directs him to do what he does, shapes what he does and how he does it. In this way Paul shows us what is at the heart of our own baptismal calling. We are called to come to know with our heart and mind Christ's love for us, and allow that love to shape what we do and how we do it. We are to give expression in our lives to Christ's love for humanity. Paul was a religious person before his meeting with Christ. However, he was only a Christ-like person after that meeting. It is possible to be religious without being loving. Paul, the apostle, shows us that authentic religion, true spirituality, shows itself in a life that reveals the love of Christ for all.

27 January, Monday, Third Week in Ordinary Time
Mark 3:22–30

The final verses of today's gospel reading seem rather harsh to our ears. Jesus speaks of a sin that is beyond forgiveness, an eternal sin. The sin in question is to attribute the work of God's Spirit in Jesus to the Spirit of Satan, which is what the scribes who came up from Jerusalem were doing. They were saying that the power beyond the good work that Jesus was doing was the power of Satan. Those who say such a thing are so closed to God's presence and activity that even God's power to forgive will not penetrate their heart. The Gospels are clear that God's mercy is boundless and that Jesus is the revelation of the boundless mercy of God. Yet even the boundless mercy of God requires some level of openness on the part of others to receive it. Those who see only evil in the obvious good that others are doing, while seeing no sin in themselves, will struggle to allow themselves to be embraced by God's merciful love. The good news is that even the slightest opening on our part is all God needs to bring us to himself. The Lord has done and is doing most of the work; all he needs is a little from us, but that little is very important. One expression of that 'little' is expressed in the prayer of the tax collector in the parable Jesus spoke, 'Lord, be merciful to me a sinner', a prayer we can all make our own.

28 January, Tuesday, Third Week in Ordinary Time
Mark 3:31–35

A few verses before our gospel reading, Mark tells us that the family of Jesus set out from Nazareth to Capernaum to restrain Jesus, to seize him, because people were saying that Jesus was out of his mind. With the best of intentions, they set out to take charge of Jesus.

According to today's gospel reading, when the mother and brothers of Jesus arrived at Capernaum asking to see Jesus, he more or less ignored them. He didn't leave what he was doing, teaching his disciples in a house, to go out to his family. Instead, he sent a message out to them declaring that he now had a new family, the family of his disciples, the family of those who listened to and lived his word, thereby doing God's will. It can't have been easy for Jesus' family, especially his mother, to hear that message. Jesus was not going to be managed or reined in. Jesus' family had to learn to let him go to God's purpose for his life. It is a lesson we all have to learn in relation to others, especially those we love. We feel we know what is best for them and we want them to respond to our promptings. Yet there comes a time when we have to acknowledge our powerlessness and let them go, even though we do not fully understand what is happening in their lives. This can be painful, as it must have been for Mary and the other members of Jesus' family. Letting go of others is but one expression of a more fundamental letting go, which is letting go to the Lord. This is what is being asked of Mary and her family in the gospel reading. Their purpose for Jesus was much narrower than Jesus' purpose for them; he wanted them to be part of his new family of disciples. The Lord's purpose for our lives is always greater than our own purposes for ourselves. We spend our lives letting go to the Lord's purpose for our lives, which alone can do justice to our full humanity.

29 January, Wednesday, Third Week in Ordinary Time
Mark 4:1–20

Many scholars hold that, whereas the parable in today's gospel reading was spoken by Jesus, the interpretation that follows reflects the experience of the early Church. In this interpretation, the focus has shifted from the sower to the various types of soil that have come to represent various responses to the preaching of the Gospel. How might Jesus have intended this parable to be heard? When Jesus saw the farmer going out to sow seeds, it reminded him of the way God was at work in his ministry. Jesus noticed that the farmer scattered the seed with abandon, not knowing on what kind of soil it would fall. Inevitably, a great deal of the seed that was scattered never germinated, yet some fell on good soil and produced an extraordinary harvest. In a similar way, God was scattering the seed of his life-giving word through Jesus' ministry. God's favour was being scattered abroad in an almost reckless manner. He gave the most unlikely places the opportunity of receiving the life-giving seed of his word. Jesus' ministry had something of that scatter-gun approach of the sower. There was nothing selective about Jesus' company. As with the farmer in the parable, much of what Jesus scattered was lost; it met with little or no response. Yet Jesus knew that some people were receiving the seed of his word, and that would be enough to bring about the harvest of God's kingdom. In speaking this parable, Jesus may have been speaking a word of encouragement to his disciples, 'Despite all the setbacks, the opposition and hostility, God is at work and that work will lead to something wonderful'. The seed of the Gospel is good and powerful. Whatever the odds against us, we must keep sowing.

30 January, Thursday, Third Week in Ordinary Time
Mark 4:21–25

Just prior to this gospel, Jesus has spoken the parable of the sower and given his interpretation of that parable. In that parable and its interpretation the focus is on the word of God that Jesus proclaims and on the need to really hear the word so that it takes root in our hearts and bears fruit in our lives. In today's gospel reading the 'lamp' is an image of God's word. It is proclaimed to all, just as a lamp is placed on a lamp stand for all to benefit from its light. The Lord proclaims his word; it is up to us to really listen to it. In the words of the gospel reading, 'if anyone has ears to hear, let him listen to this'. The gospel reading goes on to suggest that the more we give ourselves to the Lord's word, the more we will receive from it. 'The amount you measure out is the amount you will be given.' In other words, the more we invest in God's word, the more we will get. The light of God's word will shine but we have to listen to it attentively if it is to bear fruit in our lives. As we make a greater effort to really hear and understand God's word, we will receive more. 'The one who has will be given more.' If we make no effort, if we ignore the Lord's word, we risk losing what we have already gained: 'The one who has not, even what he has will be taken away.' We have to exercise our spiritual muscles, otherwise they will lose the strength they once had. The gospel reading suggests that the Lord can't do it all. We must play our part if his word is to bear the good and rich fruit in our lives that the Lord desires for us.

31 January, Friday, Third Week in Ordinary Time
Mark 4:26–34

There are times when less is better. We can want something to happen so much that we try to force it and in doing so we only manage to hold it back or even derail it. There is a time to be active and a time to be still and let be. In the first parable of today's gospel reading, the farmer needed to be active in sowing the seed, but then he needed to step back and allow the soil to interact with the seed in nature's way. Jesus says that the kingdom of God is like that. Yes, God needs labourers for his harvest. Jesus once called on those he was sending out as his messengers to pray to God to send more labourers into his harvest. However, our labour is not the decisive factor in the coming of God's kingdom into our world. It is ultimately God who will see to the coming of God's kingdom. Like the farmer in the parable there will be times when, after our labour, all we can do is step back and allow

God to do what only God can do. The farmer in the parable did not understand how the seed he had sown comes to maturity as full grain: 'how, he does not know'. There is much about how the Lord works that we will not understand either. Saint Paul said of his ministry and that of his co-worker Apollo in his first letter to the Corinthians, 'I planted, Apollo watered, but God gave the growth'. We do what we can and then we trust that the Lord will do what only he can, which is much more significant. The Lord is always at work beyond our human efforts. He will continue to work for the coming of his kingdom, even when our efforts seem insufficient to the task.

1 February, Saturday, Feast of Saint Brigid

Luke 6:32–38

Saint Brigid is the secondary patron of Ireland, after Saint Patrick. She was born around 454. When she was young, her father wished to make a suitable marriage for her but she insisted that she wanted to consecrate herself to God. She received the veil and spiritual formation, probably from Saint Mel, and she stayed for a while under his direction in Ardagh. Others followed her example and this led to her founding a double monastery in Kildare, with a section for men and a section for women. Through Brigid's reputation as a spiritual teacher the monastery became a centre of pilgrimage. She died in 524 and she is venerated not only throughout Ireland but in several European lands. She was renowned for her hospitality, almsgiving and care of the sick. The gospel reading is very suited to her feast because it calls on us to be generous, not only to those who are in a position to be generous to us, but even to our enemies. Jesus declares in that gospel reading, 'Give, and there will be gifts for you: a full measure, pressed down, shaken together, and running over, will be poured into your lap.' Jesus is saying there that if our focus is on giving, then we will discover that we receive more than we give. It could be said to the contrary that if our focus is on receiving, then we will ultimately be disappointed. It is not the case that we give with a view to receiving. It is simply that we give in various ways, in accordance with our gifts, abilities and energies, and we discover along the way that we are actually receiving more than we are giving. Our giving creates an opening for the Lord to grace us. The most generous form of giving, according to the gospel reading, is to love those who do not love us and to give to those from whom we have no hope of receiving anything in return. This kind of giving, the gospel reading reminds us, has something of God about it, because God is as kind to the ungrateful and the wicked as he is to those who are good. Such selfless giving opens up our hearts to receiving a great abundance from the Lord, what the gospel reading calls a 'full measure'.

3 February, Monday, Fourth Week in Ordinary Time

Mark 5:1–20

There is a lot of aggression in both of the readings today. In the first reading, a member of the tribe of Benjamin, the same tribe as Saul, Israel's first king, speaks very aggressively to David, Israel's second king, who had replaced Saul. The reading says that this man 'uttered curse after curse and threw stones at David'. In the gospel reading, a very disturbed person speaks very aggressively to Jesus, 'What do you want with me, Jesus, son of the Most High God? Swear by God you will not torture me!' David did not respond to the Benjaminite's aggression with aggression of his own, even though one of David's soldiers asked David for permission to cut the man's head off. David simply said in response, 'Let him curse only if the Lord has told him to'. Likewise, in the gospel reading, Jesus did not respond aggressively to the disturbed person's aggressive approach towards him. Whereas David's response was to let his aggressor alone, Jesus went much further. He engaged his aggressor in a very personal way, asking him,

'What is your name?' Up to now, people's only response to this man's aggression had been to put him in chains. However, this only served to make him more aggressive. His aggressive strength enabled him to snap his chains and break his fetters. Just before this scene in Mark's Gospel, Jesus had calmed a disturbance in nature, a storm that threatened to sink the boat in which he and his disciples were sailing. Now he calmed the disturbance in this man's spirit by relating to him as a human being, as distinct from some kind of an animal. The people of the region came and saw the man sitting beside Jesus, 'clothed and in his full senses'. The reading suggests that the Lord can take anything we throw at him and remain calm. Our disturbance does not disturb him, but, rather his calm can calm our disturbance. Prayer is a moment when we bring ourselves before the Lord, including our disturbed and angry selves, and allow the Lord of life to calm us, to give us rest, to bring us peace. We rise from prayer to bring his calming presence to others, just as, in the gospel reading, Jesus called on the man whose disturbance had been becalmed to 'go home to your people and tell them all that the Lord in his mercy has done for you'.

4 February, Tuesday, Fourth Week in Ordinary Time
Mark 5:21–43

The experience of grieving is present in both of today's readings. When David receives news that his son, Absalom, has been killed, he weeps bitterly, even though Absalom had led a revolt against him. The depth of David's grief is strikingly captured in his powerful lament, 'My son Absalom! My son! My son Absalom! Would I had died in your place! Absalom, my son, my son!' A son remains a son, even when rebellious. In the gospel reading, people grieve over the death of a twelve-year-old girl, the daughter of the synagogue leader, Jairus. The gospel reading makes reference to 'people weeping and wailing unrestrainedly'. However, in this instance, the weeping associated with death does not have the last word. Because of Jairus's faith in Jesus, Jesus comes to the recently deceased child and restores her to life. Our faith in the Lord allows him to work in a life-giving way even in the face of death. Our trusting faith in the Lord in the face of sickness and death will not ultimately be in vain. Our loved ones may die, as we all will, but Jesus, now risen Lord, will bring new life out of the experience of death. If our faith creates an opening for the Lord to work, as the faith of Jairus did, then the Lord will not allow death to have the last word. Jairus is a model of faith in the face of death. The woman with the flow of blood is another model of faith in the face of death. Because of her condition, she was suffering a kind of social death; she was considered an outsider to the community. Her faith, like the faith of Jairus, created a space for Jesus to work in a life-giving way in the face of her dying. Both of these people, a prominent, wealthy man in the community, and a penniless woman who had been ostracised from the community, have much to teach us about a faith that endures in the face of the worst life can send us.

5 February, Wednesday, Fourth Week in Ordinary Time
Mark 6:1–6

Jesus had spent the best part of thirty years in Nazareth. During that time he was known by all as the carpenter, the son of Mary. However, since leaving Nazareth, Jesus' life had taken a new direction. He had thrown himself into the work that God had given him to do. He had left Nazareth as a carpenter; he returned as a teacher and a healer. There was in fact much more to Jesus than his own townspeople had ever suspected while he was living among them. The gospel reading suggests that they could not accept this 'more'; they rejected him. They wanted him to be the person they had always known; they would not allow him to move on from that. The image they had of him, which they held on to with great tenacity, became a block to their learning more about him. There was more to Jesus than the people of Nazareth were aware of. Indeed there is always more to every human being than we are aware of. That is true even of those we would claim to know well. We can easily assume that we know someone, when, in reality, we know only one side to them. We are each made in God's image. There is a profound mystery to each one of us. We can never fully probe the mystery of another person's life. This is uniquely true of Jesus. It was Jesus' very ordinariness that made it difficult for the people of Nazareth to see him as he really was, in all his mystery. God was powerfully present to them in and through someone who was as ordinary, in many respects, as they were themselves. God continues to come to us today in and through the ordinary, in and through those who are most familiar to us. The primary way the Lord comes to us is in and through the everyday. The ordinary and familiar often reveal to us the mystery of God's presence.

6 February, Thursday, Fourth Week in Ordinary Time
Mark 6:7–13

In the instructions that Jesus gives to the twelve as he sends them out on mission, he takes it for granted that their message and ministry will not be well received everywhere. He makes reference to places that do not welcome them and to people who do not listen to them. In such situations, all they can do is walk away. Yet the prospect of their message not being welcomed and listened to by some should not deter them. They are to preach the Gospel and give expression to it in their works of healing. Jesus himself knew that his message and mission would not be welcomed by everyone but would be rejected by some in the most violent way possible. The situation with regard to preaching the Gospel today is not any different from how it was for Jesus and his first disciples. We are called to be people of faith in a context that is not always supportive of faith. When we come up against a lack of openness to faith, or indifference or even hostility, it can easily unsettle our own faith. Today, more than ever, we need a faith that is not dependent on the approval of others. Ultimately, our faith needs to be rooted in the Lord; it is a response to his faith in us, his faithfulness to us. It is the Lord's faithful presence to us that keeps us faithful, regardless of how our faith is received by others. One of the ways we experience the Lord's faithful presence is in and through the community of faith, the family of his followers. We need to belong there, to be grounded there, if we are to experience the Lord's faithful presence to the full, so as to witness to our faith even in settings that have little appreciation for it.

7 February, Friday, Fourth Week in Ordinary Time
Mark 6:14–29

We often hear the expression nowadays, 'speaking truth to power'. It could certainly be said of John the Baptist that he spoke truth to power. He told Herod Antipas, tetrarch of Galilee, that it was against the law of God for him to have married his brother's wife, Herodias. In certain parts of the world today, speaking truth to power is a very dangerous business. Many people have ended up in prison or even been killed for doing so. John the Baptist's speaking truth to power initially landed him in prison. Herodias considered prison too good for John and wanted him killed immediately. However, Herod had a certain respect for John, considering him to be a good and holy man. The gospel reading suggests that there were good instincts in Herod which he initially listened to, against the wishes of his wife. However, he abandoned those good instincts at his birthday banquet when he made a rash promise to Herodias's daughter to give her anything she wanted. When, at the prompting of her mother, she said she want-ed the head of John the Baptist on a platter, Herod acted against his better instincts to save face and ordered John to be beheaded. John the Baptist ended up paying the ultimate price for speaking truth to power. In the end Herod listened to the voice of Herodias rather than the voice of his better self. We can all find ourselves caught between conflicting voices. The voice of our better self, the voice of the Holy Spirit that prompts us to take the Lord's way, can be opposed by a very different voice that prompts us to take a very contrary way. Jesus was aware that his followers would all find themselves facing this fundamental conflict, which is why he taught us to pray, 'Lead us not into temptation, but deliver us from evil'. He encourages us to turn to God for strength when we are tempted to take a path that is not in keeping with God's will for our lives, that does not correspond to the voice of the Holy Spirit within us.

8 February, Saturday, Fourth Week in Ordinary Time
Mark 6:30–34

We are all familiar with the experience of our plans not working out. In the course of our day we might plan to get something done and our plans come to nothing. On a grander scale, some plan we might have had for our life does not materialise. We can respond in different ways to our plans not working out. In today's gospel reading, Jesus' plans for himself and his disciples did not work out. He intended taking his disciples away to a lonely place all by themselves, because they were so busy that they had no time even to eat. However, when Jesus got to the lonely place, he discovered to his surprise that it had become a crowded place; the crowd had got there ahead of him. He didn't respond with annoyance to this unexpected interruption; instead, according to the gospel reading, he had compassion on the crowd and set himself to teach them. Jesus' plans did not work out, but something else happened that served God's purpose. When our own plans fail to materialise, sometimes something better can come to pass, something that would never have happened if our plans had worked out. The Lord's purpose is always greater than our plans. Whenever we have to let of our plans, the Lord's life-giving purpose for our lives will always prevail. Our plans not working out can create an opportunity for the Lord to work in a way that surprises us.

10 February, Monday, Fifth Week in Ordinary Time
Mark 6:53–56

The question, 'Where is God to be found?' is one that has often engaged people throughout the generations. In today's first reading, Solomon recognises that God has chosen to dwell in the Temple that Solomon had built in Jerusalem, 'Yes, I have built you a dwelling, a place for you to live in for ever'. Yet God's presence can never be confined to a building, not even the most sacred building in Israel, the Temple in Jerusalem. In the gospel reading, people flocked to Jesus, bringing with them those who were sick and who couldn't come to Jesus without the help of others. They all recognised that God was to be found in a powerfully life-giving way in the person of Jesus. Galilee was far to the north of Jerusalem, where the Temple was, yet these people felt no need to go to the Temple when Jesus was in their midst, because they recognised Jesus as the one in and through whom God was powerfully present and active, bringing healing to their brokenness. We too recognise Jesus as God with us, Emmanuel, as the new Temple, the new dwelling place of God. We believe that every encounter with Jesus, now risen Lord, is an encounter with God. If Solomon was amazed that God had chosen to dwell in the Temple he had built, we can be even more amazed that God has chosen to dwell among us in an even more wonderful way. Our calling is to keep growing in our awareness of and in our attentiveness to God's presence to us through his Son, our risen Lord.

11 February, Tuesday, Fifth Week in Ordinary Time

Mark 7:1–13

Today's first reading contains a section of Solomon's prayer on the occasion of the consecration of the Temple which he had built in Jerusalem. He acknowledges that God has chosen to dwell in this Temple. 'Let your eyes watch over this house, over this place of which you have said, "My name shall be there".' God's name was a way of referring to God's presence. Yet Solomon also recognises in that prayer that the wonderful Temple he has built could not possibly contain God. 'Why, the heavens and their heavens cannot contain you. How much less this house that I have built.' No human institution, not even the Temple, can contain God. Jesus makes a similar point in the gospel reading. The Pharisees and the scribes criticise the disciples of Jesus because they do not respect 'the tradition of the elders', with respect to various ritual washings. Jesus counters their criticism of his disciples, declaring, 'You get around the commandment of God to preserve your own tradition'. Jesus is reminding us that no human tradition, including the most cherished of religious traditions, can fully express God's will. Just as the Temple cannot contain God's presence, religious tradition cannot contain God's intention for our lives. The tendency to identify religious tradition with God's will is always with us. There have been times when the Church gave more reverence to its traditions than was warranted. Jesus compared his ministry to new wine, which calls for new wineskins. The temptation to preserve old wineskins can be very strong. The Church's tradition has to keep growing and evolving if the new wine of the Lord's message is to be heard afresh. We need to keep listening to what the Spirit is saying to the Church.

12 February, Wednesday, Fifth Week in Ordinary Time
Mark 7:14–23

The words of Jesus in today's gospel reading are part of the response to the experts in the Jewish Law who criticise Jesus' disciples for 'eating with defiled hands, that is, without washing them'. This failure to follow the washings prescribed was considered to make someone ritually unclean. In his response, Jesus shifts the focus away from a concern with external, ritual cleanliness, to a focus on what lies within the human person, what Jesus calls the 'heart'. Jesus was more concerned with people's underlying attitudes and values than with whether or not they followed various human regulations that some held to be sacred. It is not that Jesus made a sharp distinction between what was internal to someone and what was external. He was well aware that what is internal will reveal itself externally. As he declares in the gospel reading, the very visible and external behaviours of fornication, theft, murder and adultery all have roots within the person. 'They come from within and make a person unclean.' What is within the heart cannot be kept hidden for long. As Jesus says elsewhere, 'a good tree cannot bear bad fruit, nor can a bad tree bear good fruit … Thus you will know them by their fruits.' If our heart is right, our lives will bear good fruit that is visible to all. Getting our heart right is as much God's work as ours. There is a conviction throughout the Scriptures that it is God who works the internal transformation that shows itself in a life of goodness. That same conviction is well expressed in the traditional prayer to the Holy Spirit, 'Come Holy Spirit, fill my heart, and kindle in me the fire of your love'.

13 February, Thursday, Fifth Week in Ordinary Time
Mark 7:24–30

Both readings today feature pagans as well as Jews. The portrayal of pagans in the first reading is decidedly negative. King Solomon had pagan wives. In this way, he could establish good relations with the pagan nations that surrounded his kingdom. However, according to our reading, his pagan wives turned his heart away from the God of Israel. He built temples for the pagan gods whom his wives worshipped, showing that his heart was not wholly with the Lord, the God of Israel. In contrast, the gospel reading has a very positive portrayal of a pagan woman. Jesus travels to the north-west of Galilee, to the region of Tyre, in modern-day Lebanon, an area that was predominantly pagan, even though not devoid of Jews. A pagan woman approached Jesus and displayed a strikingly tenacious faith in his power to heal her daughter. She holds on to her faith in Jesus, in spite of Jesus' efforts to turn her aside. Sometimes in the Gospels, people who show faith in Jesus are turned aside by Jesus' disciples, such as the blind man Bartimaeus. Here, however, it is Jesus himself who seems to turn away a person who shows faith in him, just because she is a pagan. Jesus announces to her that 'the children should be fed first'. He is declaring that the people of Israel, God's children, are his primary focus, for the moment. Jesus' reference to the unfairness of taking the food that is intended for the children and throwing it to the house dogs seems rather harsh. The woman isn't put off. She is happy to identify herself with the house dogs in Jesus' image, declaring that, in many households, while the children are eating, the house dogs can nibble on the scraps that the children let fall. The pagans shouldn't have to wait; Jews and pagans can be fed together. Jesus seems to take her point; he grants her request. Perhaps one of the messages of this striking passage is that there is nothing wrong with an argumentative faith, even when the one we are arguing with is the Lord himself.

14 February, Friday, Feast of Saints Cyril and Methodius
Luke 10:1–9

There is an Irish connection to today's feast of Saints Cyril and Methodius, who were born in Thessalonica in northern Greece in the ninth century. They became noted linguists and scholars and went on to become monks. In response to a request from the leader of Moravia to the emperor in Constantinople, Cyril and Methodius were sent to preach the Gospel in Moravia, corresponding to the modern-day Czech Republic, Slovakia and parts of Hungary. In their efforts to do this they translated the Scriptures and the liturgical texts into the local Slav language. They understood that only if the sacred texts were in the vernacular could they communicate to the local people. In the process they invented a new alphabet, from which the present Slav alphabet is derived. Today this alphabet is called Cyrillic and is used for Russian, Ukrainian, Bulgarian and Serbian. For that reason they are regarded as the founders of Slavonic literature. Because of opposition to their work, they had to leave Moravia, and at the invitation of the pope they travelled to Rome. Pope Adrian approved of their work in Moravia and created the two brothers bishops. Cyril died in Rome in 869, and is buried in the Irish Dominican church of San Clemente near the Colosseum, where an ancient fresco depicts his funeral. Methodius returned to Moravia where he preached the Gospel in spite of great opposition, including opposition from local bishops who objected to his use of the vernacular. Worn out by his labours, he died in 885. Cyril and Methodius were both labourers in the Lord's harvest, in the language of today's gospel reading. We are all called to be labourers in the Lord's harvest in one way or another. We are all called to proclaim with our lives the message that Jesus gave to the seventy-two in that gospel reading, 'The kingdom of God is very near to you.' We may not be asked to travel far from home like Cyril and Methodius, but we can labour on behalf of the Lord wherever we find ourselves. The Lord can use whatever natural gifts we have in the service of his mission to make present the kingdom of God on earth. All he asks for is something of the same responsiveness to his promptings that marked the lives of Cyril and Methodius.

15 February, Saturday, Fifth Week in Ordinary Time

Mark 8:1–10

This is the second time in Mark's Gospel that Jesus feeds a large crowd in the wilderness, the first feeding having occurred in Mark 6:34–44, less than two chapters earlier. At this point, Mark has been placing Jesus in what would have been predominantly pagan territory. The fact that the disciples had already witnessed Jesus feeding a large crowd in Jewish territory makes their somewhat despairing question on this occasion, 'Where could anyone get bread to feed these people in a deserted place like this?' all the harder to understand. It seems odd that the disciples have learned nothing from the earlier feeding. If Jesus can feed a Jewish crowd in the wilderness, why not a pagan crowd? The disciples seem to have lacked an expectant faith. The fact that God provided through Jesus in the past did not lead them to expect that God could provide through him in the present. Jesus' question, 'How many loaves have you?', in contrast to the disciples' question, revealed an expectant faith. He expected that God would provide again for this predominantly pagan crowd with the resources that were available. This would be God's work, which is why Jesus first gave thanks to God for the seven loaves and the few small fish, before feeding the multitude. Jesus teaches us to have an expectant faith, even in the face of situations that seem beyond us, humanly speaking. If we engage with such situations out of our prayerful communion with the Lord, then he will often accomplish far more than we could imagine.

17 February, Monday, Sixth Week in Ordinary Time

Mark 8:11–13

Mark's Gospel gives us the most human portrait of Jesus of all the Gospels. Mark makes more frequent reference to the human emotions of Jesus than any of the other evangelists. In today's reading, Mark states that Jesus responded to the Pharisees' request for a sign from heaven 'with a sigh that came straight from the heart'. That sigh issued forth in a question, 'Why does this generation demand a sign?' We can almost sense the frustration and weariness of Jesus in that phrase of Mark, 'with a sigh that came straight from the heart'. The religious quest often takes the form of a search for heavenly signs, a longing for the extra-ordinary and unusual. The Jesus of the Gospels, however, will always redirect us towards the ordinary, such as the sower who goes out to sow his field, the woman who looks for her lost coin, the care given to a stranger on the road from Jerusalem to Jericho, the poor day labourer who unexpectedly finds treasure in his field, the rich merchant who finds the pearl of great price he has always been looking for, children playing games in the marketplace. It is in the ordinary events of daily life that the mystery of God's kingdom is to be found, because God's good creation is full of God's glory. The preoccupation with unusual religious signs can distract us from recognising the holy ground of ordinary human experience.

18 February, Tuesday, Sixth Week in Ordinary Time
Mark 8:14–21

In today's first reading, James makes an interesting statement about God. He declares that 'God cannot be tempted to do anything wrong, and he does not tempt anybody'. God will never tempt us to do something wrong. It is in that context that we need to understand the petition in the Lord's Prayer, 'Lead us not into temptation, but deliver us from evil'. There is no implication that God would deliberately lead us into temptation. In that prayer, we are really asking God to keep us faithful when we are tempted by evil or the evil one to take a path that is contrary to God's will for our lives. In the Garden of Gethsemane Jesus called on his disciples, 'Pray that you may not enter into temptation'. He wanted them to pray, so that when their faith in him was put to the test, when they were tempted to be unfaithful, they might remain firm in the face of such temptation. On that occasion, the disciples did not pray, and when the temptation to publicly disown Jesus came their way, they succumbed to that temptation. That failure of Jesus' disciples is anticipated in today's gospel reading, where Jesus addresses them as having minds that are closed, as failing to see with their eyes and hear with their ears, as being without perception. As their teacher, Jesus was finding them to be very difficult pupils. Jesus probably finds us unresponsive at times. When our faith is put to the test we often fail, we succumb to temptation. Yet the strong message of Mark's Gospel, from which our gospel reading is taken, is that the Lord remains faithful to us even when we fail him. He keeps calling us to begin again, to set out once more on the path of being his faithful disciples.

19 February, Wednesday, Sixth Week in Ordinary Time
Mark 8:22–26
There is something very personal about the encounter between Jesus and the blind man in today's gospel reading. When the people of Bethsaida brought the blind man to Jesus, he took the man by the hand and led him out of the village, perhaps in search of privacy and quiet in which to heal him. Then, as Jesus is alone with the man, he places his own spittle on the man's eyes and lays his hands on him, both very personal and, indeed, intimate, gestures. Without presuming that the man is healed, Jesus asks him, 'Can you see anything?', thereby involving the man in his own healing. When the man indicated that he was beginning to see but could not yet see clearly, Jesus laid his hands on him again. It was only then that the man could see everything plainly and distinctly. Jesus could now send him home, without the need to take him by the hand. We can see in this healing

story an image of how the Lord wishes to relate to us today. He calls each one of us into a personal relationship with himself. To deepen this relationship, he will often lead us by the hand away from the places where we normally congregate to a quiet place where he can speak to our hearts and touch our lives. The Lord needed to touch this man more than once to bring him from darkness to light; the man's healing was not instantaneous. We need the repeated touch of the Lord's presence if we are to keep journeying towards ever greater light, the light of the Lord's life-giving love. The Lord continues to call us 'out of the village' and he looks to us to keep responding to his call.

20 February, Thursday, Sixth Week in Ordinary Time
Mark 8:27–33

The question 'Who do you say I am?' is one that we might be slow to ask. We might be a little anxious about the responses we would get, especially if we think people are going to be completely honest with us. How others see us does not always correspond to how we see ourselves. Jesus had no such anxieties. He wanted his disciples to give him an honest answer to his question. He was testing them to see how well they had come to understand him. The answer Peter gave was correct. 'You are the Christ'. However, although Peter knows the correct answer, he does not understand what it means. Peter seems to have shared the triumphalist view of the Messiah that was current at that time, a view that left no room for suffering and death. When Jesus proceeds to interpret the title 'Christ' with reference to the Son of Man who must suffer grievously and be rejected and put to death, the evangelist tells us that Peter 'rebukes' Jesus. Jesus was telling Peter who he was, and Peter could not hear it. We can all struggle to accept the Lord on the Lord's own terms, to let God be God. We can sympathise with Peter's rebuke of Jesus. We all recoil at the prospect of someone who has become significant for us suffering and dying, yet Jesus would be a suffering Messiah because he was a loving Messiah. It was his passionate love for God and for all God's people that put him on a Roman cross. The crucified Jesus does not merit our rebuke, but rather our loving response.

21 February, Friday, Sixth Week in Ordinary Time
Mark 8:34–9:1

Martin Luther once dismissed the letter of James as an epistle of straw. He had a rather dusty opinion of its emphasis on works rather than on faith, and it seemed to be in conflict with one of his favourite letters, Paul's letter to the Romans. However, all James is saying in the reading we have just heard is that real faith always finds expression in good deeds. Faith is more than an intellectual assent to a set of propositions about God. As James says in that reading, even the demons believe that there is one God. Faith is a response to God that embraces all of our lives, our intellect, our emotions, our spirit, our body, and, as a result, it shows itself in how we live, in what we do and refuse to do. There is no conflict between Paul and James on this. Indeed, Paul, in his letter to the Galatians, says, 'The only thing that counts is faith working through love'. Paul, like James, understood that real faith expresses itself in a life of love, in works of love. That, of course, was especially true of Jesus. He was a person of supreme faith; he was faithful to God, even unto death on a cross. His faith, his faithfulness, expressed itself in a life of love, in the gift of himself to us all and for us all. In calling on us, in the gospel reading, to follow him, even to the point of losing our lives, Jesus is calling for a faith or faithfulness like his own. Such a faith will always show itself in a love that in some way reflects his supremely self-emptying love.

22 February, Saturday, Feast of the Chair of Saint Peter
Matthew 16:13–19

In every cathedral of the worldwide Church, there is to be found a special chair where the bishop or archbishop of the diocese sits when he is celebrating the liturgy. The chair is a symbol of the teaching authority of the bishop. In Saint Peter's Basilica in Rome, behind the main altar at the very back of the basilica, in a very elevated position, is an ancient wooden chair encased in bronze. It is traditionally understood to be the chair of Saint Peter. He was recognised as having a special teaching authority among the faithful from the very beginning of the Church. That teaching authority was based on the gospel reading for today's feast. Jesus is portrayed as giving Peter the keys of the kingdom of heaven. Keys are a symbol of authority. It is clear that teaching authority is involved from Jesus' subsequent reference to binding and losing. It is a Jewish expression that relates to the teaching authority of the experts in the Jewish law. They had the authority to bind and loose the law, determining which elements of God's law were binding and which could be interpreted more loosely. Peter is being asked to interpret not the Jewish law but Jesus' own teaching for the other members of the Church. In this way, he is to watch over the flock of God, in the words of today's first reading. The Catholic Church has always recognised that this teaching role that Jesus assigned to Peter resides in a special way with the bishop of Rome, the pope, who is understood to be Peter's successor in this regard. We look to each pope to proclaim the teaching of Jesus in a way that speaks to the concerns of our times. Jesus was aware that his words, his teaching, would need to be reinterpreted continually for every age. Today we ask for the grace to listen to our current pope who, we believe, is especially inspired to interpret the teaching of Jesus for us for this age.

24 February, Monday, Seventh Week in Ordinary Time
Mark 9:14–29

We can easily find ourselves identifying with the father of the disturbed boy in today's gospel reading. His prayer comes easily to us. 'I do have faith. Help the little faith I have.' We can all be aware that we have faith in the Lord, but that it is not all it could be. We sense that we have a relationship with the Lord, but that it has a long way to go. We recognise that in some ways we live as the Lord's followers, but in other ways we do not. We are a work in progress. We reveal the Lord's love to people in various ways, but then we have moments when we speak and act in ways that display more self-love than love of others or love of the Lord. We can easily get discouraged by those moments of personal failure. When we don't live up to the ideals we have for ourselves, we can easily get very down. We can allow our failures to define us. We forget the first part of the father's prayer, 'I do have faith', and become focused only on our 'little faith'. We become very aware that we have sinned but forget that we are loved sinners. At those times when we are tempted to focus only on how we have failed, how we are lacking, we need to keep turning from ourselves towards the Lord. In the gospel reading, Jesus' disciples failed to help the father's seriously disturbed son. Jesus did not rebuke the disciples for their failure to heal the boy, but, rather, for their failure to turn towards the Lord in prayer. 'That is the kind that can only be driven out by prayer.' In prayer we turn towards the Lord in our weakness, and in our weakness we discover his strength.

25 February, Tuesday, Seventh Week in Ordinary Time
Mark 9:30–37

There is always room for healthy and respectful argument, even when it comes to matters of faith. The world of faith is the world of mystery and so there is great scope for lively exchanges. Such exchanges or arguments, when they are respectful and display a listening attitude, can bring everyone closer to the truth. There are other kinds of arguments that do not serve our faith well, especially when they are driven by the need to promote ourselves. This is the kind of argument that the disciples were having in today's gospel reading. They had listened to Jesus proclaim the presence of God's kingdom, and they were arguing as to which of them would be the greatest in that kingdom. It was an argument about status and identity. In response to this misplaced argument, Jesus not only says something but does something. In what has been called an acted parable, he takes a child, sets the child in front of his disciples, and says to them that anyone who welcomes one such child in his name, with his unconditional love, will be the greatest in the kingdom. In that culture, a child was just above the position of a slave on the social ladder. The child was a symbol of lowliness and powerlessness. Jesus says to his disciples and to us that the truly great in God's eyes are those who show concern for the weakest and most vulnerable in the community. Furthermore, Jesus identifies himself completely with the child, the symbol of those without status. 'Anyone who welcomes one of these little children … welcomes me.' The journey from seeking status towards serving the Lord in the most vulnerable is one we all have to keep on making.

26 February, Ash Wednesday
Matthew 6:1–6, 16–18

Almsgiving, prayer and fasting, which Jesus comments on in today's gospel reading, have been described as the three pillars of Lent. They are practices that are deeply rooted in the Jewish tradition. Jesus affirms their value in today's gospel reading, but he warns against engaging in these practices in a way that draws attention to ourselves. What seems like something virtuous can be very self-serving in reality. The Gospels show that Jesus himself fasted, prayed and engaged in various forms of almsgiving or self-giving service of others. Of the three practices, fasting can seem the most negative. Fasting is a saying 'no' to something. Prayer is a saying 'yes' to God, to the Lord. Almsgiving is a saying 'yes' to others and, for us believers, a saying 'yes' to the Lord present in others. Yet there is nothing essentially negative about fasting or self-denial. If it is a saying 'no' to something, that 'no' is always in the service of our saying a more generous 'yes' to the Lord in prayer and to others in almsgiving. Pope Francis has said the following about fasting or self-denial, 'Lent is a fitting time for self-denial; we would do well to ask ourselves what we can give up in order to help and enrich others by our poverty. Let us not forget that real poverty hurts; no self-denial is real without this dimension of penance.' Pope Francis sees self-denial or fasting as in the service of our helping and enriching others, or what we might call almsgiving. Fasting also serves our prayer, as Jesus showed by his forty days in the wilderness. There is always that other-centred dimension to our fasting and self-denial, whether the other is God directly, as in prayer, or God present in others, as in almsgiving. Lent is a time to reflect on how we might take up these three practices of almsgiving, prayer and fasting, so as to grow more fully into our baptismal calling. We take ashes on this Ash Wednesday as a sign of our desire and our commitment to grow in our response to the Lord's calling by means of these three great Lenten pillars.

27 February, Thursday after Ash Wednesday
Luke 9:22–25

There wasn't a strong belief in the afterlife during most of the period when the Jewish Scriptures were written. As a result, it was very important to live in a way that enhanced one's earthly life. The question was, 'How do we live in such a way that we become fully alive as human beings here and now?' That is the focus of today's first reading from the Book of Deuteronomy. The author puts before the people two ways, the way that leads to death and the way that leads to fullness of life in the present. The call of the reading, as of much of the Jewish Scriptures, is 'Choose life'. In the mindset of those Scriptures, and of the first reading, choosing life means choosing God, loving the Lord our God and following God's ways, commandments and laws. Because we are made in the image of God and belong to God, the path of life is the path that God sets before us in his commandments. Jesus understood himself to be the path that God sets before us. If God's path was to be found in the laws and commandments of the Jewish Scriptures, it is to be found more fully in his life and teaching. Choosing life now means following Jesus, taking him as our way and our truth, thereby finding life, both in the here and now and beyond this earthly life. That is the message of today's gospel reading. Jesus declares that those who follow him will gain life; they will preserve their very self. If the first reading calls on us to love God by keeping his commandments, the gospel reading calls on us to love Jesus by following him. In that gospel reading, Jesus recognises that following him, loving him faithfully, will often mean renouncing ourselves, which to some can look like renouncing life. However, he assures us that those who renounce themselves out of love for him will find life in the here and now and, more completely, in eternity.

28 February, Friday after Ash Wednesday
Matthew 9:14–15

In today's gospel reading, Jesus affirms the value of the Jewish practice of fasting. 'The time will come for the bridegroom to be taken away from them, and then they will fast.' Jesus is looking ahead to the time after his death and resurrection. He declares that, beyond that time, fasting will be appropriate for his disciples, but not during his public ministry, which is equivalent to the joy of a wedding feast. In today's first reading, Isaiah declares that fasting must be in the service of just relationships with others. He speaks of a fast that breaks unjust fetters, that leads to sharing our bread with the hungry and sheltering the homeless poor. Fasting can seem like something negative, a saying 'no' to something that can be good in itself, but the prophet reminds us that this 'no' is always in the service of a more generous 'yes' to the Lord and his people, especially his most vulnerable people. We deny ourselves so that others can live more fully. We have become more aware in recent times that we need to say 'no' to others, to fast, so that our natural environment can also live more fully. Pope Francis reminds us of our responsibility to our environment in his wonderful encyclical *Laudato Si'*. We deny ourselves not only for the sake of others but for the sake of our natural environment. The pope expresses this bond we have with all of creation very beautifully in that encyclical: 'Everything is related, and we human beings are united as brothers and sisters on a wonderful pilgrimage, woven together by the love God has for each of his creatures, and which also unites us in fond affection with brother sun, sister moon, brother river and mother earth.'

29 February, Saturday after Ash Wednesday
Luke 5:27–32

Tax collectors were unpopular in the time of Jesus. They collected taxes on behalf of Rome, the occupying power, and they had a reputation for enriching themselves at other people's expense. Even though they were reasonably wealthy, they were marginalised among the people, and this made them a special object of Jesus' attention. Jesus' calling a tax collector to be among his followers is an indication of the inclusive nature of the community he gathered around himself. There was a home here for those who normally felt ostracised. Jesus' call empowered Levi to leave his wealth. He sensed that in following

Jesus and joining his band of disciples he would find a different kind of wealth. He immediately used some of his remaining resources to put on a meal for Jesus and other tax collectors to celebrate this new beginning in his life. The Lord continues to call each one of us, regardless of where we are on our life's journey. We don't have to get ourselves somewhere for the Lord to call us. He calls us as he finds us. He doesn't wait for us to be 'well', in the language of today's gospel reading, before calling us. In that sense, when it comes to the Lord, we are always 'on call'. While calling us as we are, he will always call us beyond where we are. In calling us, he also empowers us to go where he is calling us. If we allow ourselves to keep responding to the Lord's loving call, we too are entitled to throw the occasional celebratory meal.

2 March, Monday, First Week of Lent

Matthew 25:31–46

It was Saint John of the Cross who said, 'in the evening of life, we will be judged on love alone'. This is a very succinct commentary on today's gospel reading. The setting is the coming of the Son of Man at the end of time, and what really matters to this kingly figure is how well we have loved or failed to love, understanding love as practical action on behalf of those in greatest need. Yet the really striking thing about this gospel reading is that that this kingly figure, who has the power to assemble all the nations before him, identifies completely with the least powerful in society, the hungry, the thirsty, the stranger, the naked, the sick and the imprisoned. In serving those in greatest need, people were serving him without realising it; in failing to serve them, they were failing to serve him without realising it. We are being reminded that every act of love for another human being brings us directly in touch with the Lord of heaven and earth. When we get into the nitty-gritty of journeying with others in their need, we are really walking on holy ground. In the weakest and most vulnerable we are coming face to face with the King of Kings and Lord of Lords. Today's gospel reading almost combines in one the two great commandments, love of God and love of neighbour. In loving our broken and suffering neighbour, we are loving the Lord, and, as Saint John of the Cross says, it is such love that will matter most in the Lord's eyes at the end of time, and at the end of our own earthly lives.

3 March, Tuesday, First Week of Lent
Matthew 6:7–15

We are very familiar with today's gospel reading, because we pray most of it every time we come to Mass and probably at other times too. It is clear from the Gospels that Jesus was a man of prayer, who often went off to some lonely place to pray. He was a prayerful person. It is not surprising then that some of his teaching, as we find it in the Gospels, relates to prayer, how to pray. It is only in today's gospel reading from Matthew, and its corresponding passage in Luke, that Jesus' teaching on prayer consists of an actual prayer. Jesus was teaching us a prayer, and, also, a way to pray. 'Pray like this' – here is a prayer and an approach to prayer. What does this prayer teach us about how to approach prayer, how to pray? It begins, as all prayer needs to, with a focus on God. The first three petitions relate directly to God: 'your name … your kingdom … your will'. We recognise that what God wants takes priority over what we want. The second part of the prayer teaches us to bring our needs rather than our wants to God. It is not just my needs that are to feature in our prayer but the needs of all God's people, all humanity: 'us … we … our'. Every day we need food to nourish not only our bodies, but also our souls. Each day we stand in need of God's forgiveness, just as we need to pass on that forgiveness to others. Every day we need the Lord's help to prevent us giving in to the temptation of evil or the evil one. The prayer

Jesus gives us invites us to come before God in prayer out of a strong awareness of these basic needs.

4 March, Wednesday, First Week of Lent
Luke 11:29–32

In today's gospel reading, Jesus declares of himself that he is greater than Solomon and greater than Jonah. We could add to that list – greater than Abraham, greater than Moses, greater than Isaiah or Jeremiah. Jesus is greater than all the leading figures of the Jewish Scriptures because he has a closer relationship with God than all who went before him. We express his close relationship with God by saying that Jesus is the Son of God. Jesus' relationship with God is unique to himself, yet he came into the world to draw us all into his own very close relationship with God. He pours his Spirit, the Holy Spirit, into our hearts, so that we, like him, can call God 'Abba, Father'. Through the Holy Spirit, we become brothers and sisters of Jesus; we come to share in his own intimate relationship with God. Our calling is to live out of that relationship, to live as brothers and sisters of Jesus, as sons and daughters of God. The season of Lent is a time to live that calling more fully. Rather than looking for signs, like the people in the gospel reading, we are called to be living signs of Jesus, the Son of God, in the world.

5 March, Thursday, First Week of Lent
Matthew 7:7–12

Saint Augustine wrote in his Confessions, 'You have made us for yourself, O Lord, and our hearts are restless until they rest in you'. Augustine had come to realise that the inner restlessness that drove him down all sorts of avenues in his younger years could only be calmed by God. All our seeking and searching is ultimately a search for God, who alone can satisfy our deepest yearnings. One of the ways we give expression to those deep yearnings for God is prayer.

Prayer is an outlet for our restless hearts, our searching spirits. At the beginning of today's gospel reading, Jesus speaks of prayer in the language of searching, asking and knocking. He acknowledges that our longing for God, our desire for God's attention, God's love, finds privileged expression in prayer. He also assures us that if we give expression to our searching spirits in prayer, we will not ultimately be disappointed. 'It will be given to you … you will find … the door will be opened to you.' Jesus is not saying that whatever we ask for in prayer we will get. He is saying that God the Father will give what the gospel reading calls 'good things' to those who seek God in prayer. Our prayer will serve us well at the deepest level of our being. When we focus our restless spirit on God, as we do in prayer, we open ourselves up to the good that God wants to give us. In prayer we always discover that we are graced by God, in a way that anticipates that full and final grace or good that awaits us in eternity.

6 March, Friday, First Week of Lent
Matthew 5:20–26
In his teaching, Jesus often shows a concern about human behaviour, what we do and what we fail to do. However, he is equally concerned about the wellspring of human behaviour, the inner emotions, attitudes and values that shape our behaviour. We find this concern in today's gospel reading. Jesus cites the Jewish law in relation to the most destructive form of human behaviour: 'You shall not kill'. He then goes beneath such destructive behaviour to the emotion that often underlies it. 'Anyone who is angry with his brother will answer for it.' The first murder in the Bible is the murder of Abel by his brother Cain. According to the book of Genesis, Abel's murder was motivated by anger. 'Cain was very angry … and rose up against his brother Abel, and killed him.' Jesus was aware of the destructive power of anger from the story of his own people. The Gospels suggest that Jesus

himself was angry at times; anger in itself is not morally wrong. On one occasion, Jesus was angry with his disciples because they tried to prevent parents from bringing their children to Jesus for him to bless them. 'When Jesus saw this, he was indignant.' Jesus went on to give an important teaching about children's entitlement to the riches of God's kingdom. Here is an example of anger being channelled in a way that is beneficial for others. Many people's commitment to working for justice is motivated by an anger at the injustices being done to others. Anger can be a force for good, but Jesus was well aware that it can be, and more often than not is, a force for harm. We all need to be reflective about our anger. We acknowledge it and we ask the Lord to help us to use its energy in a way that is life-giving for others.

7 March, Saturday, First Week of Lent
Matthew 5:43–48
If we hear that such and such a person is a perfectionist, it can conjure up in our minds someone who is very demanding and rather fussy about getting everything right, down to the last detail. When Jesus says at the end of today's gospel reading, 'Be perfect just as your heavenly Father is perfect', that is not what he means. The corresponding passage in Luke's Gospel is almost word for word the same as the passage from Matthew, which is today's gospel reading. Yet it is striking that in Luke the gospel passage ends with Jesus saying, 'Be compassionate as your heavenly Father is compassionate'. Luke has captured there what Jesus meant by 'Be perfect as your heavenly Father is perfect'. In today's gospel reading, being perfect is identified with being loving to an extraordinary degree, loving our enemy, praying for those who persecute us, who make life difficult for us. Being perfect consists in loving in the way that God loves, which is with a love that doesn't discriminate on the basis of how people relate to us. This is the pinnacle of Jesus' teaching in the Sermon on the

Mount. The fact that Jesus asks us to love as God loves suggests that he does not consider this call unrealistic. We will not be able to love in this divine way on our own, but we can do so with God's help. As Jesus will say to his disciples later on in Matthew's Gospel, 'For God, all things are possible'. The love that Jesus calls for is the fruit of the Holy Spirit in our lives. We look to the Holy Spirit to kindle the fire of God's love in our hearts.

9 March, Monday, Second Week of Lent

Luke 6:36–38

The last line in today's gospel reading is quite thought-provoking. 'The amount you measure out is the amount you will be given back.' Normally, we would think that the more we measure out of something, the less of it we will have. However, in the logic of the kingdom of God, the opposite is the case – the more we measure out, the more we will have. Jesus seems to be saying that the more generous we are with what God has given us, the more we will experience God's generosity. It is not that God waits to see how generous we are before deciding how generous to be with us. God desires to be extravagantly generous with us all. However, just as the amount of water we can draw from a tank depends on the capacity of the container we use, in a similar way, the amount of God's generous love we can draw on depends on our capacity to receive it. The more generous we are with others in love, the more we expand our capacity to receive God's love. In the words of Jesus in the gospel reading, 'Give and there will be gifts for you'. The giving that expands our capacity to receive from God can take various forms, according to the gospel reading. It can take the form of a readiness to be merciful or compassionate towards others, or a willingness not to judge or condemn others too quickly. Whatever form our giving to others in love takes, Jesus assures us that we will be the richer for it.

10 March, Tuesday, Second Week of Lent

Matthew 23:1–12

It is evident that the Church, since its earliest days, has not taken some of the words of Jesus in today's gospel reading literally. Jesus calls on his disciples not to allow themselves to be called teachers, since they have only one Teacher, the Christ. We have no difficulty in referring to those who teach, including those who teach the faith, as teachers. Jesus also calls on his disciples not to call anyone on earth their father, since they have only one Father, in heaven. Again, we have no difficulty to referring to male parents of children as fathers, and within the Roman Catholic tradition, priests are often referred to as 'father'. It is likewise the case that the teaching of Jesus elsewhere in the Gospels has not been taken literally by his followers. However, that is not to say that Jesus' words are without relevance and meaning for us today. There is a sense in which we have only one teacher, Jesus, and we have only one Father in heaven. Because Jesus is our one Teacher, we, his followers, are all his pupils, including those of us who might be teachers. We all look to him to teach us about God and about how God wants us to live. Jesus speaks in the Gospels with an authority that no earthly teacher has. Because God is our one Father, we, Jesus' disciples, are all sons and daughters of God. We share in Jesus' own relationship with God as Father, and, as a result, we are all brothers and sisters of Jesus. Regardless of our role or position in life or in the Church, we are all equally privileged to call God our Father and Jesus our brother. We were given this privilege at baptism through the power of the Holy Spirit. This shared privilege makes very relative whatever distinctions of role exist between us within the Church.

11 March, Wednesday, Second Week of Lent

Matthew 20:17–28

We often find in the Jewish Scriptures that when believers are in some dire situation they address an agonising question to God. One such example is to be found in today's first reading. In response to those who are plotting his downfall, Jeremiah asks God, 'Should evil be returned for good?' Although, in theory, we would answer 'no' to Jeremiah's question, in practice we are all aware that evil is often returned for good. Jesus exemplifies that sad reality of life more than anyone. He was God's goodness personified, yet he suffered the evil of crucifixion. In the gospel reading, Jesus attempts to get his disciples to face this prospect. 'The Son of Man is about to be handed over to the chief priests and scribes. They will condemn him to death … .' Yet the remainder of the gospel reading shows that the disciples could not imagine that evil would be returned for good, in the case of Jesus, or themselves, as his followers. James and John express their desire, through their mother, for a significant share of the presumed reward that God would give Jesus for his goodness. The other ten were probably of a similar mindset. Jesus' response to this preoccupation is sobering for his disciples, and for the Church today. Goodness itself is to be the concern of his disciples, not the reward for goodness. Jesus understands goodness here in terms of the loving service of others, after the example of the Son of Man who came not to be served but to serve. The focus of Jesus' disciples, the Church, is to embody in the here and now his self-emptying service of others. The reward for such goodness is a matter for God the Father.

12 March, Thursday, Second Week of Lent

Luke 16:19–31

The story Jesus tells sets up a sharp contrast between someone who is extraordinarily rich and someone who is desperately impoverished.

The rich man wears purple, the most expensive clothing of the time; he feasts magnificently, not just occasionally, but every day. The poor man's plight is as desperate as the rich man's condition is sumptuous. He is starving, with nothing to eat; he is seriously ill, his body covered in sores; the only solace he gets is from the dogs who lick his wounds. Here is a rich man who is totally self-indulgent, so absorbed in satisfying his own needs that he pays no attention to Lazarus, whom he must have passed on a regular basis as he lay at his gate. In the afterlife, God gives to Lazarus what he was denied in this life. Lazarus is in the bosom of Abraham; he is reclining on the breast of Abraham at the banquet of eternal life. The rich man has been refused entry to this banquet and can only look on in frustrated longing. God provided for Lazarus in the end, but it is clear that he wanted him to be provided for in this life. As Jesus states at the end of the reading, those who listen to Moses and the prophets should know this. We who listen not only to Moses and the prophets but to the teaching of Jesus certainly know this. God calls on us to provide for each other. If we have an abundance, we are to share from it with those in greatest need. This is an aspect of the Gospel message that Pope Francis has been emphasising since he became pope. None of us may be as wealthy as the rich man or as destitute as Lazarus, but we all have something we can give to those whose need is greater than ours. The parable may be suggesting that our giving begins with noticing, paying attention.

13 March, Friday, Second Week of Lent
Matthew 21:33–43, 45–46

In the parable that Jesus speaks in today's gospel reading, he would have recognised himself in the son of the vineyard owner who was killed by the tenants when he came to collect the produce of the vineyard. In his comment on the parable, where he quotes one of the psalms, Jesus would also have recognised himself in the reference to 'the stone rejected by the builders'. However, whereas the killing of the vineyard's son clearly refers to Jesus' death, the reference to the stone hints at Jesus' resurrection as well, because the stone rejected by the builders went on to become the keystone of the building. In the same way Jesus, who was rejected in the most violent way imaginable, was raised from the dead by God the Father and became the keystone of a new spiritual building, the Church. God brought great good out of the tragedy of Jesus' death, not just for Jesus but for all who turn to him in faith. God saw to it that the rejection and death of his Son did not have the last word. God worked in and through that dark moment in human history for the good of all, including the good of those responsible for the death of his Son. That is how God and his Son, now risen Lord, continue to work today. In places of great darkness and death, the Lord is always working in a life-giving, life-affirming way, and that is true of our own personal lives, of the life of the Church and of the life of the human race. Our calling is to recognise the ways in which the Lord is working for life, even at the heart of darkness, and to cooperate with this divine work.

14 March, Saturday, Second Week of Lent

Luke 15:1–5, 11–32

The traditional title for the story we have just heard is the parable of the prodigal son. Yet there are three characters in this story and the primary character is really the father. The story might better be called the parable of the compassionate father. It is the story of the passionate love of a father for his two sons. The father is certainly not slow to express his emotions in public towards his two sons. He runs towards his lost younger son as soon as he sees him on the horizon. Then, full of compassion, he clasps him in his arms, kissing him tenderly and orders a feast for him. He then has to leave the feast, which really required his presence, to plead with his older, angry son, addressing him tenderly as 'my son', assuring him that he is loved just as much as his rebellious younger brother, calling him in from the cold to join the feast. If the younger son reminds us of those who were judged to be 'sinners' with whom Jesus shared table, the older son reminds us of the Pharisees who stood in judgement on Jesus and on those with whom he shared table. Jesus is saying that God loves both groups equally –those who find themselves judged by others and those who stand in judgement on others – with the same passion and desire. God's passionate love does not discriminate; it goes out to all equally. Yet the parable suggests that we can find ourselves standing outside the embrace of God's love, like the elder son. The parable has an open ending; we are not told if the older son went in and joined the feast in response to his father's loving plea. There is a sense in which we have to write the conclusion of the parable with our own lives, by allowing ourselves to be found by God, who never gives up searching for us in love.

16 March, Monday, Third Week of Lent
Luke 4:24–30

There is no shortage of angry people in today's two readings. In the first reading, the king of Israel was angry when he received a letter about Naaman, the Syrian army commander, asking that he be cured of his leprosy. Naaman became angry when the prophet Elisha asked him to bathe seven times in the River Jordan. In the gospel reading the people of Nazareth were enraged when Jesus drew attention to how God had cured the pagan Naaman of his leprosy through the prophet Elisha, and fed a pagan woman from Sidon through the prophet Elijah. In none of the three instances was the anger really justified. We can all find ourselves getting angry for no good reason. The people of Nazareth were angry because Jesus was implying that the God of Israel cared just as much about the people beyond Israel as he did about the people of Israel itself. They didn't really want to hear this. They had their own comfortable understanding of God as the God of Israel, his favourite people, his chosen people. The God whom Jesus had come to reveal made them feel uncomfortable because it challenged their narrowness and parochialism. God is always bigger than our understanding of God, and, rather than being resentful like the people of Nazareth, we can be very grateful that God is always more generous, more embracing, more forgiving, than we could ever imagine. God's ways are not ours and God's thoughts are not ours, and that is ultimately very reassuring and comforting.

17 March, Tuesday, Feast of Saint Patrick
Matthew 13:24–32

Today we celebrate the feast of the missionary who was the first to preach the Gospel in large parts of Ireland. Two of his writings have survived. It is nothing short of a miracle that these two texts have come down to us through the turmoil of history. They allow us to hear the voice of Patrick in our own time. We must be grateful to Patrick for sharing something of his story with us, and to the scribes who made copies of the texts down through the centuries.

There is great humility in these two texts. Patrick recognises his imperfections. He says in his Confession, 'I am imperfect in many ways'. Looking back on his youth he writes that 'we had turned away from God and had not kept the commandments'. He goes on to declare, 'I did not believe in the living God … I remained in death and unbelief'. It was the experience of captivity that opened him up to God. He says that in the land of his captivity, he was 'seized by an awareness of God's presence'. Patrick seems to have come from a very privileged background. When all that was taken from him, he became sensitive to God's presence. He expresses this religious awakening with a very striking image: 'Before my humiliation, I was like a stone lying deep in mire; and the Mighty One came and in his mercy … raised me up and placed me on top of a wall'. Having been living in a kind of spiritual death, he was now raised to a new life in God. His spiritual awakening was an experience of God as Love. He writes in his Confession that 'the love of God surrounded me more and more and my faith and reverence towards God was strengthened and my spirit was moved so much that in a single day I would pray as many as a hundred times'. He was so deeply touched by God's love for him that he had a deep desire to communicate with God in prayer.

However, it is clear from his writings that this period of rejoicing in God's love did not stay with him every day ever after. He is very open about the times when his faith was put to the test. Some time after he escaped from captivity and before he arrived at his home, he endured a great assault on his relationship with God. He speaks of this experience using very vivid imagery: 'While I was sleeping, Satan assailed me violently, which I will remember as long as I am in this body. He came down upon me like a huge rock, so that none of my limbs could move.' Elsewhere he writes, 'There is a strong force which strives every day to subvert me from the faith'. He knew the darker side of faith and, also, the presence of Christ as light in the midst of the darkness.

Some time after returning home from captivity, Patrick heard the voice of the Irish calling to him to leave his home once more and return among them as a free man, as a messenger of the Lord. 'We beg you, O holy youth, to come and walk once more among us.' His subsequent mission among the Irish bore great fruit, yet it is evident from his writings that he suffered a great deal in the exercise of that mission. One of the most painful experiences was when a senior member of the Church tried to undermine his ministry by drawing attention to some sin of his youth. He writes that 'on that day I was hit so hard I could have fallen here and forever', yet he managed to keep going because, as he writes, 'the Lord … boldly came to my assistance in this trampling, as a result of which I did not fall apart badly even though shame and blame fell upon me'.

His accusers were made aware of some deed from his past, in the language of the gospel reading, and, on that basis they were prepared to undermine all the good he was doing. Patrick was very aware that he was a mixture of wheat and darnel, yet he also knew that the Lord loved him and was working powerfully through him, flawed though he was. One of the messages Jesus is giving us in that parable is that the attempt to root out evil may destroy the good as well. There is a mixture of good and evil, of virtue and sin, in each one of us and in the Church as a whole. Patrick's story teaches us that the existence of evil is not a cause for disillusionment. If we acknowledge it and open ourselves to the Lord's love in our weakness, he can strengthen what is good in us and empower us to be his messengers in the world.

18 March, Wednesday, Third Week of Lent
Matthew 5:17–19
It is clear from today's first reading that the people of Israel did not consider their laws and commandments as primarily a burden. Rather, they contain 'wisdom and understanding' that is the envy of the nations. Furthermore, according to the reading, such laws and commandments put before people a path that leads to life. In the gospel reading, therefore, it is not surprising that Jesus declares that he has not come to abolish the Jewish law but to complete it. Jesus was always open to the good in every situation. Rather than abolishing something because it was less than perfect, he worked to bring the good that was there to completion. Jesus recognised the life-giving quality of many of the laws and commandments of his people. His attitude to the Jewish law is reflected in his attitude to people. Rather than condemning people because they had failed in some way to live up to their calling, he saw the good in them and worked to

bring it to perfection. There is a lesson for all of us in Jesus' way of relating to other people and to institutions like the Jewish law. Our intolerance of imperfection can blind us to the good that is also there. Our calling is to recognise the good wherever it is to be found, even when it is hidden or clouded by other realities, and, having recognised the good, to call it forth by our loving attentiveness.

19 March, Thursday, Feast of Saint Joseph
Luke 2:41–52

In the first reading, Saint Paul refers to Abraham as 'the father of all of us'. For Paul, Abraham was the father of all believers because he was a man of faith who trusted in God's word of promise. Just as the Jewish people look back to Abraham as their father in faith, so too can we who believe in Jesus. Today, we celebrate the feast of Saint Joseph. As a man of faith, deeply rooted in the Jewish tradition, he certainly would have looked to Abraham as his father in faith. Joseph was unique among the spiritual children of Abraham in being the father of Jesus, whose relationship with God was of a different order from Abraham's relationship with God. According to the Gospels, Jesus was known as 'the carpenter's son'. There are many titles for Jesus in the gospels and in the rest of the New Testament, but 'the carpenter's son' is, perhaps, the most human. Joseph provided for Mary and his son Jesus by working as a carpenter in Nazareth. He helped to provide a stable home for the young Jesus, where he could grow in 'wisdom and in stature and in favour with God and people', according to the Gospels. Joseph seems to have died before Jesus began his public ministry, because he never features in the story of Jesus' public adult life in the Gospels. By the time Jesus began his public ministry, Joseph's work was done. Luke suggests that Mary lived on at least until the feast of Pentecost, when the Holy Spirit came down upon her and the disciples. Joseph reminds us that the Lord has some work for all of us to do. Very often, our work, like Joseph's, consists in creating a space for God to work in the life of someone else. That work will often involve a letting go of others, a letting be. That is what we find Joseph being called to do in today's gospel reading. He had to let Jesus go to God the Father's work in the life of his young son. Today's gospel reading suggests that this was a struggle for Joseph and Mary, at times. When Jesus said to Mary and Joseph, 'I must be busy with my Father's affairs', meaning God, not Joseph, 'they did not understand what he meant'. Yet, in the end, Joseph did the work that God asked him to do, a work no one else could have done. He encourages us to relate to others, including those closest to us, in ways that allow God's purpose for them to come to pass.

20 March, Friday, Third Week of Lent
Mark 12:28–34

There are times in our lives when we all struggle to get our priorities right. We can find ourselves putting our time and energy into what is not so important. In today's gospel reading, a Jewish scribe, an expert in the Jewish law, asked Jesus to help him find what was most important in the Jewish law. Which of all the many commandments that were to be found in the Jewish law did Jesus think should be given priority? Jesus' answer to that question was both simple and profound. God was to be given priority. That is why Jesus began his answer with the basic Jewish creed, 'The Lord your God is the one Lord'. Then Jesus declared that in the way we relate to God, love is to be given priority, a love that springs from our whole being, our heart, our understanding, our strength. God and the love of God are to be our first priority. However, there is a second priority, which needs to be mentioned in the same breath as the first priority, and that is love of neighbour as if the neighbour were an extension of ourselves. In many ways, that second priority is less contentious today. Even those who have no religious faith can proclaim this priority of love of neighbour. It is the first priority that people are less convinced about today. We hear much less about love of God than about love of neighbour in most of the settings in which we live and move. Jesus' answer to the question of the scribe is a challenge to that absence. Jesus reminds us that only God is worthy of our total love, a love that proceeds from the whole person. What God requires of humans, Jesus suggests, is consonant with God's own nature, which is love.

21 March, Saturday, Third Week of Lent
Luke 18:9–14

The young people of our parishes who are making their confirmation soon are celebrating the sacrament of penance these days in prepara-tion. In the short liturgical service during which they come to confes-sion, today's gospel reading is proclaimed. It is a very suitable gos-pel reading as a preparation for confession. In the parable Jesus told, both the Pharisee and the tax collector prayed. The Pharisee prayed a prayer of thanksgiving and the tax collector a prayer of petition. Both forms of prayer are very valid; it is good both to ask God for what we need and to thank God for all he has given us. What completely undermined the value of the Pharisee's prayer was his lack of love for a fellow worshipper. The Pharisee looked down on the tax collector as a sinner. The Pharisee presumed that his own relationship with God was of a much higher order than the tax collector's. He seems to have had no awareness that his judgemental attitude towards a fellow worshipper significantly damaged his relationship with God. The tax collector, in contrast, did not judge the Pharisee. He judged only him-self: 'God, be merciful to me, a sinner'. The humble recognition that his relationship with God was not all it could be created the opening for God to restore that relationship. The one who prayed as if he were closer to God than others went home at odds with God, whereas the one who prayed out of his awareness that he was at odds with God went home reconciled to God. God is always working to draw us to himself. What God needs from us is the attitude of the tax collector, a humble, contrite heart that refrains from judging others and trusts in God's mercy.

23 March, Monday, Fourth Week of Lent
John 4:43–54

Today's gospel reading puts before us the anguished prayer of a parent on behalf of his seriously ill child, 'Come down before my child dies'. It is a prayer that would resonate with every parent who has known the anguish of a seriously ill child. The prayer of the father is not answered in the way he wanted it to be answered. Jesus did not go down with him to his home. Instead, he instructed the father to go home on his own and promised him that his son would live. The father was being asked to trust the Lord's promise to him. He set off home, without Jesus, but trusting in Jesus' word of promise. His journey home was a journey of hopeful faith. In that sense, he represents us all. We are all called to journey in hopeful faith on the basis of Jesus' word of promise, a word that promises life. Jesus promises that those who believe in him will pass from death to life. We will experience the fullness of this promise only beyond this earthly life, yet, along the way, we can begin to experience the beginnings of the fulfilment of this promise, just as the father, when he arrived home, found that his son had recovered. The Lord who will bring new life out of our own personal death also works in a life-giving way in our lives during our earthly pilgrimage. That is why we are called to keep walking in hopeful faith in response to the Lord's word, like the father in today's gospel reading.

24 March, Tuesday, Fourth Week of Lent

John 5:1–3, 5–16

Jesus' question to the paralysed man in today's gospel reading may strike us as strange. 'Do you want to be well again?' Surely it goes without saying that he wanted to be well again. However, his illness had lasted thirty-eight years; perhaps the long years of fruitless waiting may have extinguished his hope of ever being healed, and, with it, the desire to be healed. The question was probing whether the man who was paralysed in body was also paralysed in spirit. His answer to Jesus' question suggests a certain lack of hope of ever being healed. 'I have no one to put me into the pool when the water is disturbed.' Yet his answer revealed some desire to be healed, and in response to that faint desire the Lord cures the man with a word, 'Get up ... and walk'. The Lord is always seeking to engage with our desire. The opening words of Jesus in John's Gospel, from which we are reading this week, takes the form of a question addressed to the disciples of John the Baptist.'What are you looking for?' In other words, 'What is your desire?' The Lord's coming among us, his presence to us, is assured, but his coming will only be life-giving for us if it meets with our desire for his coming. Elsewhere in the Gospels Jesus says, 'Seek and you will find'. If we keep entering into and acting out of our deep-seated desire for the Lord and for the life that he brings, then the Lord's presence will be truly life-giving for us.

25 March, Wednesday, Feast of the Annunciation

Luke 1:26–38

Mary's question in today's gospel reading, 'How can this come about?', is a very human one. It is the kind of question that is asked by others in the Gospels. When Jesus was with his disciples in the wilderness in the presence of a hungry crowd, they asked him, 'How can one feed these people with bread here in the desert?' When we stand before a situation which seems beyond our resources to deal with, we all find ourselves asking the same kind of question, 'How can this be?' 'How will I get through this?' The angel Gabriel's answer to Mary's question invited her to trust not in herself but in God. 'The Holy Spirit will come upon you and the power of the Most High will overshadow you.' A lot was being asked of Mary and it would make great demands on her, but she was not being asked to take on this task of being mother to God's Son on the basis of her own resources alone. With this reassurance, she surrendered to the demanding task that God was giving her. 'Let what you have said be done to me.' Mary has often been described as a model disciple. In today's gospel reading, she models a faith that trusts in God's power and, because it trusts in God's power, stands ready to do what God asks. The question, 'How can this be?' can inhibit us, hold us back, but, as in the case of Mary, it can also open us up to the working of the Holy Spirit within us and through us.

26 March, Thursday, Fourth Week of Lent

John 5:31–47

Most of us are aware of our need for human approval. If people approve of us we sense that we are worthwhile. If people do not approve of us we can easily begin to doubt our self-worth. The saying of Jesus in today's gospel is, to that extent, true to human experience. 'You look to one another for approval.' Very few of us could make our own the sentiment of Jesus in today's gospel reading, 'As for human approval, this means nothing to me'. Human approval means something to all of us and, sometimes, it can come to mean a great deal. In speaking in this way, Jesus is trying to highlight a more fundamental approval than human approval, and that is the approval that comes from God. When Jesus says to his opponents, who were already intent on killing him, that 'you look to one another for approval', he immediately goes on to say, 'You are not concerned with the approval that comes from the one God.' If they were concerned with God's approval, they would not be intent on killing Jesus who reveals God to us. Jesus suggests in today's gospel reading that a more important question than, 'Do people approve?' is 'Does God approve?' At the end of the day, it is God we are seeking to please rather than other people. Like Jesus, we are to put God's will before the will of others. The life and, especially, the death of Jesus clearly show that the lack of human approval can sometimes go hand in hand with God's unreserved approval.

27 March, Friday, Fourth Week of Lent

John 7:1–2, 10, 25–30

Occasionally, we can claim to know more than we actually know. We are not humble enough in our knowing. We fail to recognise our ignorance about some issue or some person, as well as our knowledge. What we know is only a fraction of what can be known, and that is the case with every human person and every human situation. It is even more the case with matters of faith, with what pertains to God and to his Son, Jesus. In that domain above all, it is true that, in the words of Paul's first letter to the Corinthians, 'Now I know only in part'. In today's gospel reading, the people of Jerusalem declare concerning Jesus, 'we all know where he comes from'. They were saying that they all know that Jesus comes from Nazareth, yet at a deeper level they did not know where Jesus really came from. In that gospel reading, Jesus goes on to state, 'There is one who sent me, and I really come from him, and you do not know him'. Jesus ultimately came from God his Father and not from Nazareth. The people of Jerusalem who are suspicious of him do not know God and, in that sense, do not know where Jesus came from, in spite of their claims to know. Today's gospel reminds us that when it comes to God and his Son Jesus, we will always be learners. There is always more to him than we realise. We constantly need the Lord to teach us. Later on in John's Gospel, from which today's gospel reading comes, Jesus promises to send us the Spirit of Truth who will guide us into all the truth. If we are to come to know the Lord more fully we need to keep praying, 'Come Holy Spirit, come Spirit of Truth'.

28 March, Saturday, Fourth Week of Lent
John 7:40–52

We hear a lot about peer pressure today. Young people especially seem quite susceptible to peer pressure in various ways. If something is not considered 'cool' by their peers it can be very difficult for them to take it on. When it comes to acknowledging one's faith and witnessing to it, peer pressure often works against young people. It is not easy for young people to witness to their faith in any kind of public way. That is why we all have to support those young people who are trying to do so, whether it is our young readers, our young Eucharistic ministers, the members of our youth choir. They need role models to help them resist the kind of peer pressure that mocks their faith. We all need such models. There is one such model in today's gospel reading, Nicodemus. His peers, his fellow Pharisees, had already made up their minds about Jesus. He was leading people astray. Nicodemus, who was a prominent member of the Pharisees, challenged his peers. 'Surely the Law does not allow us to pass judgment on a man without giving him a hearing and discovering what he is about?' He was saying to his fellow Pharisees, 'Don't prejudge Jesus. Give him a hearing'. Nicodemus had already come to Jesus by night and had engaged Jesus in serious conversation. Like many a person who goes against his or her peers, Nicodemus incurred the disdain of his fellow teachers of the law. 'Are you a Galilean too?' We need plenty of people like Nicodemus today who are prepared to risk isolation because of their faith, even if it is only an emerging faith, as was the case with Nicodemus. Indeed, we all need to have something of his courage and integrity today.

30 March, Monday, Fifth Week of Lent
John 8:1–11

The men who brought the woman to Jesus saw her only in terms of her immediate past, while being blind to their own past. Jesus' way of looking at her was very different; he saw the whole picture of her life, not just one little bit of it. Seeing the whole picture of her life, he also saw that she had a future as well as a past, a future that those who brought her to him would have denied her. When the Lord looks at us he sees the whole picture too; he does not become obsessed with one or two dark details of the picture. The Lord is attentive to the full story of our lives, not just to a couple of lines of that story. He also knows that the story of our lives is always an unfinished story. It is the Lord himself who will endeavour to write the final chapter of that story when, in the words of Paul's letter to the Philippians, he will come from heaven to transfigure our lowly bodies into copies of his own glorious body. Speaking through the prophet Jeremiah, the Lord says, 'I know the plans I have for you, plans for your welfare and not for harm, to give you a future full of hope'. The Lord offered the woman, and offers all of us, a 'future full of hope'. He can offer us such a future because, again in the words of Paul, 'his power at work within is able to accomplish abundantly far more than all we can ask or imagine'. We need something of the Lord's hopeful vision when we look upon ourselves and others.

31 March, Tuesday, Fifth Week of Lent
John 8:21–30

In the gospel reading the Pharisees with whom Jesus is in conversation ask him the question, 'Who are you?' It is the question of people who are puzzled by this mysterious person and who want to understand him better. In a sense it is the question of each one of us. We never fully grasp Jesus in this life. We never get a full answer to the question 'Who are you?' As a result, we have to keep on asking it. In his response to that question, Jesus goes on to say, 'When you have lifted up the Son of Man, then you will know that I am he'. In speaking of his being lifted up, Jesus is looking ahead to the moment when he will be lifted up on the cross, and lifted up in glory. It is then, Jesus seems to be saying, that he will reveal himself fully. When he appears to be at his weakest on the cross, Jesus will reveal himself as the one in whom God is present and powerfully at work. It is above all when we look upon Jesus crucified, in the light of the resurrection, that we will hear the clearest answer to the question 'Who are you?' The answer we hear is, 'This is God's love made flesh; here is the God who so loved the world that he gave his only Son'. Next week is Holy Week. It is a good week to carry in our hearts that question addressed to Jesus, 'Who are you?' It is a good week to listen to the answer to that question that comes to us as we contemplate the passion and death of Jesus in the light of his resurrection.

1 April, Wednesday, Fifth Week of Lent

John 8:31–42

We have all been trying to come to terms with some painful truths about our Church in the past while. The revelations of clerical child sex abuse and the failure of Church authorities to deal with this scandal have been very distressing for all believers who value and love the Church. In today's gospel reading Jesus declares that 'the truth will make you free'. Facing the truth is often painful but it can be liberating. What is sometimes put out as the truth is not always the full truth. One particular slant on an issue can easily be presented as the full truth. Full truth does not come our way easily; we have to keep on seeking after truth in its fullness. Indeed, in some sense full truth is always beyond us, yet it is in honestly striving for truth that we attain as much of it as is humanly possible. In seeking the truth, we will be drawn to the person of Jesus because, as he declares in John's Gospel, 'I am the truth.' In today's reading from John's Gospel Jesus states that if we make his word our home, we will learn the truth. The call to seek the truth is a call, ultimately, to grow in our relationship with Jesus. That is a call we all need to heed in these times. In so far as we grow in our relationship with the Lord, who is truth personified, we will begin to experience what Saint Paul in his letter to the Romans calls the glorious freedom of the children of God.

2 April, Thursday, Fifth Week of Lent
John 8:51–59
In today's gospel reading Jesus says that he does not seek his own glory but that his glory is conferred by his Father. In the culture of Jesus, seeking glory, honour and renown for oneself was a very important value. In this regard, as in so many other ways, Jesus stood against the culture. He did not seek glory for himself but he trusted in God to give him glory in God's own time. He was critical of those who sought glory from others, who looked for earthly honours. In today's gospel reading Jesus says in relation to God who sent him into the world, 'I faithfully keep his word'. This was the driving force of Jesus' life, not seeking glory for himself from others. He knew that if he faithfully kept God's word, he would receive glory from God. The driving force of Jesus' life is to be the driving force of all of our lives. Our primary desire as Jesus' followers is to faithfully keep God's word, as it finds expression in the message and life of Jesus. If we keep trying to be faithful to God's word, as spoken and lived by Jesus, then we are assured that we will receive glory

from God; we will be honoured by God. Today's gospel reading declares that this is the only glory and honour worth having.

3 April, Friday, Fifth Week of Lent
John 10:31–42

In today's gospel reading, Jesus risks being stoned because of the claims he makes about himself. 'You are only a man and you claim to be God,' they said. As followers of the risen Lord, we recognise that claim to be true. Jesus goes on to say of himself, 'I am the Son of God ... the Father is in me and I am in the Father'. In the teeth of the deadly hostility of his opponents, Jesus makes an unequivocal claim to have a unique relationship with God, such that whoever sees him sees God, the Father. The author of the Fourth Gospel puts it very simply when he writes that the Word who was God became flesh, became enfleshed Word. Jesus, in other words, is God in human form. That conviction is at the core of our Christian faith. Jesus is the revelation of God, and because of that, in the words of the gospel reading, the good works that he does are the work of the Father. God is doing God's work through Jesus. God will always be something of a mystery to us, but Jesus has unveiled that mystery to a great extent. Jesus has revealed that the mystery of God is, ultimately, the mystery of Love. In the words of the first letter of Saint John, 'God is Love'. In the words of the gospel, 'God so loved the world that he gave his only Son.' That is the wonderful mystery that we will be remembering and celebrating this coming Holy Week.

4 April, Saturday, Fifth Week of Lent
John 11:45–56

Pragmatism is a quality that is often admired in political leaders. In today's gospel reading we have an example of a rather deadly form of political pragmatism. Caiaphas, the high priest, was both a religious and a political leader of the Jews. He declares to the members of the Jewish ruling council, 'It is better for one man to die for the people, than for the whole nation to be destroyed.' Jesus is threatening the status quo, therefore he needs to be eliminated. This particular individual is expendable for the sake of the nation as a whole. That outlook of considering one individual as expendable for the sake of the perceived good of the majority is not unique to the time and place of Jesus; it has always been around and is still around. It is the opposite to the outlook of Jesus. For Jesus the individual was everything. Jesus is the good shepherd who calls his own by name and seeks for the one who is lost; he called Lazarus from the tomb by name; he called Zacchaeus down from his tree by name; he called Mary Magdalene outside the empty tomb by name. The individual was of infinite value to Jesus. The Lord calls each of us by name; we are each precious in his sight. He also wants us to call on him by name, just as the good thief did on the cross, when he prayed, 'Jesus, remember me'.

6 April, Monday in Holy Week

John 12:1–11

The week during which Jesus is to suffer so much begins with a friend's act of kindness towards him. In the previous chapter the evangelist had said that Jesus loved Mary and Martha and Lazarus. This was a family to whom Jesus was close and who gave him hospitality and support. In thanksgiving for delivering their brother from death, the two sisters, Mary and Martha, put on a dinner for Jesus. Mary showed her appreciation of Jesus in a very dramatic way. She anointed his feet with very costly ointment and then dried them with her hair. It was a gesture Jesus valued greatly; he recognised it as an anointing in preparation for his coming death. He was being strengthened by this gesture of love and appreciation for the ordeal that faced him. Judas, in contrast, devalued Mary's action, accusing her of wasting money that could have been given to the poor. Unlike Mary, Judas would not be a support to Jesus in his hour of need; on the contrary, he would betray Jesus. We all need support when we are vulnerable and facing down a difficult road. Mary models for us the kind of attentive love that can be a light in someone's darkness. We can anoint people by our attentive and caring presence at a time when everything is stacked against them. The Jesus of Holy Week, the suffering Son of Man, comes to us in many guises, and it is Mary, rather than Judas, who shows us how to respond to his presence.

7 April, Tuesday in Holy Week
John 13:21–33, 36–38

Today's gospel reading from John comes immediately after Jesus washed the feet of his disciples. He washed all of their feet, including the feet of Judas Iscariot. Jesus loved his disciples until the end and his love showed no discrimination. The gospel reading goes on to portray Jesus as showing Judas a special sign of affection. For a host to take a morsel of food and dip it in the sauce and give it to one of the guests was a gesture of honour and affection in that culture. Jesus' final outreach of love to Judas, enacted in the gift of the morsel, is rebuffed. On receiving the morsel, Judas promptly leaves the company of Jesus and the other disciples and goes out into the darkness of the night. The evangelist is implying that Jesus' love for Judas was never in doubt, yet he seemed helpless before the freedom of Judas to refuse his love. The Lord's love for us is never in doubt, but he can never force our loving response. Yet even Judas' dark deed would serve God's greater purpose, rooted in God's love for the world. That is why, when Judas left the room, Jesus could exclaim, 'Now has the Son of Man been glorified, and in him God has been glorified.' We are being reminded that even our failings can somehow serve God's purpose of drawing all people to himself through his Son. Even when, like Judas, we head out into the darkness, God's light is not extinguished. The light of God's love continues to shine and to pursue us.

8 April, Wednesday in Holy Week
Matthew 26:14–25

Today's gospel reading is a section of Matthew's account of the last supper that Jesus had with his disciples on the night before his crucifixion. In the equivalent passage in Mark's Gospel, after Jesus makes the dramatic announcement, 'one of you is about to betray me', the disciples ask Jesus one by one, 'Not I, surely?' In Matthew's version the question the disciples ask has a subtle difference. 'Not I, Lord, surely?' 'Lord' is how the early Church came to confess Jesus. By adding 'Lord' to the question of the disciples, Matthew is encouraging the members of his own church to ask that question for themselves. Only in Matthew does Judas alone then ask the question, 'Not I, Rabbi, surely?' It is as if Matthew will not allow the title 'Lord' to be spoken by Judas, the one who betrayed Jesus. We can all ask the question, 'Not I, Lord, surely?' Like the other eleven disciples, and unlike Judas, we have not taken steps deliberately to betray Jesus. Our presence at the Eucharist indicates that we have a desire to be his faithful disciples. We are people of faith, and yet we are aware that we are not always as faithful as we could be. We often show ourselves to be disciples of 'little faith'. The question, 'Not I, Lord, surely?' expresses both our faith in Jesus as 'Lord' and our awareness that we do not always live in ways that proclaim his lordship. Like Peter, we can sometimes deny the Lord by what we say and do, yet the message of this Holy Week is that, in the words of Saint Paul, 'if we are faithless, he remains faithful'. The conviction of the Lord's faithful love encourages us to keep returning to him, knowing that, in the words of today's responsorial psalm, 'the Lord listens to the needy'.

EASTER TRIDUUM, 9–11 APRIL

13 April, Easter Monday
Matthew 28:8–15

Today's gospel reading falls into two very distinct parts, each part standing in contrast to the other. The first part is full of the joy of Easter. Having heard the message from the empty tomb that Jesus is risen, the women are filled with awe and great joy. Their joy is deepened when the risen Lord himself meets them and commissions them to share the good news, the Gospel, with Jesus' brothers and sisters, his disciples. We have a sense of a joy that is ever expanding, beyond the circle of the women, to the wider circle of the disciples, and beyond them to that much wider circle of all those who will become the Lord's disciples. We all belong in that wider circle and we are invited to taste the joy of the good news of Easter this Easter Monday. The second part of the gospel reading has a much more sombre tone. There is a conspiracy to suppress the good news of Easter by spreading a false story, that Jesus' body was, in reality, stolen. Just as money had been used to procure Jesus' betrayal, it is used again to promote this lie. The second half of the gospel reading reminds us that there are always forces at work to suppress the Easter story, because this story is so significant and so much depends on it. Easter placed God's seal of approval on all that Jesus said and did. In raising Jesus from the dead, God raised up all that Jesus stood for. To suppress the Easter story is to suppress the whole story of Jesus from his conception to his death. We are all asked to keep bearing witness to the Easter story even in the face of those who try to suppress it. We are to keep bearing witness to all that Jesus stood for, to his attitudes and values, and we are to keep announcing God's power to transform all our tombs into places of new life.

14 April, Easter Tuesday

John 20:11–18

In the gospel reading, the risen Lord asks Mary two questions: 'Woman, why are you weeping? Who are you looking for?' Mary was weeping because she could not find Jesus, for whom she was looking. Some of the sadness in our lives comes from a sense of loss, an awareness of unfulfilled longing. We have probably all known that particular form of sadness. We long for something or someone, and because that longing goes unfulfilled, we experience a sense of deep sadness. In the gospel reading, Mary's longing for Jesus was satisfied. The risen Lord spoke her name, and her sadness was banished as she clung to him. Yet, even in that moment of great joy, she had to learn to let go of Jesus as she had come to know him. Because Jesus was returning to the Father, from now on he would relate to her and to all of his disciples in a new way. He would be as close to her and his disciples as he ever was, indeed even closer, but in a different way. The gospel reading assures us that, even if many of our longings go unsatisfied, our longing for the Lord, which is our deepest longing, will always be satisfied. The risen Lord speaks our name as he spoke Mary's name. Because of his death and resurrection, his Father is now our Father and his God is now our God. In journeying from this world to the Father, Jesus draws us into his own relationship with God, thereby making us his brothers and sisters, and brothers and sisters of each other. If we open our lives to him and search for him as Mary did, we will come to experience a deep communion with him and with each other.

15 April, Easter Wednesday

Luke 24:13–35

Like the disciples on the road to Emmaus, we are not always aware of the risen Lord's presence to us. These disciples were so absorbed by their own grief at the death of Jesus and by their disappointed hopes that they struggled to see any other reality. When some misfortune overtakes us, it is often difficult to see beyond it. It can come to define our past, present and future. The risen Lord joined the two disciples to help them to see beyond the tragedy they were struggling to come to terms with. He is constantly working in our lives to help us to see further and deeper to the signs of new life that are often present where only death seems to feature. Having listened to the sad story of the disciples, the risen Lord tells them a bigger and more hopeful story from the Scriptures, a story that did not end in death but in glory. We all need to expose our own stories, especially our sad and tragic stories, to the bigger, hopeful, life-affirming story of the Scriptures, especially the Easter story contained therein. Exposure to that bigger story made an immediate impact on the disciples. Reflecting subsequently, they could say, 'Did not our hearts burn within us as he talked to us on the road and explained the Scriptures to us?' They were already beginning to look beyond their own sad story. It was only when the stranger took, blessed, broke and gave bread to them at the table that their eyes were fully opened and they saw with Easter eyes. The Lord who is present to us through his word, is even more powerfully present to us through the Eucharist. It is above all in the setting of the Eucharist that the Lord works to open our eyes, so that we see the story of our lives in the light of the good news story of the Lord's faithful love for us.

16 April, Easter Thursday

Luke 24:35–48

Luke's account of the appearance of the risen Lord to his disciples in today's gospel reading suggests that the disciples had great difficulty believing that it was the same Jesus they had come to know and love and had been crucified who was now standing before them. The gospel reading says that 'in a state of alarm and fright, they thought they were seeing a ghost', and that 'their joy was so great that they still could not believe it, and they stood there dumbfounded'. It seems that it took the disciples a while to take in and believe the good news of Easter. They had been so traumatised by what had happened a few days earlier that they struggled to believe that Jesus was alive with a powerful new life. There is indeed something extraordinary about the good news of Easter. Even today we struggle to take it in, to really believe it. We often find it easier to identify with Jesus' death than with his resurrection. In our religious tradition images of the crucifixion are more common than images of the resurrection. We can easily connect with the suffering Jesus because of the suffering in our own lives. Like the disciples in the gospel reading we stand before the good news of Easter dumbfounded, struggling to believe. Perhaps that is why the Church gives us seven weeks of the Easter season to take it all in. We need time to recognise that the risen Lord is indeed standing among us, saying to us what he said to his disciples in the gospel reading, 'Peace be with you'. He offers us that peace of mind and heart which is the fruit of his love poured into our hearts through the Holy Spirit. As we allow ourselves to receive this gift of his reconciling love, he sends us out as agents of reconciliation, as his peacemakers, just as he sent out the disciples in the gospel reading.

17 April, Easter Friday
John 21:1–14

John's Gospel draws heavily on the imagery of light and darkness. Only four verses into the gospel we have that ringing declaration, 'The light shines in the darkness, and the darkness did not overcome it.' That image of light and darkness is there in today's gospel reading. The disciples are out on the Sea of Tiberias, fishing at night, in the darkness. After the disaster of Golgotha, they have gone back to their former occupation, yet they seem to have lost their touch. In the darkness of night, they catch nothing, they labour to no avail. Their professional failure on this occasion harks back to their personal failure during the passion of Jesus when they showed themselves unfaithful to him in various ways. The dark night of failure is something we have all experienced in different ways at different times in our lives. Yet, with the coming of the dawn, Jesus stands on the shore, although the disciples do not recognise him at first; the light is shining in the darkness. In response to the word of this stranger, the disciples cast their nets again and this time they catch a huge number of fish. The word of the Lord brings light into their darkness, and their labour bears rich fruit. We are reminded of an earlier saying of Jesus in John's Gospel: 'Those who abide in me and I in them bear much fruit, because apart from me you can do nothing.' Today's gospel reading proclaims that the Lord's light always shines in our darkness, whatever form that darkness takes. We are being assured that our failures need not have the last word. The Lord remains in communion with us, and if we seek to be in communion with him and are open to his word, he will work powerfully to bring new life out of our failures.

18 April, Easter Saturday
Mark 16:9–15

There is a striking contrast between the way that the disciples are portrayed in today's gospel reading and how they are portrayed in the first reading. In the gospel reading the disciples refused to believe Mary Magdalene and the two disciples who had left Jerusalem for Emmaus when these three people told them that Jesus was alive and had appeared to them. When Jesus himself appeared to his disbelieving disciples, he rebuked them for their refusal to believe those who had who had borne witness to his resurrection. In spite of their initial failure to believe, Jesus commissions them to go out and proclaim the good news of Easter to all creation. That is precisely what we find the disciples doing in the first reading. From being people who refused to believe the Easter Gospel, we now find them proclaiming that Gospel with conviction and with great courage. The religious leaders in Jerusalem forbade them to preach the Gospel of Jesus but the disciples, uneducated as they were, stood up to them and declared to them that they cannot stop proclaiming what they have seen and heard. The disciples are a living sign of how people can change through the power of the risen Lord. Jesus was transformed through his resurrection from the dead and he had a transforming effect on others. The same risen Lord can have a transforming effect on all of us. If we are open to his presence, he can do for us what he did for the disciples, transforming our doubt and disbelief into a faith that is public and courageous.

20 April, Monday, Second Week of Easter
John 3:1–8

Nicodemus, who features in today's gospel reading, was very much at home in his own Jewish tradition. He is described as a 'Pharisee' and a 'leading Jew', yet he is also a seeker after truth. He is not so settled in his own tradition that he doesn't continue to keep seeking God, so as to come to know him more fully. It is his searching spirit that brings him to Jesus under cover of darkness. Nicodemus can speak to the searcher in each of us. Even though we may be basically at home in our own religious tradition, our Catholic faith in our case, God is always beyond us. In that sense we are always seeking after God, striving to know God more fully and to love God more deeply. For us this involves seeking out Jesus, as Nicodemus did, because we believe Jesus to be God in human form, the enfleshed Word. There will always be an element of unease about our faith, some restlessness that moves us to keep seeking the Lord. As people of faith, we are always on a journey, a pilgrimage. We never arrive at our destination in this earthly life. When Nicodemus sought out Jesus, Jesus called him to take a step he had never taken before, to allow himself to be born from above, to be born of the Spirit. Jesus is always calling us too to take some new step on our faith journey. This step will always entail for us, as it did for Nicodemus, a greater surrender to the movement of the Holy Spirit in our lives.

21 April, Tuesday, Second Week of Easter
John 3:7–15

In today's gospel reading, Jesus speaks about the wind, a phenomenon of nature we are very familiar with in Ireland. He says, 'The wind blows where it pleases'. The wind is beyond our control; it doesn't blow where and when we want it to blow. We can harness the wind to some good purpose, but we are never in control of it. Jesus often spoke about day-to-day realities, like the wind, as a way of talking about more spiritual realities. In today's gospel, in speaking about the wind, he is, in reality, speaking about the Holy Spirit. 'This is how it is with all who are born of the Spirit.' In the language Jesus spoke, and in the language the Gospels were written in, the same word could mean either 'wind' or 'spirit'. Jesus seems to be saying to Nicodemus and to us that the Spirit of God is not something we can control. We do not take the Spirit where we want it to go; the Spirit takes us where God wants us to go. All we can do is to surrender to the breath of the Spirit within us and around us, to allow the Spirit to direct us and to lead us. Like a flag blowing in the wind, we are to move in response to the movement of the Spirit. Yet, whereas a flag has no choice but to blow with the wind, we have to decide whether or not to surrender to the movement of the Spirit. The spiritual person is the person whose life is shaped and directed by the Spirit. We are all called to be spiritual people in that sense. Discerning where the Holy Spirit is leading us and surrendering to that leading is central to our lives as followers of Jesus.

22 April, Wednesday, Second Week of Easter
John 3:16–21

A common security measure in many homes and businesses are strong lights that come on at night when somebody comes within a certain radius. It is based on the presumption that light is the enemy of anyone who might want to break into the premises. Those who might be up to no good prefer the cover of darkness. In the words of today's gospel reading, 'everybody who does wrong hates the light and avoids it, for fear his actions should be exposed'. Light exposes wrongdoing. In a sense, it condemns the wrongdoer. According to the gospel reading, God did not send his Son into the world to condemn the world. Jesus speaks of himself in this gospel as 'the light of the world'. When the gospel reading says that 'the light has come into the world', the reference is clearly to Jesus. Yet the light of Jesus is not primarily a condemnatory light whose primary purpose is to expose evil. The light of Jesus is a light of love, the light of God who so loved the world that he gave his only Son. When we step into this light, there is a sense in which our sins are exposed. To see ourselves in the light of Jesus is to recognise how far we fall short of the person God has created us to be. Yet the primary purpose of this loving light is to take away our sin. Jesus, the light of God, seeks to draw us to himself so that we may have life and have it to the full. The Lord's light is not in any way threatening. There is a fullness of life there from which we are all invited to receive.

23 April, Thursday, Second Week of Easter

John 3:31–36

In today's gospel reading, we are given words spoken by John the Baptist. In the verse just before this gospel reading begins, John the Baptist had said of Jesus, 'He must increase, but I must decrease'. He then goes on to speak of Jesus, in the opening line of today's gospel reading, as 'the one who comes from above' and who, therefore, 'is above all others'. John was very aware that Jesus was above him. He goes on to say of Jesus that he 'comes from heaven', that 'the Father gives Jesus the Spirit without reserve', that the Father 'has entrusted everything to the Son'. John was very aware that none of those things could be said about himself. He had a profound appreciation of the uniqueness of Jesus, which is why he could say, 'He must increase, but I must decrease'. There is a sense in which we never fully appreciate the uniqueness, the specialness, of Jesus in this life. The more we see of Jesus, the more we recognise what is yet to be seen. The closer we come to him, the more we realise how much deeper our relationship with him could be. There is always a sense in which we can say, with John the Baptist, 'he must increase' and 'I must decrease'. As he increases in us and we decrease, we don't cease to be ourselves. Rather, the more Jesus increases in us, the more we become our true selves, our Christ selves, the selves God is calling us to be.

24 April, Friday, Second Week of Easter

John 6:1–15

When we are faced with a challenge or a problem, the way we speak about it can be very important. We can speak about it in a way that deflates us and drains us of energy or we can speak about it in a way that makes us hopeful and inspires us. In today's gospel reading, Jesus sees crowds coming towards him. Seeing that they were in need of food, he asked Philip where food could be bought to give them something to eat. Philip's response to Jesus showed that he felt overwhelmed by the problem. The words he used were very defeatist. 'Two hundred denarii would only buy enough to give them a small piece each.' When Andrew chimed in, he too spoke in a way that conveyed a kind of hopelessness. Noticing that there was one small boy with five barley loaves and two fish, he asked, 'What is that between so many?' However, the way Jesus spoke in response to the problem was much more inspirational. He gave instructions to the disciples, he prayed aloud to God, and somehow the crowd got fed with the young boy's small fare. We can all be a little bit like the disciples before the challenges that life throws up. We can become limp before it all. The gospel reading encourages us to remain hopeful even in the face of situations that seem very unpromising. The reading suggests that the Lord can work in surprising ways before challenges that seem daunting. Saint Paul seems to have a very strong sense of how the Lord can work powerfully in weakness. That is why he could say in his letter to the Philippians, written from prison, from a very unpromising situation, 'I can do all things through him who strengthens me.'

25 April, Saturday, Feast of Saint Mark
Mark 16:15–20

Mark wrote the first of the four Gospels. Even though Mark's Gospel is placed second in the New Testament, almost all scholars agree that it was the earliest gospel to be written. It is generally dated to around about the year 70. Very ancient tradition suggests that Mark's Gospel was written in Rome and that Mark was a disciple of Peter. That is why a reading from the first letter of Peter is read on Mark's feast day. This letter was certainly written from Rome. The conclusion of the letter, which is the conclusion of today's first reading, sends greetings from 'your sister in Babylon'. 'Babylon' is often a code for Rome in the New Testament. The Babylonians destroyed Jerusalem at the beginning of the sixth century BC, resulting in the Babylonian exile, and the Romans, the new Babylon, destroyed Jerusalem in AD70. 'Your sister in Babylon' is the church in Rome. I Peter appears to have been written from the church in Rome some time after the year 70. The letter also concludes with a greeting from 'my son Mark'. The author, Peter, is probably referring to Mark as his spiritual son, his follower in the faith. One of the features of Mark's Gospel is its very negative portrayal of Jesus' first disciples, including Peter. This gospel emphasises the failure of those who were closest to Jesus. They fail to understand who Jesus is and what he says; eventually, they all desert him, Judas betrays him and Peter denies him. Yet Mark's portrayal of the failure of the disciples serves as a foil for his portrayal of Jesus' faithfulness to them, in spite of all their weaknesses. In today's gospel reading, the risen Lord keeps faith with them, sending them out to proclaim the Gospel to the whole world. Mark is assuring all of us, his disciples today, that the risen Lord keeps faith with us, even when we let him down in various ways. The Lord's faithfulness to us prompts us to keep faith with the Lord, and with each other, especially with those who are close to us.

27 April, Monday, Third Week of Easter

John 6:22–29

In today's gospel reading, Jesus speaks of two kinds of food, food that cannot last and food that endures to eternal life. He challenges the crowd to reflect on their priorities. Are they working for food that cannot last or for food that endures to eternal life? Jesus takes seriously food that cannot last. He fed the hungry multitude in the wilderness with five loaves and two fish. The basis physical needs of people were very important for him. He fed the hungry, healed the sick, called on the rich to share with the poor. People's basic human physical needs had to be met first. However, when he has fed the physical hunger of the crowd, some of that crowd now want Jesus to give them more of the same. In response to this preoccupation with Jesus as the provider of physical bread, Jesus speaks of the food that he is offering which endures to eternal life. He is calling on those who have gone looking for him to attend to the deeper hunger in their lives, their spiritual hunger. Jesus presents himself as the one who can satisfy this spiritual hunger. That is why he equates working for the food that endures to eternal life with believing in him. Believing in him is the one work that is required if that deeper hunger in our lives is to be satisfied, the hunger for a love that is unconditional, for forgiveness, for truth, for justice, for peace, ultimately, our hunger for God. We cannot ignore our physical hunger. When we are hungry, we eat. We can ignore those deeper hungers, which Jesus alone can satisfy. This is why he draws attention so strongly in today's gospel to our need to work for the food that endures to eternal life.

28 April, Tuesday, Third Week of Easter
John 6:30–35

In today's gospel reading we find one of the great 'I am' statements attributed to Jesus in the Fourth Gospel. 'I am the bread of life. Whoever comes to me will never be hungry; whoever believes in me will never thirst.' The image of bread corresponds to that of hunger, but the reference to thirst is perhaps surprising in this context. The language of 'bread', 'hunger' and 'thirst' is clearly symbolic. Jesus is declaring that he alone can satisfy the deepest hunger and thirst of the human heart. In the next chapter of John's Gospel Jesus will say, 'Let anyone who is thirsty come to me, and let the one who believes in me drink.' The language of eating and drinking in this gospel are often symbolic of believing. Jesus is declaring that all who come to him and believe in him will find that their deepest spiritual hunger and thirst will be satisfied. He is stating that he is as essential to our spiritual lives as food and drink is to our physical lives. We are always aware of our physical hunger and thirst; we cannot ignore it. We try to eat and drink on a regular basis. The deeper, spiritual, hunger and thirst in our lives, while just as real, do not always reach the same level of awareness in us. We can much more easily neglect them. If we do so, there will be something seriously out of joint within us. Today's gospel reading invites us to attend to that deeper hunger and thirst and to recognise Jesus as the one who alone can satisfy them fully.

29 April, Wednesday, Feast of Saint Catherine of Siena
Matthew 11:25–30

When Jesus declares in today's gospel reading, 'My yoke is easy and my burden light', he is saying that his teaching, his understanding of God's will, is not something burdensome. Rather, his teaching is liberating and life-enhancing. If his teaching is received and lived, it lightens the burden of oppression; it brings joy. That is not to say that Jesus' teaching is not demanding. It is demanding but not burdensome. That is because Jesus does not ask us to live his teaching out of our own strength alone. He empowers us to live his teaching. In today's gospel reading, Jesus does not say, 'Come to my teaching', but 'Come to me'. He doesn't say, 'Learn my teaching', but 'Learn from me'. He calls us into a personal relationship with himself. Earlier in the gospel reading, Jesus spoke about the intimate relationship he has with God his Father. 'No one knows the Son except the Father, just as no one knows the Father except the Son.' Yet this is not a closed relationship. Jesus wants to share with each one of us his own very intimate relationship with God; he wants to draw us into his own personal relationship with God, his Father. He wants to reveal his Father to us, to share the love of the Father with us. 'Come to me,' Jesus says, 'and through me come to the Father.' It is in coming to him and his Father that we receive his Spirit, the Holy Spirit, and so are empowered to live his teaching and, thereby, to become fully alive as human beings and his joyful servants in the world. This twofold movement of coming to Jesus and going forth in his strength express-es well the contemplative and active dimension of the Christian life. We are called to be contemplatives in action, like Catherine of Siena. Catherine was a great mystic, or contemplative, but her mysticism did not withdraw her from the world. She was deeply involved in what was happening in Europe and in the Church in her time. Cath-erine stood out as a beacon of light at a dark time in Europe and in the Church. She was such a light because of her deeply personal and mystical relationship with Jesus.

30 April, Thursday, Third Week of Easter

John 6:44–51

When we hear in today's first reading of the road from Jerusalem to Gaza it is hard not to think of the strained and tension-filled relation-ship between Jerusalem and Gaza today. Yet the story we have just heard relating to that road is a good news story. The Ethiopian on this road is a seeker. He is reading the Jewish Scriptures, a section of the prophet Isaiah. When Philip, one of the deacons of the Church, joins him, he invites Philip to accompany him in his search and to throw light on what he is reading. The probing question he asks Philip about the text gives Philip an opening to speak to him about Jesus. Philip's proclaiming of the Gospel moves the Ethiopian to ask for baptism. When Philip leaves him, the Ethiopian goes on his journey rejoicing. The Ethiopian was searching, but he needed help from someone who was a little further down the road of faith than he himself was. The story is a reminder to us that we need each other on the journey of faith. We all have something to receive from someone else. In the gospel reading, Jesus declares that no one can come to him unless he is drawn by God the Father. Our coming to Jesus is always in response to the Father drawing us to his Son, yet the Father draws us to his Son in and through each other, just as God drew the Ethiopian to Jesus in and through Philip. Sometimes we may find ourselves in the role of the Ethiopian, seeking the Lord, needing someone like Philip to guide and lead us. At other times we may find ourselves in the role of Philip, helping someone to take a new step on their journey towards Jesus. If the Father is to draw us to his Son, we need to be ready both to receive from the faith of others and to give to others from our own faith.

1 May, Friday, Third Week of Easter

John 6:52–59

The story of Paul's transformation is one of the founding stories of our Christian faith. Here was a Pharisee who, on his own admission, was a zealous persecutor of the Church, yet the Lord managed to break through to him and completely turn his life around, so that the zealous persecutor became the equally zealous preacher of the Gospel to the Gentiles. As a Pharisee, Paul could never have envisaged the way he would spend the last thirty years of his life, but the Lord was able to envisage it. Paul's story reminds us that the Lord's plans for us may be a great deal bolder than what we might have in mind for ourselves. The Lord took Paul by surprise, and he can take any of us by surprise. Our calling is to allow the Lord's vision and purpose for our lives to become more of a reality. When we receive the Lord in the Eucharist we are opening ourselves up to the Lord's vision and purpose for our lives. As Jesus says in today's gospel reading, 'Whoever eats me will draw life from me'. In receiving the Lord in the Eucharist we give him the opportunity to shape us in the way he wants to. Paul met the Lord on the road to Damascus; we meet the Lord in the Eucharist. In coming to us there, he directs us to take the path he wants us to take, just as he directed Paul.

2 May, Saturday, Third Week of Easter
John 6:60–69

Today's gospel reading captures a moment of crisis for the followers of Jesus. Some of those who have already responded to the call of Jesus to follow him, to become his disciples, are now struggling to accept the claims he has been making for himself, in particular his claim to be the Bread of Life that has come down from heaven. In response, Jesus wonders aloud what they will make of his further claim to 'ascend to where he was before', to return to the Father through his forthcoming death and resurrection. Arising from this exchange, the evangelist tells us that 'many of his disciples left him and stopped going with him'. Jesus could not and would not hold on to disciples against their will. There will always be people who will leave the community of disciples, for a variety of reasons. We have all become aware of that phenomenon, in more recent years especially. We can all feel impoverished when those who have been part of our community of faith no longer wish to remain so. At this moment of crisis, Jesus took what might seem to us to be a risk. He asked those left behind, 'What about you? Do you want to go away too?' Jesus wanted them to stay but he needed them to want to stay. The question 'Do you want to go away too?' is addressed to us all and we each have to make our own personal response to it. It would be hard to find a more appropriate response to Jesus' question than the response of Peter, which we are invited to make our own at every Eucharist: 'Lord, to whom shall we go? You have the message of eternal life, and we believe, we know that you are the Holy One of God.'

4 May, Monday, Fourth Week of Easter
John 10:11–18

In John's Gospel Jesus often uses the phrase 'I am', and then adds some image to it. 'I am the bread of life'; 'I am the light of the world';

'I am the good shepherd'; 'I am the resurrection and the life'; 'I am the way, the truth and the life'; 'I am the vine.' Most of those images are drawn from day-to-day life: bread, light, shepherd, way, vine. It was as if Jesus was saying to people that what they encounter in the course of their ordinary lives can reveal something of himself, if looked at in a certain way. In today's gospel reading, Jesus uses another of these 'I am' images drawn from day-to-day life, when he says, 'I am the gate'. A locked gate keeps people out and can also keep people in. On the other hand, an open gate creates an opening that allows people to move freely in and out of an area. When Jesus said, 'I am the gate', he meant it in that second sense; he is the gate to a place or state. He says, 'Anyone who enters through me will be safe; they will go freely in and out and be sure of finding pasture'. He is the gate, the opening, towards fullness of life, towards God, the source of life, life in the here and now and life beyond this earthly life. If Jesus is the gate, our calling is to keep passing through him. At the end of our prayers, we often say, 'through Christ our Lord'. We are not only to pray through him, but we live through him as well. All of our life is to be through him, to the glory of God the Father.

5 May, Tuesday, Fourth Week of Easter

John 10:22–30

In today's gospel reading, Jesus speaks as the shepherd who will never allow any of his sheep to be stolen from him. Jesus invites us to imagine a shepherd who will stop at nothing to prevent any would-be thief from stealing even one sheep from his flock. It is an image that speaks to us of the Lord's determination to hold on to us and prevent us becoming separated from him. It is a consolation to know that the Lord is so devoted to us and so committed to our well-being and, in particular, our ultimate well-being, our eternal well-being. As Jesus says in that gospel reading, 'I give them eternal life.' Yet we are not just passive sheep. When it comes to the Lord's relationship with us, there is a role for us as well. The Lord will do all he can to hold on to us but we also have our part to play. In that gospel reading, Jesus declares that 'the sheep who belong to me listen to my voice ... they follow me'. The Lord is very attentive to us, but we need to attend to him as well. We try to listen to his voice, especially as it comes to us in the words of the Gospels, of the New Testament as a whole, and, indeed, in all of the Scriptures. There are many voices competing for our attention today, but in the midst of them all we need to be attentive to the voice of the Lord so that we can follow him each day. We listen to him, we follow him, in the confidence that his devotion to us and to our ultimate well-being is unconditional.

6 May, Wednesday, Fourth Week of Easter

John 12:44–50

In today's first reading, the Holy Spirit prompts the church in Antioch to send two of their leading and most gifted members, Paul and Barnabas, on mission. There might have been those in the church in Antioch at the time who said, 'No, we can't let two such key people leave. They are needed here.' As communities, as individuals, there is a natural temptation to hold on to what we have. We resist deliberately making ourselves poorer, yet that is what the Holy Spirit was asking the church in Antioch to do, to make itself poorer, to let go of two of its greatest assets, so that those who had never heard the Gospel might be brought to Christ. The ways of the Holy Spirit in the Church today are probably not very different from the ways of the Holy Spirit at the beginning of the Church. The Spirit prompts us to take the way of Jesus, which is the way of self-emptying love so that others might have life. In his second letter to the Corinthians, Paul declared, 'You know the grace of our Lord Jesus Christ who, though he was rich, yet for your sakes he became poor, so that by his poverty you might become rich.' In the gospel reading, Jesus speaks of God the Father as the one who sent him. God sent his most valuable gift to us, his only Son. Every sending to others of what is precious to us reflects something of that loving sending by God of his Son.

7 May, Thursday, Fourth Week of Easter
John 13:16–20
In the gospel reading, Jesus declares blessed or happy those who 'behave accordingly'. He was referring back to the action he had just performed in washing the feet of his disciples. This was an act of self-emptying service on the part of Jesus which symbolically anticipated his self-giving on the cross the following day. Such acts of service, Jesus declares, bring people true happiness. Most people are searching for happiness, but if happiness becomes the sole goal of our search it is often missed. Jesus suggests that happiness comes to those who seek something else. Happiness comes to those who seek to serve others, or, as Jesus declares elsewhere in the Gospels, it is in giving that we receive. The action of Jesus in washing the feet of his disciples suggests that our service of others is not to be dependent on how they relate to us. At the Last Supper, Jesus washed the feet of all his disciples, including Judas. He makes reference to Judas in the gospel reading. 'Someone who shares my table rebels against me.' Jesus washed the feet of the one who rebelled against him. As Jesus declares in Luke's Gospel, 'If you love those who love you, what credit is that to you?' Jesus gives expression to a much more self-emptying kind of love. He calls us to live in the same way and gives us the Holy Spirit to help us to love as he loves.

8 May, Friday, Fourth Week of Easter

John 14:1–6

Thomas is one of the disciples who features in the John's Gospel a couple of times. We associate him with the scene in that gospel where he refuses to believe the other disciples who announce to him that they have seen Jesus. He is clearly not afraid to speak his mind. He is portrayed in a somewhat similar way in today's gospel reading. When Jesus says to his disciples, 'You know the way to the place where I am going', Thomas pipes up, 'Lord, we do not know where you are going, so how can we know the way?' Jesus had just declared that he was going to his Father's house, where there were many rooms. On the night before he dies Jesus declares that he is on his way to the Father, from whom he came. This journey he is about to travel is a journey that is open to all his disciples. 'I shall return to take you with me.' His ultimate destination is also our ultimate destination, and the way to that destination is Jesus himself. 'I am the way.' One of the earliest terms for Christians was 'followers of the Way'. We are those who take Jesus as our Way. In taking Jesus as our Way, we will find truth and life, we will find God, both in this life and in eternity. Every day we try to orientate ourselves towards Jesus. Our daily calling is to keep taking Jesus as our Way. Thomas's question, 'How can we know the way?' is a valid one, but Jesus has answered that question with his statement, 'I am the way'.

9 May, Saturday, Fourth Week of Easter

John 14:7–14

It can be interesting to try and identify with the questions and the requests of the disciples in the gospels. In today's gospel reading we find Philip making a request of Jesus. 'Lord, let us see the Father and then we shall be satisfied.' What is it that really satisfies us? We can so easily go looking for satisfaction in the wrong places. We have huge longings in our hearts and we mistakenly think that something or someone can satisfy them. We pursue what we think will satisfy those longings only to be bitterly disappointed. Philip had the insight to recognise that only God can satisfy our deepest longings. 'Let us see the Father.' He turned to Jesus, trusting that Jesus could enable them to see God. Jesus' answer to Philip's request was very simple and very profound. 'To have seen me is to have seen the Father.' The first letter of John declares that beyond this life 'we shall see God as he is'. That is our ultimate destiny, to see God who is Love and in so doing to become like God, as loving as God is loving. John's Gospel declares that we can anticipate that vision of God in this life by seeing Jesus, who is God in human form. In seeing Jesus with the eyes of faith and in responding to him as the revelation of God's love, we are given a foretaste of that ultimate destiny that awaits us, when we will see God as he is and all our deepest longings are fully and finally satisfied.

11 May, Monday, Fifth Week of Easter
John 14:21–26

There has always been a human tendency to worship something less than God. A movement, an ideology, an institution or an individual can acquire an almost divine status that demands and sometimes receives a quality of allegiance that is due to God alone. Idolatry is the fundamental sin which is the root of other sins. The very attractiveness of some reality can be the catalyst for relating to it as godlike. In today's first reading, some people of Lycaonia came to the conclusion that Paul and Barnabas were gods because they had cured a cripple. They wanted to treat them as they did their other gods, offering sacrifice to them. Paul had to restrain them in no uncertain terms. 'What do you think you are doing? We are only human beings like you.' He wanted them to worship the living God who had been revealed in the person of Jesus, God's Son. The Lycaonians' zeal to worship Paul and Barnabas was unenlightened. They needed instruction on the folly of what they were doing. In the gospel reading, Jesus acknowledges our continuing need for instruction, for enlightenment. He declares to his disciples on the night of the Last Supper that beyond the time of his death and resurrection, his heavenly Father will send the Advocate, the Holy Spirit, to 'teach you everything and remind you of all I have said to you'. It is the Holy Spirit who keeps leading us to a deeper appreciation of Jesus as the face of the one, true God, and to a closer following of him. Just as the Spirit leads us to Jesus, Jesus leads us to the Father, the living and true God.

12 May, Tuesday, Fifth Week of Easter
John 14:27–31

The first reading begins with an example of the trials and tribulations Paul experienced in the course of his missionary work. Some people stoned him and dragged him outside their town, thinking he was dead. Paul was far from dead. He got up, went back to the town and the next day he set off for another town. There, Luke tells us, he 'put fresh heart into the disciples, encouraging them to persevere in the faith'. If most of us were treated the way Paul was, it would take the heart out of us. Paul, in contrast, was able to put fresh heart into others, shortly after his own dreadful treatment. In the gospel reading, Jesus announces to his disciples that 'the prince of this world is on his way'. This prince of darkness, working through human agents, would put Jesus on a Roman cross. Yet, even as this is about to transpire, Jesus is putting fresh heart into his fearful and troubled disciples, giving them the gift of his own peace, a peace the world cannot give. Both Paul and Jesus had a peace that, even in the face of great hostility and rejection, allowed them to bring peace and encouragement to others. This peace could only be of God. It was the fruit of their love for

God and their deep awareness of God's love for them. In the gospel reading, Jesus declares, 'I love the Father.' He will go on to say, 'The Father has loved me'. Jesus wants us to experience the same love of the Father through him. 'As the Father has loved me, so I have loved you.' In opening ourselves to this love, we too will know a peace the world cannot give, and we will become peacemakers, bringing fresh heart to those we meet.

13 May, Wednesday, Fifth Week of Easter
John 15:1–8

Those who have roses will know that they need to be pruned if you are to get the best out of them. What is true of roses is true of most plants; pruning brings on new life. Jesus refers to that procedure of pruning in today's gospel reading. He suggests that in various ways God prunes our lives to make them even more fruitful than they are. There are some things we may need to shed if we are to become all that God is calling us to be. Some experiences of letting go, which can be very painful at the time, can help us to grow in our relationship with God and with others. Yet during those painful experiences of pruning in our lives the Lord is in communion with us. In the words of the gospel reading, he makes his home in us, he remains in us. We don't have to face into that experience of being pruned on our own, or on the strength of our own resources alone. The Lord who makes his home in us will sustain us in those times, and will lead us through the painful experience of pruning into a new and more fruitful life, because, as he says in the gospel reading, it is to the glory of his Father that our lives bear much fruit, the rich fruit of the Spirit. However, to experience the Lord's sustaining and guiding presence, we need to remain in him as he remains in us; we need to keep in communion with him, as he is in communion with us.

14 May, Thursday, Feast of Saint Matthias

John 15:9–17

In today's first reading, the early Church meets to find a replacement for Judas, so that the group of twelve can be restored to its integrity. They engage in a process of discernment. They must select from among those who were with Jesus from the time of his baptism in the River Jordan to the time of his ascension into heaven. Having decided on two candidates, they bring both to the Lord in prayer, and they invite the Lord to show them which of the two he has chosen. As a result, Matthias came to replace Judas. The discernment process involved both work and prayer. In making this important decision the members of the early Church didn't leave everything to the Lord and, at the same time, they didn't take the whole process upon themselves alone. Their efforts to find a replacement for Judas were important, but the fruit of those efforts needed to be brought to prayer so that the Lord could have the final and most important say. Saint Augustine once wrote, 'Pray as though everything depended on God. Work as though everything depended on you.' This twofold movement of prayer and work is reflected in today's gospel reading. Jesus calls on us to remain in his love. The Lord's love for us is primary; we are to remain in that love, receiving it, welcoming it. This is the movement of prayer. Having remained in the Lord's love for us, we then go out and bear fruit that will last, by loving one another as the Lord has loved us. This is the work of love that we are to engage in, yet it is significant that Jesus first calls on us to remain in his love before calling on us to love one another as he has loved us. Our prayerful openness to the Lord's love is the foundation for the work of loving others as the Lord has loved us.

15 May, Friday, Fifth Week of Easter

John 15:12–17

In today's first reading we have a good example of how the members of the very early Church supported and built up one another. The church in Jerusalem sent a delegation to the church in Antioch with a letter to be read out. When this letter from the church in Jerusalem was read aloud, the reading says that the members of the church in Antioch 'were delighted with the encouragement it gave them'. The ministry of encouragement seems to have been a very important one in the early Church. In the earliest letter of Paul that has come down to us, his first letter to the Thessalonians, he twice says, 'encourage one another'. In the gospel reading, Jesus engages in that ministry of encouragement towards his own disciples. It is the night of the Last Supper and the disciples are fearful and troubled. Jesus encourages them; he assures them that his forthcoming death is an expression of his love for them. 'A man can have no greater love than to lay down his life for his friends.' He declares to them that he no longer calls them servants but, 'I call you friends'. He tells them that his choice of them is prior to and more fundamental than their choice of him. 'You did not choose me, no, I chose you.' Jesus not only encourages them in these ways, but he also calls on them to live from the grace of this encouragement. They are to love one another, as he has loved them, to befriend one another as he has befriended them, to encourage one another as he has encouraged them. The Lord encourages us so that we can encourage one another. We firstly need to open ourselves to the Lord's encouraging presence and in the strength of that grace go forth and encourage all that is good in each other.

16 May, Saturday, Fifth Week of Easter

John 15:18–21

Saint Patrick writes in his Confession that some time after he returned to Britain, having escaped from captivity in Ireland, he had a vision one night in which he saw a man named Victor who had come from Ireland with a large number of letters. In the vision this man gave Patrick one of the letters and Patrick read the opening words of the letter which were, 'the voice of the Irish'. At the same time, Patrick began to hear the voice of those who lived near where he had been held captive and they shouted, 'We ask you, boy, come and walk once more among us'. I was reminded of that section of Patrick's Confession by today's first reading. According to our reading, one night Paul had a vision while in Troas, which is in north-western Turkey. In that vision a Macedonian appeared and appealed to him, 'Come across to Macedonia and help us'. Macedonia is in northern Greece. Both Patrick and Paul responded to the calls they heard and as a result those who had never heard the Gospel came to know Christ. We are all called by the Lord to bring the Gospel to others; we are always trying to discern what that call might mean in concrete terms in our lives. In so far as we respond to the Lord's call to us, the lives of others will be greatly blessed. In the gospel reading, Jesus tells his disciples that they 'do not belong to the world'. The term 'world' here means the world in so far as it is hostile to Jesus. Yet Jesus called his disciples to proclaim the Gospel in that world. We too are called to proclaim the Gospel by our lives in a world that will often be hostile to it. We proclaim it in the conviction that the world needs to hear it.

18 May, Monday, Sixth Week of Easter

John 15:26–16:4

The question of Europe has been very much in the news for the last two years and more, mostly in the context of the United Kingdom leaving the European Union. In today's first reading, Paul crosses over from modern-day Turkey to modern-day Greece to preach the Gospel there for the first time. This could be seen as the coming of the Gospel to Europe. It is hard to know where Europe begins or ends today, but, in the time of Paul, Turkey would have been considered Asia. In crossing over to Greece, Paul first landed in Neapolis, which was the port of the city of Philippi. He then made his way to Philippi, the first European city in which the Gospel was preached. According to our reading, it was to a group of women in this city that Paul first preached the Gospel. One of them Lydia, was a dealer in purple cloth, the most expensive cloth at the time. She was clearly of woman of some means. When she and her household were baptised, she offered Paul accommodation in her house. Women were to the fore at the beginning of the Church in Europe, and, of course, they have remained to the fore in the Church in Europe ever since. In the gospel reading, Jesus warns his disciples that they will be expelled from synagogues and that anyone who kills them will think they are doing God's work. That prophecy certainly came true for Paul. He was expelled from synagogues; those who sought to kill him thought they were serving God. Yet Paul was the greatest witness to the risen Lord in the early Church; his missionary work bore rich fruit. We are being reminded that hostility to the Lord's message and values is no obstacle to the Lord's good work being done, provided we show some courage and rely on the Holy Spirit, whom Jesus refers to in the gospel reading as the 'Advocate', the one who comes to our defence.

19 May, Tuesday, Sixth Week of Easter
John 16:5–11

At the beginning of today's first reading, we find Paul and Silas singing God's praises even though they had been beaten and thrown into prison. None of us would find it easy to sing God's praises in such circumstances. It is more likely that a desperate prayer for help would come to our lips rather than a prayer of praise to God. Paul's prayer of praise in prison was a powerful witness to his conviction that God was stronger than the forces that had imprisoned him and Silas. If God had raised Jesus from the dead, God could rescue Paul from this seemingly hopeless situation. Indeed, at the end of the reading, Paul's jailer and his family respond to Paul's preaching of the Gospel and are baptised. Paul's jailer went on to become his host at a meal to celebrate the jailer and his family coming to faith in Jesus. It seems that the risen Lord can indeed work powerfully in the most unpromising of situations. This is also the message of Jesus in the gospel reading. His disciples are sad because on this night of the Last Supper Jesus has been speaking about going away and leaving them. All seems lost, yet Jesus assures them that his leaving them, his death, will create an opening for God to work in a new and life-giving way. The going of Jesus will make possible the coming of the Advocate, the Holy Spirit, and this Spirit of the risen Lord, working through the disciples, will demonstrate how wrong the world that rejected Jesus has been about the most fundamental realities, sin, goodness and judgement. Those who rejected Jesus thought Jesus was the sinner, that they were in the right and that Jesus was being judged. The Holy Spirit, who will flow from Jesus' death and resurrection, will demonstrate how misguided all these convictions are. We continue to trust that the Lord is working powerfully at those very times when we, his followers, seem to be at our most vulnerable and fragile.

20 May, Wednesday, Sixth Week of Easter
John 16:12–15

The gospels these days have a certain focus on the coming of the Paraclete and today's gospel reading is no exception. It is an appropriate focus as we approach the feast of Pentecost, which is Sunday week. In the gospel reading Jesus declares that the Holy Spirit will lead the disciples to the complete truth. A little earlier in John's Gospel Jesus had declared 'I am the truth'. He is the truth because he is the revelation of God and of God's purpose for our lives. One of the roles of the Spirit is to help us to enter more deeply into the rich mystery of the person of Jesus who is the truth. The Spirit helps us to know the truth, to know the Lord, not just with our heads but with our hearts. We tend to know best those whom we love. The Spirit works to deepen our loving friendship with the Lord, our love of the Lord, so that we come to know him in that deep sense, in the sense in which the Lord knows us, because he loves us. As we approach the feast of Pentecost, we ask the Spirit to renew our relationship, our friendship, with the Lord, and so lead us ever more closely to the complete truth.

21 May, Thursday, Sixth Week of Easter
John 16:16–20

When we are sorrowful or feeling low, it can be difficult to imagine a time when things will be better. We wonder if we will always be like this. We might even speak of not being able to see a light at the end of the tunnel. We are in a dark tunnel and it seems endless. In today's gospel reading, on the night of the Last Supper, Jesus tells his disciples, 'I tell you most solemnly, you will be weeping and wailing'. They would indeed weep and wail when Jesus was taken from them and put to death on a Roman cross. In the wake of Jesus' crucifixion, perhaps his disciples could see only bleak darkness without end. Yet, having spoken the hard truth to his disciples about the darkness that lies ahead, Jesus immediately says to them, 'Your sorrow will turn into joy.' Golgotha would give way to Easter Sunday morning, when their hearts would rejoice. We are in the season of Easter. Indeed, every day is an Easter day for us, regardless of the time of year, because the Lord is always risen. The risen Lord is always a light in our darkness. We don't need to look for a light at the end of the tunnel; there is always a light in any tunnel, the light of the risen Lord. Jesus once said, 'I am the light of the world. Whoever follows me will never walk in darkness but will have the light of life'. The light of the risen Lord often comes to us through others. Paul makes this discovery in today's first reading. He arrives in Corinth for the first time, a bustling, overpowering city, and he meets a Jewish Christian couple who immediately offer him hospitality. The Lord will not abandon us in our hour of need; he will touch our lives in one way or another. We just need an expectant and aware faith to notice his coming to us.

22 May, Friday, Sixth Week of Easter

John 16:20–23

In the gospel reading Jesus refers to the forthcoming weeping and wailing of his disciples. He speaks of their being sorrowful, of their sorrow. These are natural and unavoidable emotions in the face of loss. Jesus will soon be put to death. His disciples will be plunged into grief. We have all known the sadness and sorrow that Jesus speaks about. Everyone's grief is very personal to them. It is good to be able to name our grief, to acknowledge it to ourselves and others. Jesus names the disciples' grief. There can be no escaping the sorrow to come, yet Jesus also declares that their sorrow and weeping will not last indefinitely. It will turn to joy, because Jesus' death will give way to his resurrection. 'I shall see you again, and your hearts will be full of joy.' Their sorrow will pass. Sometimes when we are in the midst of great loss and sorrow we need to be able to say to ourselves, 'This sorrow too will pass'. This sorrow will not have the last word. As followers of a risen Lord, we can say that with a special conviction. Jesus' promise to his disciples, 'I will see you again', is addressed to each one of us. In times of loss and sorrow, the risen Lord sees us. He is present to us; the light of his risen presence shines upon us. He journeys with us through the valley of darkness. Even in the midst of sorrow, he helps us to find moments of joy, a sharing in his own risen joy.

23 May, Saturday, Sixth Week of Easter

John 16:23–28

At the end of today's gospel reading, Jesus declares on the night of the Last Supper, 'I came from the Father and have come into the world and now I leave the world to go to the Father.' Jesus is speaking of his own personal mission. He has come from God to reveal the light of God's love to the world and he is about to leave the world to return to God the Father. There is a sense in which what Jesus says of himself is true of every human being, and, in particular, of his followers. We came from God the Father and have come into the world, and we will leave the world to go to the Father. All human life is from God and returns to God. This is the essential truth about human life that Jesus has come to reveal to us. It is because we believe that all human life has come from God and returns to God that we consider all human life to be sacred from the moment of conception to the moment of death, and why we have a responsibility to protect and care for life at every moment of life's journey. We are all on a journey from God towards God, and Jesus as the Way shows us how to travel this journey. We are to love one another as he has loved us. In today's first reading, we have a portrayal of such love in action. In the church of Ephesus, a married couple, Priscilla and Aquila, who were a significant presence in the early Church, took an interest in a promising young Egyptian convert from Judaism, Apollos, and gave him further instruction in the Way. As a result of their support of him, Apollos, we are told, was able to help the church in Corinth considerably. We are all called to be a support to each other on our shared journey from God towards God.

25 May, Monday, Seventh Week of Easter

John 16:29–33

There is a realism about Jesus' words to his disciples in today's gospel reading. Although they seem very sure of their faith – 'we believe that you came from God' – Jesus tells his disciples bluntly that a time is coming when they will be scattered, each going his own way. Jesus warns them that in the world, much of which is hostile to the values of the Gospel, they will have trouble. Their faith will be put to the test, and they are about to fail the particular test that the passion and death of Jesus will bring to pass. Jesus is reminding all of us that we cannot take our faith for granted. It will be put to the test and we, too, will be tempted to go our own way rather than the Way of Jesus. Yet he also reassures his disciples and all of us that he is stronger than the forces that will put our faith to the test. 'I have conquered the world.' If we remain in communion with Jesus, we will draw strength from him. Indeed Jesus assures us that even in the midst of the trouble that the world of unbelief brings to us we will know his peace, 'I have told you all this so that you may find peace in me.' The words of Jesus in today's gospel reading encourage us to face the challenges to our faith, to the Church, with confidence and courage, knowing that the Lord, through his death and resurrection, has already triumphed over the forces that are opposed to the Gospel.

26 May, Tuesday, Seventh Week of Easter

John 17:1–11

People often ask us to pray for them, and we often ask people to pray for us. The prayer of intercession has always been central to the Church's prayer life. The Gospels suggest that it was central to Jesus' prayer life too. In Luke's Gospel, in the setting of the Last Supper, Jesus turns to Peter and says to him, 'I have prayed for you, Peter, that your faith may not fail'. Today's gospel reading from John is also set in the context of the Last Supper. Jesus begins by praying for himself. 'Father, the hour has come: glorify your Son.' Jesus asks his Father to bring him through the death that is imminent into the glory of eternal life. He then goes on to pray for his disciples. 'I pray for them ... for those you have given me.' He prays for his disciples, he intercedes for them, in the awareness that 'they are in the world'. Jesus is leaving the world, which has been largely hostile to him, but his disciples will remain in this world and there they will experience the same hostility that Jesus experienced. Jesus feels the need to pray for them. Although it is not said explicitly in our gospel reading, Jesus is praying that their faith in him may not fail in this hostile world. In his letter to the Romans, Paul makes reference to Christ Jesus, 'who is at the right hand of God, who indeed intercedes for us'. The letter to the Hebrews declares that Jesus, the high priest, 'always lives to make intercession for' those who approach God through him. It is re-assuring to know that the risen Lord prays for us all, just as he prayed for his first disciples. His prayer for us, in keeping with his prayer for his first disciples, is surely that our faith may not fail when it is put to the test by a hostile world.

27 May, Wednesday, Seventh Week of Easter
John 17:11–19

In today's gospel we have an extract from the prayer of Jesus for his disciples, set in the context of the Last Supper. In that prayer Jesus declares that since first calling his disciples to himself he has watched over them and kept them true to God's name. Now in prayer he calls on his Father to keep them true to God's name. His prayer to the Father on their behalf is a further expression of the commitment he has shown to his disciples since first calling them. His intercessory prayer is an extension of the many ways he had served them since they first began to follow him. In a similar way, our prayer for others is an expression of our commitment to them, our care for them; it is one of the ways we serve others. By his own intercessory prayer for his disciples – and that includes all of us – Jesus teaches us the value of all intercessory prayer. Intercessory prayer, prayer for others, has been at the heart of the Church's prayer life since the time of Jesus. Paul in his letters frequently refers to his intercessory prayers for his churches and he often calls on his churches to pray for him. Both Jesus and Paul were heirs to a Jewish tradition that greatly valued this form of prayer. Praying for others is one of the ways we give expression to our communion with others in the Lord.

28 May, Thursday, Seventh Week of Easter

John 17:20–26

Today's first reading reminds us that in the time of Jesus and the early Church, there were strong differences of opinion among leading Jews regarding matters of faith. The Pharisees believed in the resurrection of the dead, in angels and spirits. The Sadducees did not share any of these beliefs. In that reading, Paul refers to himself as a Pharisee and the son of a Pharisee. His belief while a Pharisee in the resurrection of the dead, in angels and spirits, was enriched and deepened through his encounter with the risen Lord. Jesus himself was at one with the Pharisees in these matters of belief and opposed to the Sadducees. That is evident from today's gospel reading. Jesus continues to pray in intercession for his disciples, and for all future disciples, those who will believe through the witness of the first disciples. He prays that they would be one, as he and his Father are one. This prayer of Jesus has been an inspiration to the ecumenical movement in recent decades. He also prays that his disciples would be 'with me where I am, so that they may always see the glory you have given me'. He prays that his disciples would be with him in all his glory, in eternal life. Jesus articulates here our ultimate destiny beyond this earthly life, a sharing in his own glorious destiny. As we journey towards this destiny, he prays that 'the love with which you loved me may be in them, and so that I may be in them'. As we journey towards communion with the Lord in eternity, the Lord wants to be in communion with us now, living in and through us, loving others in and through us.

29 May, Friday, Seventh Week of Easter
John 21:15–19

It was after the risen Lord had eaten breakfast with his disciples that he asked Peter the question, 'Do you love me more than these others do?' The risen Lord first entered into communion with his disciples over a meal. In that way, he was demonstrating his love for them even though they had failed him in the hour of his passion and death. The Lord was showing Peter, in particular, that he had not broken his loving communion with him, even after Peter had denied him publicly three times. The Lord's love of his disciples was not dependent upon their love of him; his faithfulness to them was not conditional upon their faithfulness to him. Having had this experience of the Lord's faithful love, Peter hears the Lord ask him, 'Do you love me?' The Lord's love for Peter was not in doubt; what needs clarifying is Peter's love for the Lord. Three times the risen Lord asks this question and three times Peter replies, 'You know I love you', thereby overcoming his earlier threefold denial. Once Peter's loving commitment to the Lord has been renewed, the Lord can entrust him with the pastoral care of the other disciples. 'Feed my sheep.' Peter's loving relationship with the Lord had first to be renewed before he could reveal the love of the Good Shepherd to others. There is a pattern there that applies to all of our lives. The Lord continues to love us even when we fail him; he continues to draw us into communion with himself, even after we have broken communion with him. He keeps asking us to renew our love for him, in response to his love for us. If we do so, the Lord will send us forth to reveal his love to all those we encounter. He calls us to be good shepherds of each other, as he has been a good shepherd to us, laying down his life in love for us.

30 May, Saturday, Seventh Week of Easter
John 21:20–25

Today's gospel reading gives us the concluding verses of the Fourth Gospel, from which we have been reading for the past seven weeks of the Easter season. The reading features two disciples, Peter and the nameless disciple who is only ever referred to in this gospel as 'the disciple Jesus loved'. The gospel reading claims that this nameless disciple is the one who inspired the writing of the Fourth Gospel. 'This disciple is the one who vouches for these things and has written them down, and we know that his testimony is true.' The risen Jesus had just commissioned Peter to 'feed my sheep'. Peter was to be the chief shepherd who would have the primary pastoral care of Jesus' flock. After Peter had received this commission, he turned to the other disciple, the one Jesus loved, and asked Jesus, 'What about him, Lord?' The Lord had a different purpose in mind for this disciple. His task would be to take some of the traditions about Jesus and help to mould them into a coherent story about Jesus. We are being reminded that the Lord works through different disciples in different ways. We each have our own unique contribution to make to the Lord's work. Grace always builds on nature. The Lord has a distinct role for each one of us on the basis of our own particular gifts and limitations, our own temperament and set of experiences. We might be tempted to ask, with Peter, 'What about him or her, Lord?' Perhaps a better question is, 'What about me, Lord? What are you asking of me at this time? How do you want me to serve your people?'

1 June, Monday, Mary, Mother of the Church

Mark 12:1–12

It is clear that Jesus recognised himself in the vineyard owner's son of today's parable. Having initially sent his servants, who were mistreated and killed, the vineyard owner sent his son to collect the produce of the vineyard from the tenants. The tenants killed him as well, and threw him out of the vineyard. Jesus spoke this parable in the city of Jerusalem, shortly before his passion and death. He would soon be taken outside the city and killed. Immediately after telling the parable, Jesus uses another image to describe his forthcoming death. He was the stone rejected by the builders. However, that second image has a note of hope in it, because, as Jesus says, quoting one of the psalms, the stone rejected by the builders became the cornerstone. Having been rejected and crucified, Jesus would be raised from the dead and would become the cornerstone of a spiritual temple, the Church, the community of his disciples. God brought great good out of the dark and painful experience of Jesus' rejection and death, because Jesus had remained faithful to God in the midst of all that darkness and suffering. In our own lives, as we seek to follow the Lord's way, we may at times feel like the rejected stone. We sense that the gospel values that are so significant for us are not shared by many others. We can feel somewhat demoralised and discouraged as a result. Today's gospel reading calls on us to remain faithful to the Lord at those times. The Lord's image of the rejected stone becoming the cornerstone reminds us that the Lord can work powerfully in and through those difficult experiences, if we keep faithful and keep turning to the Lord as our refuge and stronghold, in the words of today's responsorial psalm.

2 June, Tuesday, Ninth Week in Ordinary Time

Mark 12:13–17

The question of paying taxes to Rome was a live one in the time of Jesus and in the time when Mark's Gospel was written. A poll tax or head tax had been introduced to Judea and Samaria in AD6 when Rome appointed a governor to rule that area. Those who were opposed to Roman rule were also strongly opposed to paying this tax. Those who wanted to preserve the peace with Rome, such as the chief priests and the other members of the Sanhedrin, were strongly in favour of paying it. Jesus does not give a 'yes' or 'no' answer to the question he is asked. As is often his way in the Gospels, he responds in a manner that requires his hearers to think through the meaning of what he is saying. 'Give back to Caesar what belongs to Caesar, and to God what belongs to God.' At one level, he seems to be saying that paying taxes to the governing authorities is quite legitimate. However, in saying 'Give to God what belongs to God', Jesus is qualifying what is owed to any human authority. He will shortly go on to say that God is to be loved with all our hearts, souls, minds and strength. We are to give back to God everything that God has given to us, our whole being. No human authority, political or religious, is owed what is owed to God alone. The giving to God of all our love determines all our other human relationships, including our relationship with those in political authority. Only God is deserving of our full allegiance. In today's gospel, Jesus is saying that God is God and Caesar is Caesar. In other words, Caesar is not God, in spite of Caesar's claims to the contrary.

3 June, Wednesday, Ninth Week in Ordinary Time

Mark 12:18–27

In today's first reading Saint Paul declares that Jesus 'abolished death, and proclaimed life and immortality through the Good News'.

This was one of the ways Paul understood the ministry of Jesus, as the proclamation of eternal life and immortality through the Good News or Gospel. In today's gospel reading the Sadducees who question Jesus were a Jewish group who did not believe in eternal life or immortality. They rejected Jesus' proclamation, and by means of their questioning they tried to show how foolish belief in life after death is. A woman had seven husbands. Whose wife will she be in the afterlife? Their question presupposes that life after death is some form of extension of this earthly life. In his answer, Jesus indicates that our existence after death will be very different from our present existence, and that this life cannot simply be transposed onto the next life. As Jesus says, we will be like the angels in heaven. We cannot say what that will be like. As Paul says in his first letter to the Corinthians, 'Eye has not seen, nor ear heard, nor the human heart conceived, what God has prepared for those who love him'. When Paul does try to speak about this life beyond death he often speaks of it in terms of an experience of communion, a communion with the Lord and with each other. In one of his letters he simply says, 'We will be with the Lord for ever'. Perhaps that is as much as we need to know.

4 June, Thursday, Ninth Week in Ordinary Time

Mark 12:28–34

Paul's second letter to Timothy contains a number of traditional sayings, which are introduced with the statement, 'Here is a saying you can rely on'. They represent traditional material from the early Church, almost like mini creeds, that are older than the letter and which Paul inserts into his letters at various points. We find one of those pieces of traditional material in today's first reading: 'Here is a saying you can rely on: "If we have died with him, then we shall rise with him … ".' It concludes with the statement, 'We may be unfaithful, but he is always faithful, for he cannot disown his own self.' The first disciples, and Peter, in particular, had come to know the truth of this saying from personal experience. Peter was unfaithful. He publicly denied his association with Jesus three times, yet Jesus remained faithful to him. As risen Lord, he appeared to Peter and entrusted him with the task of the pastoral care of the other disciples. We will often be unfaithful to the Lord in our own lives. We are not always true to his values, but when that happens, the Lord remains faithful to us. His faithful love is not in doubt. The love that Jesus calls for in the gospel reading is always a response to the Lord's faithful love of us. It is because we experience the Lord's faithful love of us that we want to love him with all our hearts, understanding and strength, and to love others with something of the Lord's own love. In the words of the first letter of Saint John, 'We love because he first loved us'.

5 June, Friday, Ninth Week in Ordinary Time
Mark 12:35–37

In today's first reading Saint Paul reminds Timothy of the value of the Scriptures, how they can teach us the wisdom that leads to salvation because they are inspired by God, how they can guide our lives. When Paul speaks of the Scriptures there, he is of course referring to what we call the Old Testament, the Jewish Scriptures, because at that time there was no New Testament, no Christian books that had become canonical or authoritative. The first believers greatly valued the Jewish Scriptures; they were the only Scriptures they had. In this, they were following in the path of Jesus, who was steeped in the Jewish Scriptures. In the gospel reading, Jesus quotes from one of the psalms to show that the Messiah is more than the Son of David; he is also David's Lord. Because Jesus and his first followers valued the Jewish Scriptures so much, the Church has always valued them. That is why the first reading on Sunday and on weekdays is regularly drawn from the Jewish Scriptures. They may not speak to us as powerfully at times as they spoke to Jesus and his first followers, because they are further from us in time and in culture. However, as Christians we venerate them because, like Jesus and the early Church, we recognise that there is a great wisdom there, in the words of our first reading, 'the wisdom that leads to salvation'.

6 June, Saturday, Ninth Week in Ordinary Time
Mark 12:38–44

There is a striking contrast in today's gospel reading between the scribes, whom Jesus describes as 'men who swallow the property of widows', and the widow Jesus holds up as an example of total self-giving to God. She is described as a 'poor widow'. Perhaps she is one of those widows whose property has been swallowed up by the scribes, the recognised experts in the Jewish law. Yet, this widow gives generously to the Temple treasury, believing that in doing so she is giving to God. She gave everything she possessed to God. She exemplifies what Jesus calls the first commandment, to love God with all one's heart, soul, strength and mind. She fulfils the essence of the law, whereas the so-called experts in the law undermine its core value by taking advantage of the most vulnerable. Knowledge does not always lead to virtue. To know the good does not automatically lead to doing the good. The widow understood the heart of the Jewish law without having studied it. Jesus holds her up as an example to his disciples. This woman, who would have gone unnoticed in the culture, was noticed by Jesus, and he wanted others to notice her. Jesus may have recognised something of himself in this widow. The woman gave everything she possessed to God. As Jesus stood in the Temple of Jerusalem shortly before his passion and death, he would soon give everything he possessed, his very life, to God and to humanity. The widow brings home to us that sometimes the smallest of actions can have something of that same self-giving that Jesus displayed on the cross.

8 June, Monday, Tenth Week in Ordinary Time

Matthew 5:1–12

The gospel reading is one of the most familiar texts in the Gospels. Jesus declares blessed those who live according to certain values and attitudes. They are blessed, not so much because of their present situation, but because of a future destiny that God will bring about for them. The poor in spirit are those who are aware of their own lack of resources and look to God for salvation. The 'gentle' are the opposite of those who are grasping; they are unselfish rather than on the make. Those who mourn are those who are disturbed by the present state of the world and long for its liberation from poverty, violence and disease. Those who hunger and thirst for what is right are people who have a longing for the justice that God desires for all people and who actively pursue it. The merciful are those who bring God's merciful love to the broken in body, mind and spirit. The pure in heart are those who are single-minded in their pursuit of what God wants for the world. The peacemakers actively work for a peace based on God's justice. Having declared all of the above categories of people blessed, Jesus concluded by declaring blessed those who are prepared to suffer persecution in the pursuit of what is right, of what God desires for his world. It has been said that the one person who gives full expression to all of the attitudes and values expressed in the beatitudes is Jesus himself. At the same time, Jesus is offering us in the beatitudes a vision for human living to which he calls us all to aspire. If the beatitudes are Jesus' own self-portrait, they are also a portrait of his disciple. Later on in Matthew's Gospel Jesus will say, 'Learn from me'. We can learn from him how to live the beatitudes and he gives us his Spirit to empower us to live them.

9 June, Tuesday, Feast of Saint Columcille

Matthew 8:18–27

Columcille was born in Gartan, County Donegal, in 521 and was of royal lineage, belonging to a branch of the O'Neill dynasty. He studied under Saint Mobhi, in the monastery of Glasnevin. He went on to establish monasteries in Derry, Durrow and possibly Kells. In 563 he left Ireland with twelve companions and founded a monastery on the island of Iona off the south-west coast of Scotland, which was given to him by the ruler of the Irish Dal Riada for the purpose of establishing a monastery. The monastery became a place of learning and of the copying and illumination of manuscripts. Columcille remained in Scotland, mainly Iona, for the rest of his life, returning to Ireland only for occasional visits. He died on 9 June 597. Columcille and his companions preached the Gospel in the western part of Scotland. After his death, monks from Iona went to evangelise Northumbria, where they established monasteries at Lindisfarne and Whitby. Columcille and his companions made the word of God fully known wherever they went. During their ministry, they went through many a stormy time, like the disciples in today's gospel reading. Yet, just as Jesus was with the disciples in the storm at sea and brought them through it, he was with Columcille and his companions through all their difficult moments, and they came to discover, like those disciples, that the Lord was stronger than the storm. Our own following of the Lord won't always be easy; the storms and trials of life will often put our faith to the test. Just as Jesus was asleep in the boat, it can seem to us at such times that the Lord is asleep on our watch. However, the Lord is always attentive to us. One of the psalms expresses that conviction very well: 'He will not let your foot be moved; he who keeps you will not slumber. He who keeps Israel will neither slumber nor sleep.' The Lord is ever watchful and faithful. It is we who can become faithless or, in the rebuke of Jesus to the disciples in the boat, people of 'little faith'. It is because we are all prone to 'little faith' that we need to keep making our own that prayer of the father of a seriously ill boy which we find in one of the gospel stories, 'Lord, I believe, help my unbelief'.

9 June, Tuesday, Tenth Week in Ordinary Time
Matthew 5:13–16

The first reading is the story of a widow who had a very small amount of food for herself and her son to eat in a time of famine. The prophet asked her to share some of the little she had. Understandably she was very slow to do so but eventually she did what Elijah asked. She shared the very little food that she had. In doing so she discovered that the Lord provided for her in abundance. We are reminded of another widow in the Gospels; she put a very small amount into the Temple treasury but in doing so was praised by Jesus because she gave all she had to live on. Both widows gave generously from the little they had. Both widows remind us that generosity is measured not by the amount we give but by what we give in proportion to what we have. Those who give a little can be much more generous than those who give a lot. Real generosity leaves us vulnerable. That was the generosity that characterised the life of Jesus. He gave of himself unto death, death on a cross. When we display in our lives something of his generosity we become what Jesus calls us to be in today's gospel reading, the salt of the earth and the light of the world. Generosity can take many forms, generosity of heart, of spirit and of mind, as well as generosity with what we possess, whether it be our material resources or our time or our gifts. The first reading suggests that whenever we are generous even with the little we have, we create an opening in our lives for the Lord to be generous with us.

10 June, Wednesday, Tenth Week in Ordinary Time
Matthew 5:17–19

In many respects Jesus was a great innovator. He used the image of new wine for his ministry, declaring that his new wine required new wineskins. In other words, the traditional way of doing things would no longer do. However, Jesus also had great respect for his tradition, for his own Jewish tradition. The scriptures of his people nourished and inspired him. In today's gospel reading he declares that he has come not to abolish the law and the prophets, the two most authoritative sections of the Jewish Scriptures, but to complete them. He did not pretend to be starting from scratch. There was much in the tradition of his own people which he valued, but he wanted to bring that tradition to a greater richness and fullness; he came to renew Israel's tradition, not to replace it. Jesus' attitude to his own religious tradition suggests that we don't simply jettison our religious tradition but we don't just canonise it either. It is true that the Church is always in need of reform and renewal; the new wine of the Holy Spirit will always require new wineskins. Yet this work of renewal will always involve honouring what is best in our tradition by allowing its rich potential to be fully realised. Likewise, the Holy Spirit renews our own personal lives by honouring what is best in our own unique story while moving us towards new horizons.

11 June, Thursday, Feast of Saint Barnabas
Matthew 10:7–13

According to an earlier verse in the Acts of the Apostles, Barnabas's real name was Joseph, but he was given the name Barnabas, which means 'son of encouragement', as a kind of a nickname by the apostles. In today's first reading we can see Barnabas living up to his nickname. News reached Jerusalem of a new development in Antioch. The Gospel had been preached to non-Jews for the first time, resulting in the formation of a mixed church of Jewish and Gentile Christians. When the church in Jerusalem sent Barnabas to Antioch to check on this, he saw immediately that this new development was God's doing and he encouraged all involved. He went further and encouraged Paul to come from Tarsus and to get involved in this new departure. As a result, Paul made a great contribution to the life of this mixed church of Antioch, and this church, in turn, became a spiritual home for Paul and a base for his missionary work. You could say that Barnabas was a facilitator, an enabler; he supported the good that people were doing and he opened doors for people's gifts. We always need people like Barnabas around and we can all become a Barnabas for others. The ministry of encouragement is one in which we can all share, and it is one of the most needed ministries today. When we engage in this ministry, we are responding to Jesus' call in today's gospel reading to 'proclaim that the kingdom of heaven is close at hand'. On this his feast day, we pray for something of the spirit of Barnabas in our own lives and in the life of our Church.

12 June, Friday, Tenth Week in Ordinary Time
Matthew 5:27–32

Today's gospel reading has a sharp edge to it. The language Jesus uses is strange to our ears. 'If your right eye should cause you to sin, tear it out and throw it away … .' Jesus is speaking in a exaggerated way to get our attention; he clearly does not intend to be taken literally. This image of tearing out our right eye links back to his understanding of adultery not just as a physical act but as an intention or a desire. 'Whoever looks at a woman lustfully … .' Jesus goes behind the actions that the Ten Commandments prohibit to the roots of those actions in the human heart. This is the deeper virtue that he referred to a few verses earlier. Jesus calls not just for a change of behaviour but for a change of heart, a purifying of desire and intention. This interior transformation is understood elsewhere in the Scriptures to be the work of the Spirit. It is the Spirit of God who renews the human heart. It is above all in prayer that we open ourselves to the Spirit of God. As Elijah in the first reading sought out the mountain of God, we need to seek out the mountain of prayer. On the mountain, Elijah experienced the presence of the Lord in 'the sound of a gentle breeze', or, as another translation expresses it, 'in the sound of sheer silence'. It is above all in silence that we seek the Lord's face, in the words of today's responsorial psalm, and open ourselves to the coming of the Lord's Spirit, who works within us to create in us a heart that reflects the heart of Jesus.

13 June, Saturday, Tenth Week in Ordinary Time
Matthew 5:33–37
I am struck by Jesus' saying in today's gospel reading: 'All you need say is "yes" if you mean yes, "no" if you mean no.' In one of his letters, Paul says that in Christ 'it is always "yes"', because 'in him every one of God's promises is a "yes"'. Jesus is God's 'yes' to us all; he embodies God's faithful love for us all. Jesus is also our 'yes' to God. He is the one human being who, on our behalf, said a total, loving 'yes' to God's will for his life. As God's 'yes' to us and our 'yes' to God, Jesus had to say 'no' to anything that was in conflict with living out that fundamental 'yes' of his life. He said 'no' to the various temptations that came his way, initially in the wilderness after his baptism, and, also, at other times of his ministry, as when Peter tempted him to avoid the cross. As followers of the Lord, in whom the Lord seeks to dwell, each one of us is called to be an expression of God's loving 'yes' to others, and also to make our own daily 'yes' to God's desire and purpose for our lives. Just as for Jesus, so for us, that will often entail saying 'no' to various paths we may be tempted to take that inhibit us from revealing God's faithful love to others and

prevent us from making our own loving 'yes' to God. As Christians, our fundamental response to God and to each other is 'yes', a loving 'yes'. There is nothing negative about our faith, in that sense, even though it is often portrayed in that way. Our 'no' is always in the service of that great 'yes' to God, to each other, to life.

15 June, Monday, Eleventh Week in Ordinary Time
Matthew 5:38–42

The first reading provides us with a disturbing instance of the corrupt use of power. The wife of the king of Israel, Jezebel, had an innocent man, Naboth, killed so that the king could have Naboth's vineyard. Deadly violence was inflicted on someone by someone with power in the land for purely selfish gain. The story of Naboth's vineyard happens in every generation and in every culture. It is a reminder of how power is often used unscrupulously to benefit the powerful. The author of the first Book of Kings in which we find this story was very clear that the crime of Ahab and Jezebel was a crime not just against Naboth but against God. Immediately after this crime, God sent the prophet Elijah to Naboth to warn him of the consequences of his crime. In any situation of injustice, such as the one we have just read about, God is always on the side of those who suffer the injustice. Injustice done to others is done to God, and those responsible for the injustice will be held accountable by God. In the gospel reading Jesus addresses a situation where his own disciples will suffer injustice. They too will be the victims of self-serving violence; they too will have to come to terms with what the gospel reading calls 'the wicked man'. Jesus declares that when they find themselves the victims of unjust violence they are not to retaliate in kind; they are not to meet evil with evil. The practice of eye for eye and tooth for tooth no longer applies within the realm of the kingdom of God present through Jesus. Instead, the disciples are to remain generous and self-giving, even when confronted with evil in its various forms. This is the way of Jesus, which he would display in the hour of his passion and death when praying for his enemies, and which we are all called to follow.

16 June, Tuesday, Eleventh Week in Ordinary Time
Matthew 5:43–48

In today's gospel reading Jesus' call on his disciples to 'love your enemies and to pray for those who persecute you' would have been shocking at the time. It retains its shock value today. Jesus is calling on his disciples, calling on us, to be loving people, full stop. We are to be as loving towards those who hate us and wish us harm as we are towards those who love us and wish us well. The kind of people we are is to be shaped not by how people relate to us but by how God relates to us and to all humankind, the God who causes his sun to shine on good and bad alike. There was a bishop in southern Mexico between 1960 and 2000, Don Samuel Ruiz. He was well known for having empowered the indigenous people of his diocese and for his role as mediator in the conflict between the Zapatista rebels and the Mexican government. For this work, he had received many death threats. In an interview he gave before his death in 2011 he was asked how he had come to live so completely the command to love one's enemies, when he had so many. He replied, 'I have no enemies. There are some who want to make themselves enemy to me, but I have no enemies.' This was certainly someone who related to people out of something much deeper than how they related to him; he related to all, even his enemies, with a divine kind of love. He lived to the full the calling of Jesus at the end of today's gospel reading to be perfect as our heavenly Father is perfect.

17 June, Wednesday, Eleventh Week in Ordinary Time
Matthew 6:1–6, 16–18

Today's gospel reading is taken from the Sermon on the Mount. It begins with Jesus saying, 'Be careful not to parade your good deeds before others to attract their notice'. Yet, a little earlier in the same Sermon on the Mount, Jesus appears to have said the very opposite of that: 'Let your light shine before others, so that they may see your good deeds and give glory to your Father in heaven.' There seems to be a tension between both of these sayings, but there is truth in both. We are not to hide the light of our faith, keeping it under a bushel. Rather, we are to publicly proclaim our faith, our relationship with the Lord, by the lives that we lead, by the deeds that we do. On the other hand, we don't publicly proclaim our faith in order to attract notice, in order to draw attention to ourselves, to bring praise or glory on ourselves. Rather, our public living of our faith is with a view to bringing glory to God. Today's gospel reading invites us to ask, 'Who is being honoured by my public living of my relationship with the Lord? Is it myself or is it God?' Another way of asking that question is, 'Who is being served by my good deeds? Is it myself or is it the Lord?' The opening petitions of the Lord's Prayer points us in the right direction. 'Hallowed be your name, your kingdom come'.

18 June, Thursday, Eleventh Week in Ordinary Time
Matthew 6:7–15

In the gospel reading Jesus makes a distinction between the prayer of the pagans and the prayer of his followers. He speaks of pagan prayer as babbling, as using many words, the implication being that, by using many words, the pagans are trying to force God to listen. Pagan prayer is an attempt to put pressure on God, to manipulate God into doing what those who are praying want. The prayer Jesus taught his disciples is the complete opposite of that kind of prayer. Rather than trying to force God's hand, the Lord's Prayer, as we have come to call it, begins in a spirit of surrender to God and to what God wants –'your name be held holy, your will be done, your kingdom come'. Jesus would pray a version of those opening petitions of the Lord's Prayer in the garden of Gethsemane. 'My Father, if it is possible, let this cup pass from me; yet not what I will, but what you will.' Although Jesus recoiled before the prospect of a violent death, he did not try to force God's hand in prayer. Rather, he surrendered to what God wanted. His prayer of petition was secondary to his prayer of surrender. The Lord's Prayer begins in that same spirit of surrender to God, and only then does it invite us to petition God on our own behalf. The petitions of the Lord's Prayer are all in the first person plural, not 'me' and 'mine' but 'us' and 'our'. They express our basic material and spiritual needs as a faith community, our need for sustenance, both physical and spiritual, our need for forgiveness and our need for deliverance when our faith is tested by evil. Jesus gave us this prayer so that all our prayers may be shaped by this model prayer.

19 June, Friday, Feast of the Most Sacred Heart of Jesus
Matthew 11:25–30

The traditional image of the Sacred Heart of Jesus shows Jesus with a pierced heart. Such an image is influenced by the reference in John's Gospel to the piercing of Jesus' side with a lance as he hung from the cross, resulting in a flow of blood and water. This scene is an echo of an earlier passage in that gospel, where, on the last day of the feast of Tabernacles in Jerusalem, Jesus cries out, 'Let anyone who is thirsty come to me, and let the one who believes in me drink. As the scripture has said, "Out of his heart shall flow rivers of living water".' The fourth evangelist then comments on this saying of Jesus: 'Now he said this about the Spirit, which believers in him were to receive'. The fourth evangelist understood the flow of blood and water from the side of Jesus as a symbol of the life-giving Spirit, the Spirit of God's love. When Jesus was lifted up on the cross, he poured out this Spirit of God's love on all humanity, and those who look upon the crucified Jesus with the eyes of faith receive this gift of God's love into their lives. The death of Jesus reveals the love of the good shepherd for his own and also the love of God for all humanity. Jesus' death not only reveals God's love for the world but makes that love tangible and personal for each one through the outpouring of the Holy Spirit into our hearts. In his letter to the Romans Saint Paul expresses this wonderful truth of Jesus' death very succinctly. He declares that 'God proves his love for us in that while we were still sinners Christ died for us', and he also states that 'God's love has been poured into our hearts through the Holy Spirit that has been given to us.' Today's feast is a feast of love. It is the feast of God's love, revealed in Jesus, especially in his death, and given personally to each one of us through the Holy Spirit. Jesus' love finds expression in his invitation in today's gospel to all who labour and are overburdened to come to him and find rest. The Lord's love is a given; it is ours to receive and respond to.

20 June, Saturday, Eleventh Week in Ordinary Time
Matthew 6:24–34

We all worry from time to time. Worrying is part of the human condition. Parents worry about their children. Family members worry about each other. Young people worry about their future. Jesus must have worried about his disciples, about the lack of response on the part of some of his contemporaries to his message, about where his mission was leading him. In today's gospel reading Jesus is not saying, 'Don't ever worry about anything'. The focus of worry in that gospel reading is food, drink and clothing, and the worry in question is excessive worry or preoccupation. Jesus makes reference to 'the pagans who set their hearts on all these things'. The concern of Jesus is setting our hearts on what is not of ultimate importance. The gospel reading invites us to ask, 'What am I giving my heart to?' To that extent, it is really about getting our priorities right, bringing them into line with God's priorities. That is why, towards the end of the reading, Jesus declares, 'Set your hearts on God's kingdom first, and on his righteousness'. Don't be so preoccupied with food, drink and clothing, Jesus is saying, that there is no room in your heart for concern about the coming of God's kingdom or the doing of God's will. The first three petitions of the Lord's Prayer relate to what might be termed God's priorities: 'Hallowed be thy name, thy kingdom come, thy will be done'. These were Jesus' priorities and he calls on his disciples to make them their own as well. The prayer 'thy kingdom come' impels us to work for the coming of God's kingdom for all of God's people here and now.

22 June, Monday, Twelfth Week in Ordinary Time

Matthew 7:1–5

Much of the Sermon on the Mount concerns how we relate to each other. Today's gospel reading, which comes from the Sermon on the Mount, is no exception. Jesus says to us, 'Do not judge', by which is meant 'Do not condemn'. Obviously, the state law will condemn people who break the law, but Jesus is not speaking in that context. The remainder of today's gospel reading clarifies what Jesus' real intent is. He is aware that we can be prone to seeing what is wrong with others more easily than seeing what is wrong with ourselves. We can condemn the other while being blind to our own failings. We can try to take the splinter out of someone's eye while failing to see the plank in our own. We can presume to make others see without being aware of our own blindness. Jesus wants us to focus more on ourselves than on others. 'Take the plank out of your own eye first'. We need to examine ourselves and be aware of our own failings. Only then will we relate to others in a true spirit of humility. Jesus is suggesting that we should be slow to set ourselves up as the moral superiors of others. We always have a lot to be working on in our own lives and that comes first. As we grow closer to the Lord ourselves, we will see others more clearly, with the eyes of the Lord.

23 June, Tuesday, Twelfth Week in Ordinary Time
Matthew 7:6, 12–14

The roads around the city have improved greatly in recent years. Many of the roads in and out of the city are wide and spacious. They are a far cry from the narrow and winding roads of the past. The wide and spacious roads mean that more cars can travel on them at greater speed. However, we know from experience that there can be a value in getting off the wide and spacious roads and taking the narrower, less busy roads. In taking such roads we can often come upon a view we wouldn't get if we stayed on the main roadways. In the gospel reading Jesus suggests that taking his teaching to heart, trying to live by his values, is equivalent to taking the more difficult road as against the wide and spacious road. He thereby acknowledges that the way he puts before us in his teaching and in his own life is not the way that most people would be inclined to take if left to themselves. His way is not the broad and spacious road that most people head for; his way is one that many would instinctively avoid because it seems too difficult and fraught. Following the Lord will always be countercultural to some extent; it will always involve going against the grain. However, Jesus also assures us that his way, for all its difficulty, is the way that leads to life. Today we ask the Lord to keep us faithful to his way, especially when we are tempted to take an easier way. In the words of the Lord's Prayer, 'Lead us not into temptation but deliver us from evil'.

24 June, Wednesday, Feast of the Birth of John the Baptist
Luke 1:57–66, 80

There was something special about John the Baptist. The gospel reading suggests that his being given the name 'John' was itself special or unusual. Neighbours and relations objected to this name. 'No one in your family has that name,' they said. John's parents understood that God wanted their child to be called 'John'. In Hebrew the name 'John' means 'the Lord has shown favour'. God was inaugurating a new era of favour through this child. After the resistance of the neighbours and relations to this unconventional name had been overcome, they went on to ask, 'What will this child turn out to be?' That question of the neighbours and relations could be asked of any of us at every stage of our lives, 'What will we turn out to be?' To put the question in other terms, 'Who is God calling us to be?' Our calling is to surrender to what today's second reading calls God's 'whole purpose' for our lives, as John did. God's purpose for John's life and God's purpose for all our lives have a great deal in common. God wants all of us to do what John did, to point out the Saviour, to make way for Jesus, to lead others to him by what we say and do. John the Baptist has something to teach us about how we might keep faithful to this God-given calling. He was a man of the desert, a man of prayer. We all need to find our own desert place of prayer if we are to remain true to our calling, if we are to turn out as God wants us to.

25 June, Thursday, Twelfth Week in Ordinary Time
Matthew 7:21–29

We have been reading from the Sermon on the Mount for the past couple of weeks and today's gospel reading brings the sermon to a close. There are three activities mentioned in the gospel reading that followers of Jesus engage in: speaking, listening and doing. All three activities are important. When we gather for public prayer we speak;

in the words of the gospel reading, we address Jesus as 'Lord, Lord'. When we gather for public worship and at times of private prayer we listen; we listen to the word of the Lord and allow it to sink into our hearts. These two activities of speaking and listening will always be central to the life of a disciple. However, Jesus says in the gospel reading that unless our speaking and our listening flow over into concrete action their value is undermined. It is not enough to say, 'Lord, Lord', we are to do the will of the Father in heaven. It is not enough to listen to the words of Jesus, we have to then act on them. We must act in accordance with what we say and what we hear. When our speaking to the Lord and our listening to his word bear fruit in good works, the kind of works that characterised the life of Jesus, then our lives will be solidly grounded, like a house built on rock. According to our gospel reading, if our words to the Lord and his words to us shape our behavior, then we will more easily withstand the storms that come our way in life. Our life will have a firm foundation.

26 June, Friday, Twelfth Week in Ordinary Time
Matthew 8:1–4

In the gospel reading a leper approaches Jesus in faith, bowing low before him, as if in worship, and expressing great trust in the power of Jesus' words. 'If you want to, you can cure me'. In approaching Jesus in this way, the leper was breaking social and religious norms. The Jewish law required that those suffering from leprosy keep their distance from everyone, except other lepers. However, the leper's great need and his faith in the power of Jesus' word drove him to take a step that could have left him open to great hostility and censure. When we publicly give expression to our own faith in the Lord today, we too can risk censure and ridicule. The leper teaches us and inspires us to witness publicly to our faith in the Lord, regardless of the social consequences. When the leper took his courageous step towards the Lord, he discovered that the Lord was happy to take a step towards him. All others would have run from the leper's approach. Jesus, in contrast, stretched out his hand to touch the leper and, in touching him, healed him of his disease. Whenever we draw near to the Lord with courage and faith, we too will discover that the Lord draws near to us. In bowing before the Lord we create an opening for the Lord to touch our lives with his healing and life-giving presence.

27 June, Saturday, Twelfth Week in Ordinary Time
Matthew 8:5–17

Today's first reading is from the Book of Lamentations. The title of the book aptly describes its tone and content. The book is a series of laments that rise up from the people of Israel as they try to come to terms with the destruction of the city of Jerusalem and their land and the resulting experience of exile in Babylon. The most frequent type of psalm in the Book of Psalms is the psalm of lament. There are more prayers of lamentation in the Book of Psalms that any other type of prayer. That statistic may be saying something about the human condition; it may also suggest that we tend to approach God more in times of need than in times of plenty. In the gospel reading we have the story of someone who approaches Jesus in his time of need, not a member of the people of Israel but a Roman centurion, a pagan. He comes before Jesus with a cry of lament. 'My servant is lying at home paralysed, and in great pain.' He doesn't make an explicit request of Jesus, but his lament before Jesus has an implicit request: 'Help my servant; help me.' Every lament is, at its core, a cry for help. This particular pagan displayed extraordinary sensitivity to Jesus as well as tremendous faith in him. He presumed that Jesus, a Jew, would be hesitant to enter the house of a pagan, and he believed that Jesus could heal his servant at a distance with his word. His initial lament found expression in a wonderful prayer of petition, 'I am not worthy ... '. A version of this centurion's prayer of petition has become part of the text of the Mass. As we prepare to receive the Eucharist today we might take a moment to make this version of the centurion's prayer our own, trusting, as he did, that this is a prayer that Jesus will indeed answer.

29 June, Monday, Feast of Saints Peter and Paul
Matthew 16:13–19

Rome has been a place of pilgrimage since the very early years of the Church. In earliest times, Christians went on pilgrimage to Rome to visit the tombs of the martyrs, in particular, the tombs of Peter and Paul. Both of these great apostles were martyred in Rome during the persecution of the Church under the Emperor Nero in AD64. The two basilicas, Saint Peter's and Saint Paul outside the Walls, were built over their tombs. Those basilicas, especially Saint Peter's, remain places of pilgrimage to this day. If Peter and Paul were alike in death, both martyred in Rome, they were quite unalike in life. Peter was a fisherman from Bethsaida on the Sea of Galilee; Paul was a very well-educated Pharisee from the university city of Tarsus. Peter was called by Jesus as he was fishing by the Sea of Galilee. Paul was called by the risen Lord as he approached Damascus in pursuit of his mission to persecute the Church. Peter was to be the rock on which Jesus would build his Church; he was to be the focal point of the Church's unity. Paul was commissioned to proclaim the Gospel to pagans throughout the Roman Empire. Yet, for all their differences, what they had in common, apart from the circumstances of their death, was their faith in the Lord, their willingness to give their lives in his service. The gospel reading gives us Peter's great confession of faith in Jesus, 'You are the Christ, the Son of the living God'. Paul expresses his faith in the Lord in today's second reading. 'I have fought the good fight to the end; I have run the race to the finish; I have kept the faith.' The feast of these two great followers of the Lord reminds us that our faith in the Lord can bind together people who might otherwise have little in common. Our background, gifts and personalities can all be very different, yet we can be one in the Lord. Paul uses the image of the human body to express this unity in diversity of the Church. We give expression to our faith, our relationship with the Lord, in a way that is unique to each of us. Uniformity is not a mark of the Church. The Lord's rich and mysterious identity can only begin to find expression in the many and varied members of his body. As we celebrate the feast of Saint Peter and Saint Paul, we give thanks for our own distinctive faith journey, which the Lord is always calling us to take.

30 June, Tuesday, Thirteenth Week in Ordinary Time
Matthew 8:23–27

For the first readers of Matthew's Gospel the story of the storm at sea which we have just heard would have resonated with their own experience. The members of Matthew's church would often have found themselves praying the prayer of the disciples in the boat, 'Save us, Lord, we are going down'. We may have prayed a version of that prayer ourselves, either in relation to our own personal lives or in relation to the life of the Church as a whole. In the gospel reading, Jesus addresses his fearful disciples as people of 'little faith'. They are somewhere between no faith and full faith. Many of us can find ourselves in that in-between place, people of little faith, especially when the storms threaten to engulf us. We can easily identify with the prayer of the man in the Gospels, 'Lord, I believe, help my unbelief'. Jesus, who had been asleep in the storm, brought the fragile boat with its fearful disciples through the storm into a place of calm. In stormy times that expose our vulnerability and frailty, the Lord remains with the Church and with each of us as individuals, keeping us steady and guiding us to our destination. This passage would have reassured Matthew's church and can reassure us today that the Lord is always stronger than the storm that threatens to overwhelm us and undermine our faith.

1 July, Wednesday, Thirteenth Week in Ordinary Time
Matthew 8:28–34

There is a strange ending to today's gospel reading. Jesus had just healed two very disturbed people. They were described as so fierce that nobody could pass near them. They address Jesus very aggressively. 'What do you want with us, Son of God?' Their fierceness and aggression did not deter Jesus from ministering to them. He released them from the spirit that had left them so disturbed. He restored their humanity. However, in response to Jesus' life-giving work, the whole town implored him to leave their neighbourhood. It seems that the local people were more comfortable with having two very disturbed people about than with a display of God's healing power. Jesus' liberating ministry did not always meet with welcome and faith. The same is often true of the ministry of the Church. The Church's work on behalf of the well-being of the most vulnerable does not always meet with a welcoming response. Sometimes our own efforts to do what is best for the well-being of others don't meet with a welcoming response either. Our efforts to share in the Lord's liberating ministry will often leave us exposed to the same negative response as he experienced. Yet the Lord remained faithful to the good work that God had sent him to do. We, as members of the Church, are called to that same faithfulness. We try to keep doing the Lord's life-giving work, regardless of how it is received by others.

2 July, Thursday, Thirteenth Week in Ordinary Time
Matthew 9:1–8

When some people listen to or read the passage they have just heard they wonder why the first words that Jesus spoke to the paralysed man were, 'Courage, my child, your sins are forgiven'. Why didn't Jesus say immediately to him what he went on to say to him, 'Get up, pick up your bed and go off home'? Why this focus on the man's sin? At the time of Jesus, many people understood that there was a direct correlation between a person's illness or disability and that person's sin. Jesus rejected any such connection. On one occasion Jesus and his disciples came upon a man who had been blind from birth and his disciples asked him, 'Who sinned, this man or his parents?' Jesus rejected the premise of their question. 'Neither this man nor his parents sinned.' Perhaps the paralysed man in today's gospel reading had been made to feel that his disability was because of some sin in his life, and that God was punishing him. Jesus wanted to reassure him that was not the case. 'My child, your sins are forgiven.' If he is a sinner, he is a forgiven sinner, and in that regard he is the same as everyone else. The misfortunes that befall us, whatever form they take, are never a sign of God's displeasure. The Lord is always with us in our misfortunes and struggles, supporting us and strengthening us. He can display his presence through the goodness and kindness of friends and neighbours, just as God displayed his presence to the paralysed man through the goodness of his friends who carried him to Jesus. The God in whom we believe is a God of light and life who is always at work to bring us into a fuller life and a greater light, and who needs all of us to give practical expression to his work.

3 July, Friday, Saint Thomas, Apostle

John 20:24–29

We may find it easy to identify with Thomas in today's gospel reading. When the other disciples approached him with the good news of Easter – 'We have seen the Lord' – their message did not resonate with him in any way. The darkness of Good Friday was still too real for him and prevented his being moved by their Easter proclamation. His own reasoning did not allow him to believe that the crucified Jesus was now the risen Lord. Thomas stood in the light of Easter, yet that light did not dispel his darkness. If his fellow disciples were full of Easter faith, he was full of doubt. They claimed to have seen the risen Lord; Thomas declared that he would not believe until he not only saw the Lord but touched his wounds. In his doubting, Thomas may be like many other disciples today. Many believers can be troubled by their sense that the light of Easter does not seem to have penetrated their lives sufficiently. We can be distressed at the degree of doubt that we experience within ourselves. Like Thomas, we can struggle to identify fully with those whose faith seems so much more assured than ours. Today's gospel reading assures us that the Lord understands a doubting, questioning, faith. When the Lord appeared to Thomas, he did not rebuke him. His first words to him were, 'Peace be with you'. He invited Thomas to touch his wounds as he had requested, and then called on him to 'doubt no longer but believe'. The gospel reading does not state that Thomas actually touched the wounds of Jesus. Seeing the risen Lord was enough to dispel his doubt. Then, out of the mouth of the great sceptic came one of the most complete professions of faith in the Gospels, 'My Lord and my God'. We are being reminded that serious doubt and great faith can reside in one and the same person.

4 July, Saturday, Thirteenth Week in Ordinary Time
Matthew 9:14–17

In the Gospels people are often critical of Jesus because he was speaking and acting in a way that was new. In today's gospel reading, the disciples of John the Baptist ask why Jesus and his disciples do not fast in the way that they and the Pharisees fast. There was a celebratory element to Jesus' ministry that was somewhat at odds with the way of life of John the Baptist and his disciples, and also the way of life of the Pharisees. Jesus came to proclaim the good news of God's unconditional love for all, especially for those who felt alienated from God, those considered 'sinners' by the virtuous. Jesus shared table with those regarded as sinners, celebrating God's mercy given and received. In the gospel reading, Jesus compares his ministry to the joy of a wedding feast, with himself being the bridegroom. Who was the bride? The bride was all those who responded to his message, the good news of God's loving and merciful presence in the ministry of Jesus. This was indeed something celebratory and quite new. As Jesus goes on to say, it was like new wine. Such new wine simply could not be contained in the old wineskins that had served people up until then. Everything had to shift, including the traditional understanding of feasting. There remains a wonderful newness to Jesus' life and message today. He continues to offer himself to us as new wine, and we, his followers, have to keep adjusting the wineskins so that they can adequately hold his new wine. The Spirit of the risen Lord is a very dynamic reality that will always be leading us in new directions, ones that are in living continuity with the past but are not bound by the past. We need to keep discerning where the Spirit is leading us, as a Church, and as individual disciples. What new wineskins does the Lord ask us to create so as to adequately hold the new wine of his loving and life-giving presence?

6 July, Monday, Fourteenth Week in Ordinary Time

Matthew 9:18–26

There is a very striking image of God's relationship with his people in today's first reading from the prophet Hosea, the image of God as the husband of his people. God betrothed himself to his people, giving himself in marriage to them, and, in so doing, displayed qualities of integrity, justice, tenderness, love and faithfulness. It was Jesus who fully revealed this faithful love of God for his people. In the Gospels, Jesus once referred to himself as the bridegroom. He reveals the love of the divine bridegroom, not just for the people of Israel but for all humanity. We know from our own human experience that true love always brings life to those who are loved. This was true in a special way of Jesus' love. His love for people brought them life to a unique degree. In today's gospel reading, Jesus brings life to a synagogue official's young daughter who had died. Jesus took her by the hand and she stood up. In that way, Jesus was showing us all that his love for us is stronger than death. When death comes to us, Jesus will take us by the hand and we will stand up in our risen life, a sharing in the Lord's own risen life. However, this side of death we can also experience the life-giving power of the Lord's love for us. Like the woman who suffered from a haemorrhage in the gospel reading, we can reach out and touch the Lord's presence to us here and now. Unlike the official's very public journey to Jesus, bowing low in front of him, this woman's journey to Jesus was a very private one, coming up to Jesus from behind him. In whatever way we approach the Lord, we will find that he is always there to receive us. If we entrust ourselves to him with the faith of the woman, and the faith of the synagogue official, we will experience his healing and life-giving presence.

7 July, Tuesday, Fourteenth Week in Ordinary Time
Matthew 9:32–38

The labour of Jesus is evident from even today's short gospel reading. It begins with Jesus enabling a dumb man to speak. There follows a summary statement of Jesus' labours in all the towns and villages of Galilee, teaching in synagogues, proclaiming the good news of the kingdom of heaven and curing the sick and diseased. When he looked out upon a crowd he saw the potential for more labour. He felt compassion for them because they were like sheep without a shepherd. Although not stated on this occasion, Jesus' compassionate response to the lost always leads him to labour further, to work more. Yet, although God was working powerfully through the labours of Jesus, he was well aware that he needed other labourers to work alongside him. That is why he calls on his disciples to 'ask the Lord of the harvest to send labourers to his harvest'. He wants his disciples to labour alongside him, but they are also to pray, petitioning God to send even more labourers. That call of Jesus to his disciples to ask the Lord of the harvest for more labourers has often been heard as a call to pray for more vocations to the priesthood and religious life. Today, however, we recognise more clearly that this is too narrow an interpretation of this invitation of Jesus. The risen Lord needs all kinds of labourers today to work in God's harvest. Every disciple is needed. All the baptised need to put their shoulders to the wheel. The harvest remains rich and a varied and full workforce is required. We all have some responsibility to ensure that Jesus' work of proclaiming God's kingdom in word and deed remains a living reality today. We are all the Lord's co-workers and we need all hands on deck today more than ever.

8 July, Wednesday, Fourteenth Week in Ordinary Time
Matthew 10:1–7

Jesus has been gathering a growing number of disciples since the beginning of his public ministry. According to today's gospel reading, from this larger group Jesus called twelve to whom he gave authority and power to share in his healing ministry. The number twelve was significant, suggesting the twelve tribes of Israel. This group of twelve were to symbolise the renewed Israel that Jesus was working to form. Jesus chose these twelve very deliberately. They were to receive intensive training and instruction so as to share in his ministry in a special way. Yet, by the end of the gospel story, everyone in this group had deserted him. The first mentioned, Peter, had denied him publicly, and the last mentioned, Judas Iscariot, had betrayed him to his enemies. In spite of the fact that these twelve had been given special authority and power and had spent more time in his company than others, listening to him and seeing what he did, they failed him when the cross came into view. They showed themselves to be people of little faith. In the words of today's first reading, their hearts were divided. Although Jesus calls people, calls each one of us, he cannot force us to respond to his call. Although he has a purpose for our lives, he is somewhat helpless before our refusal to cooperate with his purpose for us. Yet, in the Gospel story, the failure of the twelve was not the end of their relationship with Jesus. After he rose from the dead, he appeared to them in Galilee and renewed his relationship with them, sending them out to preach the Gospel to all nations. The Lord may be helpless before our failure but he remains faithful to us in spite of our unfaithfulness to him and he is always at work to bring some good out of our failures. All he asks is that, in the words of today's first reading, we continue to 'go seeking the Lord'.

9 July, Thursday, Fourteenth Week in Ordinary Time

Matthew 10:7–15

In my earlier years as a priest I used to go along regularly to a charismatic renewal prayer meeting that took place every Tuesday night in the parish hall. The opening lines of one of the hymns that was regularly sung went, 'Freely, freely, you have received; freely, freely give'. It was clearly inspired by a verse in today's gospel reading, 'You received without charge, give without charge'. These words were originally spoken to the twelve, as Jesus sent them out on mission. It is a saying of Jesus that continues to speak to believers today. The sequence of the sentence is important. Jesus' statement that 'you received', comes before his call, 'give'. There are times when we can reduce the Gospel to the moral call to 'give'. However, the call to give ceases to be Gospel if isolated from the core of the Gospel: 'You received without charge'. God in Jesus has loved us and continues to love us unconditionally. God has bestowed his grace and favour upon us through the life, death and resurrection of Jesus, and the sending of the Spirit, without looking for some payment from us in advance. The only response God asks us to make initially to this gift of his gracious love is to receive it. We open our hearts in our poverty to receive God's unmerited love. Such receiving does not always come easily to us. We wonder, 'What have I done to deserve this?' and we can struggle to live with the answer: 'Nothing'. It is only in responding to the Lord's call to receive that we can then go on to give as we have received, 'without charge'.

10 July, Friday, Fourteenth Week in Ordinary Time

Matthew 10:16–23

In today's gospel reading, Jesus paints a stark picture of the hostility that his followers can expect from the surrounding society. They will be dragged before both Jewish and pagan authorities; some of them will be betrayed to those authorities by members of their own families. This was the reality of life for many of Jesus' followers in the early decades, indeed the first two centuries, of the Church's existence. The sombre picture Jesus paints in that gospel reading may seem very far from our own experience today. Yet, in every age, in every generation, there are Christians who are experiencing the kind of hostility that Jesus describes in the gospel reading. There are several regimes in today's world that will not tolerate a vibrant Church that witnesses to the vision that Jesus had for human living. Even in our own tolerant, pluralist, society, those of us who believe in all that Jesus said and did and who try to give expression to that belief in our way of life can find ourselves somewhat isolated, even barely tolerated at times. There will always be some tension between the values of the Gospel and the values of the culture in which we try to live the Gospel. This gospel reading continues to speak to us today. In the words of that reading, Jesus calls on us to stand firm to the end. In other words, we are to be courageous in our living of our faith in him. The less supportive the culture is of our faith and the way of life it inspires, the more courageous we need to be. In the gospel reading, Jesus assures his disciples that in the difficult days to come, the Holy Spirit, whom Jesus calls 'the Spirit of your Father', will be available to them. That same Holy Spirit remains our resource today. It is above all when our faith is put to the test by the culture we inhabit that we need to make our own that lovely prayer in today's responsorial psalm, 'Do not cast me away from your presence, nor deprive me of your holy spirit'.

11 July, Saturday, St Benedict, Abbot, Patron of Europe
Matthew 19:27–29

Benedict was born to a distinguished family and was educated in Rome. He abandoned his studies and his inheritance and devoted himself to the quest for God. This initially took the form of a period of solitude in a cave at Subiaco, just to the east of Rome. His solitude was interrupted by those who were drawn to his way of life and wanted to gather round him. Much against his will, he organised these followers into a group of monasteries and he himself took on the leadership of one of those monasteries, Monte Cassino, which is now considered the birthplace of the Benedictine order. There he wrote his monastic rule, which set a standard for the future western monastic tradition. His rule was marked by moderation, balance and humanity. Community was a key feature of his monastic vision, and he stressed the value of community life as a school for holiness. He saw the community as a place of equality where each person was helped by everyone else along the path of holiness. The monks' primary occupation was liturgical prayer, complemented by the reading of the Scriptures and manual work of various kinds. Benedict was made patron of Europe in 1964. Peter's question to Jesus in today's gospel reading, 'What are we to have, then?' has a somewhat self-regarding tone. It is a very human and honest question on the lips of one who, as he says, 'left everything' to follow Jesus. Peter went on to give his life for Jesus. Peter's question is one we can all be tempted to ask as followers of Jesus. 'If I am to take this difficult path, what is in it for me?' Saints like Benedict prompt us to turn away from such questions. He gave to the Lord and to others without regard for personal gain. As a result of such a generous spirit, in the words of the gospel reading he was 'repaid a hundred times over' with communities of work and prayer that helped to renew the Church of his time and ever since, and he also inherited 'eternal life'. If we give to the Lord and to others, without calculating the likely benefits to ourselves, we too will be 'repaid a hundred times over, and also inherit eternal life'.

13 July, Monday, Fifteenth Week in Ordinary Time
Matthew 10:34–11:1

In Ireland we are not used to prolonged spells of warm weather. At such times we feel the need to drink more than we usually do. A cup of cold water becomes more of a luxury when the heat makes us thirsty. In the time and place of Jesus, where the weather is generally a lot warmer and for longer periods, a cup of cold water can be highly prized. It is against that background that Jesus declares in today's gospel reading, 'If anyone gives as much as a cup of cold water to one of these little ones because he is a disciple, then, I tell you solemnly, he will most certainly not lose his reward'. The reference by Jesus to his disciples as 'little ones' may point ahead to a later saying of Jesus in Matthew's Gospel, according to which, unless disciples become like children, they will never enter the kingdom of heaven. Disciples are to live out of an awareness of their dependence on God for all that is needful. According to the first beatitude, it is to such 'poor in spirit' that the kingdom of God belongs. Jesus declares in our gospel reading that the smallest acts of kindness towards one of his followers, 'one of these little ones', such as the giving of a cup of cold water, will not go unrewarded. Within the family of disciples, the Church, we need to be attentive to each other. Small acts of kindness can be as valuable as the heroic deed in the eyes of God the Father, of whom Jesus said that not even a sparrow falls to the ground without him knowing it.

14 July, Tuesday, Fifteenth Week in Ordinary Time
Matthew 11:20–24

The last line of today's first reading is very thought-provoking. 'If you do not stand by me, you will not stand at all.' The prophet Isaiah was addressing Ahaz, the king of Judah, at a time of national crisis, because Ahaz was attempting to address the crisis without reference to the Lord. The words of Isaiah to Ahaz are echoed in the words of

Psalm 127: 'Unless the Lord builds the house, those who build it labour in vain. Unless the Lord guards the city, the guard keeps watch in vain.' In a similar vein, Jesus declares in John's Gospel, 'Apart from me you can do nothing'. We can all be tempted to go it alone, failing to recognise our dependence on the Lord for everything. The words of Jesus in today's gospel reading express his frustration at three of the towns of Galilee for their failure to acknowledge their dependence on what he had come to offer them. 'Alas for you, Chorazin! Alas for you, Bethsaida … And as for you, Capernaum … .' Jesus' words addressed to these towns may seem harsh to our ears, but they express the anguish of the shepherd who sees his flock turn away from the green pastures they need. In spite of all the mighty works Jesus had done among them, they refused to repent, to turn towards him. The Lord wishes to stand by us, but he needs us to stand by him, if we are to flourish in the way he desires for us. There may well be times in our lives when we will stand apart from the Lord, but the Lord never ceases to call us to stand by him, to rely on him, so as to allow him to do the work in our lives that only he can do.

15 July, Wednesday, Fifteenth Week in Ordinary Time
Matthew 11:25–27

In today's first reading from Isaiah, the emperor of Assyria is portrayed as full of self-importance and pride. He proclaims the power of his own strength, intelligence and understanding. He boasts of picking up the whole earth as people pick up deserted eggs. He fails to recognise his place within God's greater purpose. This is the attitude that lies behind those to whom Jesus refers as 'the learned and the clever' in today's gospel reading. They are so full of their own intelligence and understanding that they are closed to the great wisdom from God that Jesus has come to reveal. It is those to whom Jesus refers in the gospel reading as 'children' who are open to receiving this wonderful revelation that Jesus brings from God. Jesus is referring here to his disciples, those whom he asked to become like little children so as to enter the kingdom of heaven. They know their dependence on God, their need of God, their poverty before God; they are poor in spirit. In so far as we imbibe this fundamental attitude, Jesus will be able to reveal to us everything that has been entrusted to him by God the Father. Jesus wants to draw us into his own relationship with God the Father. He wants us to know the Father as intimately as he knows the Father and as the Father knows him. The relationship between Jesus and his Father is not a closed relationship. Jesus wants to open it up to all of us, but we need something of the openness of children towards him if this great grace of sharing in Jesus' relationship with God is to come to pass for us.

16 July, Thursday, Fifteenth Week in Ordinary Time
Matthew 11:28–30

Today's gospel reading has spoken very personally to believers of every generation. There is something about that invitation of Jesus, 'Come to me, all you who labour and are overburdened', that makes us feel as if it is addressed to each one of us personally. In its original setting, Jesus was addressing himself to those who had come to feel overburdened by the very strict interpretation of the Jewish law that the religious authorities were attempting to impose on them. However, that invitation of Jesus speaks to us all whenever we feel burdened for whatever reason. As we hear Jesus' invitation, 'Come to me', and respond to it, we also hear the promise that he makes to us: 'I will give you rest'. When we hear the word 'rest' the experience of sleep might come to mind, or, at least, inactivity. However, on the lips of Jesus, the word 'rest' would conjure up the experience of suddenly coming upon an oasis of refreshment, having travelled through a desert terrain. It is the experience that is referred to in the psalm, 'The

Lord is my Shepherd' – 'Near restful waters he leads me to revive my drooping spirit'. The Lord is promising that if we come to him, we will experience a renewal of our spirits, a greater fullness of life, which is a foretaste of that fullness of life, that eternal rest, that awaits us beyond this earthly life. Jesus speaks of himself as gentle and humble in heart, qualities that will prove truly refreshing and life-giving for those who labour and are overburdened. Of course, Jesus' way of life is demanding, but Jesus is suggesting that it is not burdensome because he travels this way with us. He calls us to walk in his way out of the strength we receive from the deeply personal relationship he desires to have with each one of us.

17 July, Friday, Fifteenth Week in Ordinary Time
Matthew 12:1–8

The Temple Mount is the huge platform built by Herod the Great on which the magnificent temple that he had built rested. In its day that temple was considered to be one of the Seven Wonders of the World. In today's gospel reading, Jesus says to the Pharisees, 'Here, I tell you, is something greater than the Temple.' When he spoke those words, he was, no doubt, pointing to himself. He was claiming to be greater than even the magnificent temple that Herod had built. That temple, in particular the Holy of Holies at the heart of the temple, was considered to be the place where God was present on earth. In the gospel reading Jesus is claiming that he is now the one where God is present on earth. God is no longer present in a building but in a person, the person of Jesus of Nazareth. Jesus is Emmanuel, God-with-us. Where Jesus is present, God is present. For us as Christians, where the risen Lord is present, God is present. We believe that the risen Lord is present with us in a special way in the Eucharist; in venerating the Eucharist, we are venerating Emmanuel, God with us. The risen Lord is also present in each one of us, in the members of his body, the Church. Indeed, he is present in some sense in every human being who is suffering. The holy ground of the Temple is all around us. In honouring and respecting each other, we are honouring the Lord.

18 July, Saturday, Fifteenth Week in Ordinary Time
Matthew 12:14–21

Today's gospel reading begins on a very ominous note. 'The Pharisees went out and began to plot against him, discussing how to destroy him.' Jesus had just healed a man with a withered hand on the Sabbath, and this was their reaction. Because Jesus worked on the Sabbath, he was considered to be acting contrary to God's law. To protect the integrity of God's law, they decided that Jesus needed to be destroyed. There are certain forms of religious zeal that can be quite destructive of others, as we know only too well from our own times. Jesus was also zealous to do God's will. In John's Gospel he declares that his food is to do the will of the one who sent him. Jesus' religious zeal always brought life and healing to others, never death. In response to his opponents' deadly plotting against him, the gospel reading says that Jesus withdrew from the district and cured many of those who followed him. There would come a time when Jesus would face his enemies and suffer the consequences, but this was not the time. He still had God's life-giving work to do. Sometimes, the right response to hostility is a dignified withdrawal. Matthew interprets this life-giving ministry of Jesus through the long quotation from the prophet Isaiah that he inserts into his gospel at this point. This quotation depicts someone whom God has chosen as his servant. There is a gentle quality to this servant – 'he will not brawl or shout'. His primary concern is for those who are afflicted and vulnerable, the 'crushed reeds' and the 'smouldering wicks' of this world. Matthew sees Jesus as the embodiment of this servant figure. Jesus had spoken of himself as 'gentle and humble of heart' and his primary ministry is to those in greatest need, both physically and spiritually. Jesus is the human face of God's zeal for us, a zeal that works to bring a greater fullness of life to all. It is a zeal that embraces us all, a zeal to which we are all called to give expression in our dealings with others.

20 July, Monday, Sixteenth Week in Ordinary Time
Matthew 12:38–42

When a request is made of Jesus in the gospel reading, 'We should like to see a sign from you', the implication of the request is, 'We will believe in you if you show us a powerful enough sign'. It is a request that Jesus always refused to answer. Faith is never a response to proof. There is always an element of not knowing in faith, which is why faith always implies trust. We may not see clearly but we trust in the Lord because of what he has already shown us. While faith is not a response to proof, it is not blind either. The Lord does not ask us to take a leap into the dark. In the gospel reading, Jesus tells his petitioners that he will give them a sign, what he calls the sign of the prophet Jonah. Jesus is referring to his forthcoming death and resurrection. Just as Jonah was in the belly of the whale for three days and three nights, so the Son of Man will be in the heart of the earth for three days and three nights. He will rise on the third day. This is the ultimate sign that we have all been given, the resurrection of the Lord from the dead. It does not amount to scientific proof, but it is enough to base our faith upon. If the Lord had not been raised from the dead, the Church would never have begun, the Gospels and other texts of the New Testament would never have been written and we would not be celebrating the Eucharist. The resurrection of the Lord is a powerful sign from God. We spend our lives as believers delving into its implications and absorbing its power.

21 July, Tuesday, Sixteenth week in Ordinary Time
Matthew 12:46–50

We all value our families. As we get older we might not see them as often as we once did, but they still matter a great deal to us. They say blood is thicker than water. When a family member is in difficulty, we will generally gather around to provide support. The Gospels don't really tell us a great deal about Jesus' family, yet, whenever the gospel writers do mention his family, they give the impression that there was often tension between Jesus and his blood family. In today's gospel reading, Jesus' family, including his mother, were standing outside where Jesus was speaking, anxious to have a word with him. They were trying to get his attention, trying to get him home, away from the crowds that were always pursuing him. However, on this occasion Jesus stood his ground; he didn't go with his family. Rather, he redefined who his family really were. He identifies his disciples as his family, and declares that all those who do the will of his heavenly Father are now his family. As disciples we are all brothers and sisters of the Lord, and of each other, and sons and daughters of God. This is the new family that Jesus came to form, and what distinguishes this family is the desire to do the will of God as Jesus has revealed it to us by his words and by his life. That is why, together, as members of the Lord's family, Jesus invites us to pray the prayer he often prayed, 'Thy will be done, on earth as it is in heaven'.

22 July, Wednesday, Feast of Saint Mary Magdalene
John 20:1–2, 11–18

Mary Magdalene speaks to the seeker in all of us. In the gospel reading for her feast, the risen Lord asks her two questions: 'Woman, why are you weeping? Who are you looking for?' Mary was weeping because she could not find Jesus, whom she was seeking. In the words of the first reading, 'I sought but did not find him.' Some of the sadness in our lives comes from a sense of loss, an awareness of unfulfilled longing. We have probably all known that particular form of sadness. We long for something or someone, and because that longing goes unfulfilled, we experience a sense of deep sadness. In the gospel reading, Mary's longing for Jesus was satisfied. When the risen Lord spoke her name, she recognised the true identity of the one she thought was the gardener and her sadness was banished. Yet, even in that moment of great joy, she had to learn to let go of Jesus as she had known him. Jesus had to call on her not to cling to him. Because Jesus was returning to the Father, from now on he would relate to her and to all of his disciples in a new way. He would be as close to her and his disciples as he ever was, indeed even closer, but in a different way. The gospel reading assures us that, even if many of our longings go unsatisfied, our longing for the Lord, which is our deepest longing, will always be satisfied. The Lord speaks our name as he spoke Mary's name. Because of his death and resurrection, his Father is now our Father and his God is now our God. In journeying from this world to the Father, the Lord draws us into his own intimate relationship with God, thereby making us his brothers and sisters, and brothers and sisters of each other. If we keep searching for him, like Mary Magdalene, we will come to experience him as the good shepherd who calls his own by name.

23 July, Thursday, Feast of Saint Bridget of Sweden

John 15:1–8

Today's gospel reading for the feast of Saint Bridget of Sweden is taken from John's account of what Jesus said to his disciples on the night before he died. Jesus is taking his leave of his disciples but, before doing so, he wants to assure them that beyond his death and resurrection he will remain in communion with them. The image of the vine and the branches expresses the depth of the communion he desires to have with his disciples, with all of us. The Lord wants to be in communion with all of us, but for that to happen we must seek to remain in communion with him by allowing his words to remain in us and to shape our lives. We can slip out of our communion with him; we can cut ourselves off from the Lord. However, his invitation is always there to return to him and to remain with him or in him. It is in returning to him, in remaining in him, in allowing his words to remain in us, that our lives bear rich fruit, what Paul calls the fruit of the Spirit. According to the last verse of our gospel reading, it is lives rich in the fruit of the Spirit that give glory to God. According to Saint Irenaeus, it is the human person fully alive – alive with the fruit of the Spirit – that gives glory to God. The fourteenth-century saint, Bridget of Sweden, was such a person fully alive. As a wife and mother of six children, she was noted for her works of charity towards those in greatest need, particularly unwed mothers and their children. After the death of her husband, she became a member of the third order of Saint Francis, and devoted herself to a life of prayer and caring for the poor and sick. She went on to found a religious community which became known as the Bridgettines. Her life is a living witness to the words of Jesus in today's gospel reading, 'Whoever remains in me … bears fruit in plenty'.

24 July, Friday, Sixteenth Week in Ordinary Time
Matthew 13:18–23

Jesus was very observant of ordinary everyday life in Galilee. His parables all reflect what he sees and hears all around him. The parable of the sower reflects the practice in Galilee of the farmer scattering seed liberally in a fairly casual fashion. It follows that not all of the seed will land on good soil. A lot of the seed could land in the three situations mentioned in the parable, on the edge of the path, on patches of rock and among thorns. This would have been quite normal.

What is extraordinary is the huge yield given by the seed that falls on good soil. A hundredfold, in particular, is an almost unimaginable yield. Jesus sows or scatters the word of God's kingdom in the same almost casual, indiscriminate way that the farmer scatters his seed. The Gospel is not for a select few; it is offered to all. Because it is offered to all, the word of the Gospel will encounter the same kinds of obstacle encountered by the seed sown by the farmer. In the interpretation of the parable that Jesus give, which is today's gospel reading, the three unproductive terrains, the path, the rocky soil and the thorns, become images of why many do not respond to the Gospel message. Jesus highlights three obstacles to receiving his word: a lack of understanding of the faith, an unwillingness to remain faithful to the word when it becomes costly, and allowing oneself to be overtaken by the worries and the riches of life. These all remain obstacles to the Lord's working in our lives today, but they need not remain insurmountable. Any one of us can become good soil at any time, with the Lord's help. The Lord does not give up on us. He continues to sow his word in our hearts and he continues to support us in our response to his word. If there is any openness in us towards him, we will be able to say, with Saint Paul, 'His grace towards me has not been in vain'.

25 July, Saturday, Feast of Saint James, Apostle
Matthew 20:20–28

According to the Gospels of Mark and Matthew, James, along with his brother John, were among the first disciples that Jesus called to follow him. Their father, Zebedee, seems to have had a successful fishing business by the Sea of Galilee, as he had 'hired men' working for him alongside his two sons (Mark 1:20). According to Mark, James and his brother were present at key events in the public ministry of Jesus, such as his raising of the daughter of Jairus, his transfiguration on the mountain, his announcement on the Mount of Olives of the coming destruction of the Temple and his distraught prayer in the Garden of Gethsemane. According to Luke in the Acts of the Apostles, King Herod Agrippa 'had James, the brother of John, killed with the sword' (Acts 12:2). He was the first member of the twelve to die for his faith in the Lord. According to an ancient tradition his bones were brought from Jerusalem to Compostella in north-western Spain, and the Shrine of Saint James in Compostella has been a place of pilgrimage for the past thousand years or more. Of all the passages in the New Testament where James features, today's gospel reading shows him in the least favourable light. In Mark's Gospel, James and John ask Jesus directly for seats on his right and left in his kingdom. Matthew, in today's gospel reading, appears to mitigate this embarrassing request of these leading disciples by having their mother do the asking. James's preoccupation with worldly honour draws forth Jesus' powerful teaching on what constitutes honour in his kingdom. 'Anyone who wants to be great among you must be your servant.' James went on to be a great servant of the Church and of the Lord, even to the point of drinking the cup of suffering that Jesus drank. At this point in the gospel story, James was a work in progress. God had begun a good work in him and would bring it to completion. James is an encouragement to us all. Sometimes, like James in today's gospel reading, we can display a side to ourselves that falls short of what the Lord desires. However, such failures need not hold us back from continuing to take the path the Lord is calling us to take or prevent us becoming the faithful servant the Lord desires us to be.

27 July, Monday, Seventeenth Week in Ordinary Time
Matthew 13:31–35
In today's gospel reading from Matthew, Jesus speaks two parables, one which features a man and the other a woman, a farmer who sows mustard seed and a woman who bakes bread. In Luke's Gospel, Jesus

again speaks two parables that feature a man and a woman, a shepherd who looks for his lost sheep and a woman who searches for her lost coin. The experiences of men and women were important to Jesus; both sets of experience could speak to him about the ways of God in the world. In both of today's parables there is a focus on the power of something very small. A tiny mustard seed can produce a large shrub in which birds can make their nest. A tiny piece of leaven, when mixed in with three measures of flour, can produce enough bread, it has been estimated, to feed a hundred people. Jesus may have been saying to his disciples that his own ministry might seem very small and limited. Galilee was a tiny region of the vast Roman Empire. Jesus had access to only a relatively small proportion of the people of Galilee itself. Even among those he had access to, he was already beginning to encounter opposition. Such beginnings could seem very unpromising, but Jesus assures his disciples that such small beginnings will bring forth something wonderful that will leave huge numbers blessed, as we can all vouch for. The two parables also speak to our own small efforts to do what is right and good. Jesus is reminding us that if we allow the Lord to work through us in even the smallest of ways, we will be surprised at the great good that will come from such small beginnings.

28 July, Tuesday, Seventeenth Week in Ordinary Time
Matthew 13:36–43

The explanation of the parable of the wheat and darnel in today's gospel reading suggests that, within our world, good will always sit alongside evil until the end of time. It is only beyond this present age that, in the words of the gospel reading, 'the virtuous will shine like the sun', with no darkness to obscure the light of their goodness. We are only too well aware of the presence of evil in our world, and, indeed, within the Church and in our own hearts. Various religious movements have attempted to create a perfect society, an oasis of goodness in an evil world. Such movements can end up doing more harm than good to the people who get involved; they can easily project the darkness that is within themselves onto the world outside the movement. However, matters are never that black and white. The Church is not a cult. In the language of the Second Vatican Council, we are a pilgrim people. We are on a journey towards that glorious virtuous state spoken of in the gospel reading. In this earthly life, we never reach the end of that journey. At every step of the journey we can make our own the confession of the first reading from the prophet Jeremiah, 'Lord, we do confess our wickedness and our father's guilt: we have indeed sinned against you.' Such a recognition of the lack of goodness in our lives does not discourage us because we are confident that, in the words of today's responsorial psalm, the Lord's compassion hastens to meet us. Indeed, our realisation and recognition that we are still on the way creates a space in our lives for the Lord to bring to completion the good work that he has begun in us. The Gospels suggest that Jesus found it much easier to engage with those who were aware of their need of God's mercy than with those who thought of themselves as morally superior to others.

29 July, Wednesday, Feast of Saint Martha

John 11:19–27

Today we celebrate the feast of Saint Martha. She appears in two of the Gospels, Luke and John, in each case in the company of her sister Mary. In today's gospel reading from John, Martha is portrayed as a woman in grief, because of the death of her brother Lazarus. Martha, her sister Mary and her brother Lazarus are referred to as loved by Jesus, as friends of Jesus. This is a family of disciples who have experienced the love of God present in Jesus and have responded to that love. Martha's grief at the death of her brother Lazarus is the grief of a disciple, of a believer. Her opening words to Jesus on his arrival seem to express her disappointment at Jesus' absence at the time of her brother's death. 'If you had been here, my brother would not have died.' She symbolises every believer who struggles to come to terms with the apparent absence of the Lord in the face of the stark reality of the death of a loved one. Yet her grief does not leave her hopeless, as is evident from her subsequent words to Jesus. 'I know that, even now, whatever you ask of God, he will grant you.' To the grieving, yet hopeful Martha, Jesus reveals himself as the resurrection and the life and he then makes a wonderful promise that has spoken to grieving believers down through the centuries. The promise declares that all who believe in Jesus already share in Jesus' risen life, and that the moment of physical death will not break that life-giving communion with Jesus. The question Jesus addresses to Martha, 'Do you believe this?', is addressed to every believer, and we are all asked to make our own Martha's response to Jesus' question. 'Yes, Lord, I believe … .'

30 July, Thursday, Seventeenth Week in Ordinary Time
Matthew 13:47–53

The parable in today's gospel reading is based on one of the standard ways of fishing in the Sea of Galilee at the time of Jesus. Two boats pull a very large dragnet between them. As a result, all sorts of fish are caught. Some of the fish would not be suitable for selling at the local fish market, and, so, when the catch is brought to land, these fish would have to be separated out from the fish that could be sold. In what way is the kingdom of heaven like that everyday reality by the Sea of Galilee? Perhaps Jesus is suggesting that as he goes about his ministry, he casts the net of God's loving presence very broadly. The Gospel is preached to all and sundry; Jesus does not discriminate. Everyone needs to hear the Gospel of God's unconditional love for all. No one is considered unworthy of the Gospel. As Jesus says elsewhere in Matthew's Gospel, using a different image, God makes his sun to shine and his rain to fall on good and bad alike. However, Jesus is aware that not everyone will respond to his proclamation of the reign of God's merciful and faithful love. Just as the fishermen have to separate out fish that can be sold from fish that can't, so there will come a moment, at the end of time, when God will separate out those who tried to respond to Jesus' proclamation of God's loving presence and those who refused to do so. In the meantime, the Lord continues to throw the net of God's love over our lives and his grace at work within us continues to move us to respond. The Lord does not give up on us, even if our initial response leaves a lot to be desired. He is like the potter in the first reading who keeps shaping our lives, taking even what is wrong in our lives and making something new and good from it. We, of course, are not passive clay in the Lord's hands. We can help the efforts of the potter by continuing to open ourselves to his loving work in our lives.

31 July, Friday, Seventeenth Week in Ordinary Time
Matthew 13:54–58

The journey of faith is one on which we can find ourselves asking questions. At whatever stage of our faith journey we are, a questioning spirit, mind and heart can leave us open to a deeper and more rooted faith in the Lord. In today's gospel reading, we find the people of Nazareth asking questions about Jesus. Their first question seems a really good one: 'Where did the man get this wisdom and these miraculous powers?' They are astonished both at what he said, his wisdom, and what he did, his miraculous powers. They knew Jesus as 'the carpenter's son'. The implication of their question is that Jesus did not get his wisdom and his miraculous powers in Nazareth, working at carpentry with his father, Joseph. His background, his upbringing wasn't all that different from anybody else's background and upbringing in Nazareth, and nobody else had Jesus' wisdom and miraculous powers. So, where did he get them? It is an obvious question and a good question. It is a question that had the potential to lead those who asked it to faith in Jesus as God's representative on earth, God's Son. However, that is not where their question led. The gospel reading simply states, 'They did not accept him'. Jesus goes on to lament their inability to see him as more than the carpenter's son. The Lord can lead us to himself through our questions. However, sometimes, as in the case of the people of Nazareth, our questions can leave us thinking that we know more than we do, and then our questions become an obstacle, a stumbling stone, between the Lord and ourselves. Today's gospel reading invites us to allow our questions to become stepping stones to the Lord, rather than stumbling stones between us and him. In that sense, we are to question on our knees, in a spirit of prayerful openness to the Lord's leading and guiding.

1 August, Saturday, Seventeenth Week in Ordinary Time
Matthew 14:1–12

In today's first reading, Jeremiah warns the people of Jerusalem that if they put him to death they will be bringing innocent blood on themselves, on the city and its citizens. The people heeded Jeremiah's warning, declaring, 'This man does not deserve to die'. In the gospel reading, Herod Antipas has no qualms about bringing innocent blood down on himself. He had John the Baptist arrested and imprisoned because John's preaching was not to his liking and, in particular, was not to the liking of his wife Herodias. During the celebrations for Herod's birthday, the daughter of Herodias from a previous marriage so beguiled Herod that he made a rash promise to her in public. She could have anything she asked. When, at her mother's prompting, she asked for the head of John the Baptist on a dish, Herod felt obliged to honour his public promise so as to avoid the shame of losing face. Yet the gospel reading says that it distressed Herod to grant his wife's request. There was something about John that appealed to Herod's better nature. He heard some call in John's preaching. However, he silenced that call rather than bring down dishonour on himself by refusing to keep his publicly made promise. His need to protect his honour led him to shed innocent blood. The dilemma of Herod is a very human one. The Lord calls out to what is best in us but we don't always allow ourselves to hear his call or respond to it. Other more self-regarding concerns can have greater influence over us, such as the concern to protect our honour, how we appear to others. Yet the Lord's call never goes away. The Lord never gives up on our response, even though we may seem deaf to his call. The Lord keeps pursuing us in his love, appealing to what is deepest and best in us.

3 August, Monday, Eighteenth Week in Ordinary Time
Matthew 14:22–36

In the gospel reading, in response to Peter's invitation, Jesus called Peter to step out of the boat and to come towards him across the water. Surely it would have been safer for Peter to stay in the boat, given that the sea was rough and the wind was strong. Why would Peter want to step out of the relative safety of his boat and walk towards Jesus, and why would Jesus encourage him to do so, calling on him to 'come'? Perhaps the evangelist is reminding us through this story that following Jesus will sometimes mean stepping out of our boat, the place where we feel relatively secure, and launching ourselves out into the deep. Today's gospel reading invites us to reflect on the ways that the Lord may be calling us to take some new step in our relationship with him. The Lord is always calling us to 'come'; he is constantly inviting us to grow in our lived witness to him. The Lord's call to 'come' will take different forms for different people. Today's gospel reading assures us that whenever we respond to the Lord's invitation to 'come', he will be there to support us when the journey becomes difficult. He will reach out to us when, like Peter, we cry out to him, 'Lord save me'. The Lord who calls us to journey towards him journeys with us as our strength in times of weakness.

4 August, Tuesday, Eighteenth Week in Ordinary Time
Matthew 15:1–2, 1—14

In the gospel reading the Pharisees criticises the disciples of Jesus for their lack of reverence for the body of traditions that had grown up around the Jewish law, in particular the various regulations relating to the washing of hands before eating food. Jesus defends his disciples, however, by declaring that these regulations are not decisive in God's scheme of things. What comes out of people's mouths, what comes from their hearts, is more important before God than the food that goes into their mouths. What comes from a person's heart is what defines the person, not what they eat or how they eat. It is the heart that counts; we often say of people that their heart is in the right place. On one occasion in Matthew's Gospel Jesus says, 'Learn from me, for I am gentle and humble of heart'. He calls on us to have something of his own heart within us. In the beatitudes he declares blessed those who are pure in heart, those whose heart is focused on what God wants, just as the heart of Jesus was. Jesus seems to suggest that if we get the heart right, if it is like his heart, then all else will follow. Getting the heart right is above all the work of the Holy Spirit. It is the Spirit who creates within us a heart that is truly Christ-like. One of the most beautiful prayers in the Church's tradition is 'Come Holy Spirit, fill my heart, and kindle in me the fire of your love'.

5 August, Wednesday, Eighteenth Week in Ordinary Time

Matthew 15:21–28

Many of us find that gospel story just a little disturbing. Jesus' way of responding to the pagan woman seems so out of character. This mother's desperate pleas for her sick daughter initially meet with silence from Jesus. 'He answered her not a word.' As we know from our experience silence from others can be as difficult to deal with as anything they might say. Indeed, sometimes silence can be harder to deal with than even difficult words. The woman, however, was determined to break through Jesus' silence; she continued to shout after Jesus and his disciples. When Jesus finally did break his silence, it would not have given this mother much hope. 'I was sent only to the lost sheep of the house of Israel.' Matthew's Gospel in particular, from which our reading is taken, portrays Jesus' ministry as addressed primarily to his own people. The people of Israel needed to experience the Gospel first; Israel needed renewing, and it would be a renewed Israel who would bring the Gospel to the pagans. It is only in the last verses of Matthew's Gospel that the risen Lord finally sends his disciples, the core of a renewed Israel, to preach the Gospel to all the nations. The implication was that this distraught mother would have to wait a little longer. But, she wasn't prepared to wait. In response to her dogged persistence, Jesus speaks a mini parable, which sounds harsh to our ears today. Just as children have priority over house dogs when it comes to food, the people of Israel have priority over pagans when it comes to Jesus' ministry, at least for the moment. The woman's witty response to Jesus' mini parable shows that she recognises the priority that the people of Israel have in Jesus' ministry, but she suggests that pagans like herself can at least have some of their scraps. Jesus must have felt he had met his match, because he immediately granted her request. There is something about this woman that we find very appealing. We like her gutsy faith that won't take no for an answer, not even from Jesus. We probably need that kind of stubborn faith in these times, a faith that does not give up even when the Lord seems silent and unresponsive.

6 August, Thursday, The Transfiguration of the Lord
Mark 9:2–10

There are very few incidents in the life of Jesus that have a feast of their own. We have the feast of the Presentation of Jesus in the Temple, the feast of his baptism; we remember his crucifixion on Good Friday and his resurrection on Easter Sunday. The transfiguration of Jesus on the mountain in the presence of three of his disciples also has its own feast, which we celebrate today. It suggests the importance of this incident in the life of Jesus and in our own understanding of him. Just before Jesus' transfiguration, he had spoken to his disciples for the first time about his forthcoming passion and death. The disciples, and Peter in particular, struggled to accept and understand what Jesus had to say. Perhaps, through this experience of Jesus' transfiguration on the mountain, Jesus wanted to give his disciples a glimpse of what lay beyond the passion and death that awaited him in Jerusalem. In the words of the voice from heaven, Jesus was God's beloved Son. He remained God's beloved Son as he hung from the cross. The loving hands of God would reverse what human hands had done to Jesus. God would bring Jesus, his beloved Son, through the suffering and death that had been inflicted on him, into a new and glorious life, of which the disciples on the mountain were now given a glimpse. The disciples were transfixed by what they saw on that occasion; Peter, in particular, wanted to prolong this vision of the glorified Jesus, this vision of heaven. I suppose if any of us had such a vision of heaven, we wouldn't want to let it go either. If Jesus is God's beloved Son in a unique sense, we are all God's beloved sons and daughters. As Jesus declares in John's Gospel, 'as the Father has loved me, so I have loved you'. Just as God ensured that suffering and death would not have the last word in relation to Jesus, he will ensure that suffering and death will not have the last word in our regard either. When we look upon the transfigured Jesus, we are also looking upon our own ultimate destiny. Saint Paul, in his second letter to the Corinthians, suggests that something of this glorious destiny that awaits us can become a reality in our lives here and now. 'All of us ... seeing the glory of the Lord as though reflected in a mirror, are being transformed into the same image from one degree of glory to another'.

7 August, Friday, Eighteenth Week in Ordinary Time
Matthew 16:24–28

Jesus often speaks in ways that strike us as strange, such as in today's gospel reading when he declares that 'anyone who wants to save his life will lose it'. We might find ourselves wondering, 'How could this be true?' 'What does Jesus mean by this?' It is one of those sayings that requires a certain amount of teasing out. When Jesus speaks about the 'one who wants to save his life', he is probably referring to those who selfishly seek self-fulfilment, who grasp at life in a very self-centred and self-regarding way. Jesus is declaring that such people will not live truly fulfilled lives; at the end of the day, they will lose their lives. In contrast, those who lose their lives for the sake of Jesus will find their lives; those who are prepared to give their lives away in love, because this is what Jesus did for us and asks of us, will receive the fullness of life as a gift of God. They will receive this fullness of life in eternity, but they will begin to experience it already here and now in this earthly life. Jesus is saying that we don't find ourselves, our true selves, by focusing on ourselves. Rather, we find ourselves by focusing beyond ourselves, by focusing on others in love, by focusing on the Lord present in others and calling out to us through others. Jesus declares that it is possible to gain the whole world and to lose our very selves, our true selves, the selves that are made in God's image. The reverse is also true. We can lose everything, out of love for God and others, and yet find life to the full. It is above all the life and death of Jesus that reveals this to be so.

8 August, Saturday, Eighteenth Week in Ordinary Time
Matthew 17:14–20

In today's gospel reading, the disciples of Jesus find themselves powerless before the desperate plight of the father of a young boy. A distraught father had brought his son to the disciples for them to heal him, and they were unable to do so. Much to the distress of the father, the disciples found themselves helpless before this tragedy. There can be times in our own lives when we feel that some situation is beyond us. It seems too demanding for our resources. We feel powerless and helpless. We are brought face to face with our limitations. It seems to have come as a surprise to the disciples that their power to help this father's son was so limited. They asked Jesus, 'Why were we unable to cast it out?' They had just witnessed Jesus doing what they were unable to do, heal this father's seriously disturbed son, and they wondered why they could not have done what Jesus did. When we come face to face with our limitations, it can sometimes come as a surprise to us, especially if we have been used to getting things done. We can find ourselves asking the question the disciples asked, 'Why couldn't we have done more?' In reality, we can only do so much on our own. Jesus' answer to the disciples' question suggests that they were trying to heal this boy on their own, rather than in union with Jesus. Jesus addresses them as people of little faith. In other words, their relationship with Jesus was weak. He assures them that if this relationship was stronger, if their faith was stronger, they could have done so much more. 'Nothing would be impossible for you.' If we remain in communion with the Lord, through faith, the Lord will be able to do so much more through us than we could ever be able to do on our own. As Jesus says elsewhere in the Gospels, 'For God, all things are possible'.

10 August, Monday, Saint Lawrence, Deacon and Martyr
John 12:24–26

Lawrence was a deacon in Rome who was martyred for his faith in Christ in the year 258. There has been continuous devotion to him since shortly after his death. The Emperor Constantine, the first Christian emperor, publicly honoured his grave with a chapel. The Basilica of Saint Lawrence Outside the Walls in Rome stands over the site today. Today's gospel reading is very suited to the feast of this early Christian martyr. There Jesus refers to himself as the wheat grain which falls to the ground and dies, and in dying yields a rich harvest. The rich harvest that came from his death and resurrection was the community of believers, the Church. Jesus' self-giving love, even though it led him to death on a cross, was life-giving for himself and for all humanity. He did not try to preserve his life at all costs; he was prepared to empty himself out of love for others and in doing so he gained life for himself and others. Jesus goes on to state that this pattern of life through death applies equally to his followers. If we love our lives above all else, if our primary goal in life is to preserve and protect ourselves, then we risk losing ourselves. We fail to become our true selves, the selves that are the image of the Lord. If, like Jesus, we are willing to lose ourselves, to give of ourselves, in the service of the Lord and his people, then we will become alive with the life of God and our presence will be life-giving for others. This is the paradox at the heart of the Christian life. It is in giving that we receive and, as Paul reminds us in the first reading, our giving is always to be cheerful: 'God loves a cheerful giver.'

11 August, Tuesday, Nineteenth Week in Ordinary Time
Matthew 18:—5, 10, 12–14

The question the disciples ask Jesus, 'Who is the greatest in the kingdom of heaven?' reveals a preoccupation with status and honour. In his response, Jesus cuts across this preoccupation, which is far removed from his own concerns. He does not answer the question directly but declares that the disciples will not even enter the kingdom of God unless they become like little children. In that culture, children, although loved by their parents, were considered to have no rights, no status, no honour. They were completely dependent on others for everything. In calling on all of his disciples to become like little children, he is calling on us to cast off all notions of status and honour and to recognise our complete dependence on God for everything, our poverty before God. As Jesus says elsewhere, it is those who humble themselves who will be exalted (by God). Humility is not about putting oneself down but about being grounded or earthed in the reality of our creaturely status ('humus' is Latin for 'earth'). The humble are those who recognise the truth of their reality as beggars before God, dependent upon God for all that is good. As a result, the humble will not promote themselves over others but will recognise the common humanity that they share with all people. They will recognise and welcome the Lord in the weakest, those without status or position, such as children. The conclusion of the gospel reading suggests they will go further and set off in search of such 'little ones' when they stray.

12 August, Wednesday, Nineteenth Week in Ordinary Time
Matthew 18:15–20

We can often be impressed by numbers, and that is true even within the context of the Church. We look to see how many are coming to Mass or how many are signing up to this parish event or to that parish ministry. Jesus' way of looking at things is somewhat different from ours. Numbers did not seem to be an issue for him. He understood the value of the one; he spoke of the shepherd who left the ninety-nine sheep to go in the search of the one who was lost. In today's gospel reading he declares that where two or three are gathered in his name, he is there in the midst of them. The smallest gathering in a tiny church is just as significant as the huge congregation in one of the great cathedrals or basilicas of the world. In these days of declining numbers within the Church, the gospel reading teaches us to appreciate the significance of those present, regardless of how few, rather than allowing ourselves to become too discouraged by those who are not present. The Lord is present where two or three are gathered in his name, and if we are open and responsive to the Lord's presence among us, few though we may be, he will draw others to himself through us.

13 August, Thursday, Nineteenth Week in Ordinary Time
Matthew 18:21–19:1

In today's gospel reading, Peter asks Jesus a very concrete question: 'How often must I forgive my brother if he wrongs me?' He goes on to suggest an answer. 'Seven times!' The number 'seven' was a symbol of perfection in the culture of Jesus, so to forgive someone seven times would seem like perfect forgiveness. Jesus would have shocked his hearers with his answer to Peter's question. 'Not seven ... but seventy-seven times.' Jesus seems to call for limitless forgiveness. We might be tempted to ask, 'Is Jesus' call for unlimited forgiveness not impossible to achieve?' His teaching flies in the face of how most people think and behave today. We don't live in a very forgiving culture. The parable that Jesus goes on to speak seeks to justify his call for forgiveness without limit. In the first part of the parable, a man, probably a high-ranking official, owed an astronomical debt to a pagan king. The 10,000 talents owed would be equivalent to the vast international debts under which some developing countries labour today. He asks the king for time to pay it back. In reality, he could never have repaid such a debt, no matter how much time he was given. In an extraordinary act of generosity, the king simply cancelled the whole debt. Jesus is reminding us that God's forgiveness is limitless; it doesn't make sense from a merely human point of view. This forgiveness has been poured out on us through the life, death and resurrection of Jesus. The second part of the parable is a little more challenging, because it calls on us to allow this boundless forgiveness we receive to so shape our lives that it flows through us to those who offend and hurt us. It doesn't mean that forgiving another will ever come easily to us, but the more aware we become of ourselves as graced by God's boundless mercy, as forgiven sinners, the freer we will be to forgive those who sin against us.

14 August, Friday, Nineteenth Week in Ordinary Time
Matthew 19:3–12
The Gospels show that Jesus was often tested by his opponents. They sought in various ways to trip him up. We have an example of that in today's gospel reading. The Pharisees put a thorny question to Jesus: 'Is it against the law for a man to divorce his wife on any pretext whatever?' In the time of Jesus, there was a school of teachers of the law who held this view; a man could divorce his wife for any reason. There was another school of teachers who held that a man could divorce his wife only on certain grounds. Jesus was being tested as to which school he favoured. It is simply presumed that it is the man who divorces the woman. There was no provision in Jewish law for a woman to divorce her husband, which left married women rather vulnerable. As so often when Jesus is asked a testing question,

he doesn't answer directly. Instead, he goes behind the divorce law, which is to be found in the Book of Deuteronomy, to God's original intention for marriage, which is be found in the Book of Genesis, the first book of the Bible. When a man and woman marry, they are one body, one flesh. In other words, a husband is to treat his wife as if she were himself, and the wife is to treat her husband as if he were herself. Man and woman are equal in marriage; they belong to each other equally. This original intention of God for marriage was much more enlightened than the divorce law that was current at the time, regardless of how that law was interpreted by the two schools. Jesus speaks here as the authoritative interpreter of God's will for marriage. We can broaden that out and say that Jesus is the authoritative interpreter of God's will for our lives in regard to every issue he speaks about. He is the one who lights up God's purpose for our lives and our world. That is why, as followers of Jesus, we always read the Jewish Scriptures in the light of Jesus' teaching and way of life.

15 August, Saturday, The Assumption of the Blessed Virgin Mary
Luke 1:39–56

Today's feast celebrates the good news that because Mary belonged to Jesus in a special way throughout her earthly life, she now shares in a special way in his risen life. This feast does not celebrate a privilege of Mary alone, because where Mary now is, God wants all of us to be. We are all destined to share fully in the Lord's risen and glorious life. In the words of Saint Paul in today's second reading, 'all will be brought to life in Christ'. The opening words of today's first reading from the Book of Revelation have been understood as an imaginative depiction of Mary's glorious life: 'a woman, adorned with the sun, standing on the moon, and with the twelve stars on her head for a crown'. At the same time, that first reading also brings home to us that Mary's glorious destiny belongs to us all.

Whereas the woman in that reading has been regarded as referring to Mary, the woman can also be understood as an image of the Church. The reading depicts a conflict between the woman and the dragon. The dragon's seven heads would have suggested the seven hills of Rome. At the time the Book of Revelation was written, the Church was under great pressure from Roman society to worship the Roman emperor as the agent of the Roman gods. Because the members of the Church refused to do so, they were always at risk of persecution. The woman, the Church, is trying to give birth to Christ in that Roman world, but the dragon, the evil power that is behind the Roman Empire, stands ready to devour this child, this Christ who claims to be the ruler of the nations. It is an image of the Church confronted by forces that are opposed to God's purpose for the world. The woman signifies both Mary, who gave birth to Jesus, and the Church, which continues to give birth to Jesus in every age through the lives of its members.

Mary, in that sense, is an image of the Church and, so, when we look to Mary, we can learn a lot about ourselves as Church. In Luke's Gospel, from which our gospel reading is taken, Mary is portrayed as the ideal disciple. She embodies what we, as Church, as disciples of the Lord, are called to become. Mary not only shows us our ultimate destiny, but also what it means to be a disciple of the risen Lord now. In the gospel reading, Elizabeth addresses Mary as 'the mother of my Lord'. In that regard, Mary is unique. However, Elizabeth then goes on to declare Mary blessed because she believed the promise made to her by the Lord. In that regard, we can be like her. She was a woman of faith; she entrusted herself to the Lord's word. 'Let it be to me according to your word.' We are all called to entrust ourselves to the Lord's word so that it shapes our lives, as it shaped the life of Mary. In that gospel reading, Mary shows us what a life shaped by God's word looks like. She went as quickly as she could to her older cousin Elizabeth, whose need was greater than Mary's. It was a journey of love. Mary's faith was expressing itself in the loving service of someone more vulnerable than herself.

The second half of the gospel reading shows us that Mary's faith also found expression in prayer. It reached out to others in love and it reached out to God in prayer. If our faith finds expression in love, it will also find expression in prayer. In her prayer, Mary comes before the Lord in her poverty, as his lowly servant, ready to receive from God all the great things that God wants to give. Mary teaches us that when we pray we always come before God in our need, with open hearts ready to receive all God has to offer us. Mary's prayer also shows another side of her faith. It is a faith that hungers for God's justice to become a reality on earth. She sings of a God who pulls down oppressive princes from their thrones and lifts us, the lowly, the downtrodden. She sings of a God who works to fill the hungry with good things at the expense of the self-satisfied rich. Today's feast celebrates Mary as one who not only shows us the glorious destiny that awaits us at the end of our life's journey but also how we are to travel that journey as disciples of the Lord.

17 August, Monday, Twentieth Week in Ordinary Time
Matthew 19:16–22

Many of the questions that are put to Jesus in the Gospels are with a view to testing him. However, the question that a young man puts to Jesus in today's gospel reading is very sincere. 'Master, what good deed must I do to possess eternal life?' It is the question of someone who wants to do what is good, thereby securing his ultimate salvation. The question, 'What is the path to life?' is an important question for all of us. Jesus answers this man's serious question from within the Jewish tradition that they share; he quotes the second half of the Ten Commandments, which deal with how we relate to others, and he then adds to them the second of the two great commandments, 'You must love your neighbour as yourself'. Jesus is saying to this man that the way to life is the way of love. For us as Christians, it is Jesus who shows us what the way of love looks like by his teaching and his life. When we ask a serious question of someone, the answer will not always satisfy us. Clearly, this young man was not satisfied by Jesus' answer. 'What more do I need to do?' he asks. In response to this second question, Jesus calls the young man to follow him on his journey, just as Peter, James, John, Matthew and others have done. This would have involved this young man leaving his many possessions so as to follow physically in the footsteps of someone who had nowhere to lay his head. He couldn't bring himself to do that; he was too attached to his possessions. His possessions possessed him. The realisation that he wasn't free to answer the call of Jesus left him sad. He was a good man, but he discovered he wasn't free to do what the Lord wanted of him. Many of us may find ourselves in that same place. We are fundamentally good people, but some excessive attachment in our lives holds us back from answering the Lord's call as generously as we might. Before that realisation, we need to keep praying for a greater share in the freedom of the Holy Spirit, the freedom that Jesus displayed to the full, the freedom to go where the Lord is calling us to go.

18 August, Tuesday, Twentieth Week in Ordinary Time
Matthew 19:23–30

'High hopes and hubris left in debris.' This was the headline in one of our newspapers recently in relation to a football team who had lost an important game. It is not often you see a Greek word in a newspaper headline. Even though 'hubris' is a Greek word, we all know what it means. It refers to an excessive self-confidence, a certain over-valu-ing of ourselves, a failure to recognise our place, our limitations, an excessive pride. The prophet Ezekiel accuses the ruler of the great city of Tyre of hubris in today's first reading. 'Being swollen with pride, you have said: I am a god'. To say, 'I am a god', is the most extreme form of hubris. Tyre had become very wealthy, and, according to Ezekiel, as it became wealthier, its heart became more arrogant. Too much wealth can sometimes lead to arrogant self-sufficiency, to hubris. This is why Jesus says in today's gospel reading, 'It is easier for a camel to pass through the eye of a needle, than for a rich man to enter the kingdom of heaven'. When we have less, whether that is less wealth, less health, less energy, less security, less independence, we can be much more aware of our dependence on God,. This recognition of our dependence on God is the attitude of humility, the attitude of the poor in spirit. It is the attitude that says, in the words of today's gospel reading, 'For God everything is possible', rather than the attitude which says, 'For me everything is possible'. It doesn't so much say, 'I have done great things', but, like Mary, it says, 'The Almighty has done great things for me, for us'.

19 August, Wednesday, Twentieth Week in Ordinary Time
Matthew 20:1–16
The reaction of the workers to the landowner's very generous treatment of the men who worked for only the last hour of the working day has echoes of the reaction of the older son in the parable of the prodigal son to his father's very generous treatment of the younger son. In both parables the reaction is one of righteous indignation that someone was receiving far more than they deserved. The younger son had wasted his father's property in a self-indulgent lifestyle, yet he was treated like the lord of the manor. The last group of workers had worked for only one hour and yet they were given a whole day's wages. In both parables we find it easy to identify with the reaction of the older son and the reaction of those who did a heavy day's work in

all the heat. Somehow both parables seem to offend our sense of justice, our feel for what is right and fair. The father in the first parable was extremely generous towards his wayward son; the landowner in today's gospel reading is extremely generous towards the men who worked only one hour. In both parables, there is a quality of generosity and mercy that seems to shatter our sense of justice. Yet this is precisely the message of these parables. God's generosity, God's mercy, is not simply a bigger version of human generosity and mercy. It has a completely different quality, one that leaves us scratching our heads. At the end of the day that is good news for us all.

20 August, Thursday, Twentieth Week in Ordinary Time
Matthew 22:1–14

In today's parable Jesus speaks of the kingdom of God as a wedding feast to which people are invited. The great feast is a frequent image of the kingdom of God in the Gospels. It is an image which suggests God's gracious and generous hospitality. The Eucharist can be understood as an anticipation of the banquet in the kingdom of heaven. At the Eucharist we not only look back to the Last Supper but we also look forward to the banquet of eternal life. At the Last Supper Jesus said to his disciples, 'I tell you, I will never again drink of this fruit of the vine until that day when I drink it new with you in my Father's kingdom'. In the parable in today's gospel reading, many of those who had been invited to the wedding banquet and who had already agreed to come turned down the invitation at the last minute, just when everything was ready. Even some of those who did respond to the invitation did not take the event seriously, as was clear from their inappropriate dress. God invites and he persistently invites, even after many refusals. It is up to us to respond. Our presence at the Eucharist is a sign that we are responding to the Lord's invitation. Yet we have to keep clothing ourselves in the right way, clothing ourselves with

Christ, as Paul says. We are sent out from the Eucharist to put on Christ, to put on the one whom we have received and who desires to live in and through us.

21 August, Friday, Twentieth Week in Ordinary Time
Matthew 22:34–40

The question that is put to Jesus in today's gospel reading – 'Which is the greatest commandment of the law?' – was asked with a view to disconcerting him. Jesus was being put to the test. Yet, in spite of the man's questionable motivation, Jesus took the question seriously and gave his questioner and all of us an answer that is worth pondering. Although he was asked about the greatest commandment, Jesus' answer put two commandments side by side. The first commandment was the core of the prayer recited by observant Jews several times a day, called the 'Shema'. The Hebrew word '*shema*' means 'hear'. The prayer is called after its first word. 'Hear O Israel the Lord your God is one ...'. In a similar way, the prayer that we might pray several times a day as Christians, the Lord's Prayer, is often referred to by its first two words, 'Our Father'. The combining of this commandment with the commandment to love our neighbour as ourselves seems distinctive to Jesus. For Jesus, to love God with all one's heart and soul and mind is inseparable from the love of neighbour in the way that God loves. Elsewhere Jesus defines 'neighbour' in a very inclusive way as embracing all of humanity, including even our enemy. Jesus declares that the whole law and the prophets hang on these two commandments. Love is the key to interpreting all the requirements of the law and the prophets. Jesus shows us by his life and death what loving God with all our being and loving our neighbour as we love ourselves looks like. He not only shows us what such love looks like, he also pours the Holy Spirit into our hearts so that we may be empowered to love in the way that he does.

22 August, Saturday, Queenship of Mary

Luke 1:26–28

During the Middle Ages Mary was venerated as queen of the angels and saints. Pope Pius XII proclaimed the Queenship of Mary as a memorial of the universal Church at the close of the Marian Year of 1955. The memorial is placed on this date, 22 August, to stress its connection with the feast of the Assumption, exactly a week earlier. The gospel reading for today's feast tells us that if Mary now reigns with her Son in heaven, it is because she gave herself over to God's purpose for her earthly life, as did Jesus her Son. There are many 'call' stories in the Gospels and in the Bible as a whole. Today's gospel reading is the story of the call of Mary. According to the passage, Mary displayed a whole range of responses to God's approach to her. Initially, she was 'deeply disturbed', and then she asked, 'How can this come about?' It was only after this interior journey that she finally surrendered to what God was asking of her. 'Let what you have said be done to me.' The reading suggests that Mary's response came at the end of a period of struggle. There will always be an element of struggle in our own dealings with the Lord, in our own efforts to respond to the Lord's call. Mary's response of total surrender to God's purpose for her life did not come easily to her and does not come easily to us. However, in our struggle to live in harmony with God's purpose for our lives, we all have the assurance of Gabriel's words to Mary. 'Nothing is impossible to God'. What may seem impossible to us is always possible with God's help. We can all come to make our own the words of Saint Paul, 'By the grace of God I am what I am, and his grace toward me has not been in vain' (1 Corinthians 15:10).

24 August, Monday, Feast of Saint Bartholomew

John 1:45–51

Bartholomew has been traditionally identified with Nathanael, who features in today's gospel reading. Jesus pays him a lovely compliment. 'Here is an Israelite, incapable of deceit.' Or, in another translation, 'in whom there is no guile'. Jesus admired Nathanael's openness and honesty. Even his dusty opinion about Nazareth, 'Can anything good come out of Nazareth?', was, at least, an honest opinion; it was what he believed. Nathanael went on to recognise that his honest opinion about Nazareth was a mistaken one. He came to see that Jesus from Nazareth was none other than the Son of God and the king of Israel. It takes a generosity of heart and spirit to recognise when we have got it wrong, to acknowledge that our opinion of some person or place has been shaped by our prejudices rather than by reality. Nathanael's honesty and generosity of heart can be an inspiration to us on this his feast day. The final word of the gospel reading, however, is given to Jesus, not to Nathanael. It takes the form of that wonderful promise Jesus makes to him. 'You will see greater things ... You will see heaven laid open and, above the Son of Man, the angels of God ascending and descending'. We may have a certain insight into Jesus, a certain appreciation of him, like Nathanael, but Jesus assures us that there is so much more to see and appreciate. In our relationship with Jesus, we are always only towards the beginning of our journey. There are always 'greater things' to see.

25 August, Tuesday, Twenty-First Week in Ordinary Time

Matthew 23:23–26

In today's gospel reading Jesus criticises the Pharisees for being so preoccupied with unimportant details relating to the tithing of herbs while neglecting the core values that the Jewish law sought to uphold, such as justice, mercy and faith. The background to the three values that Jesus lists here may be the prophet Micah's threefold listing of what God desires of us: 'to do justice, to love mercy, and to walk humbly with your God'. The context of Micah's statement was the people's concern about what kind of animal sacrifice should be offered to God. Micah was saying to the people that their preoccupation is wide of the mark; it does not correspond to what God really wants. Jesus stands in the line of the prophets who sought to bring people back to what was really important, what really mattered to God. As disciples of Jesus, we have to keep on returning to the essentials, to what is at the heart of the message of Jesus, what is at the heart of God. It would be hard to find a better statement of those essentials than that trinity of values given to us by Micah and by Jesus, the exercise of justice and mercy towards others and a humble, trusting faith in God. These were the values that Jesus embodied in his life and in his death. To live by them is, in the language of Paul, to put on Christ, which is the core of our baptismal calling.

26 August, Wednesday, Twenty-First Week in Ordinary Time
Matthew 23:27–32

In today's gospel reading, Jesus criticises the scribes and Pharisees for being more preoccupied with appearances, what is on the outside, than with what is within, what Scripture calls the heart. Today, even more than in the time of Jesus, appearances and image have become all important. People who have a certain image receive the most adulation, have the biggest following and, often, get the biggest salaries. We are easily taken in by appearances. Jesus invites us to look at little deeper, which is how God looks. As one of the books of the Jewish Scriptures says, 'We look at appearances, God looks at the heart'. The 'heart' in the Jewish Scriptures and in the New Testament is the seat of the emotions, the intellect and the will. What matters to God is the heart, how we feel, how we think, how and what we desire. We are to bring our feeling, our thoughts and our desires in line with how God feels, how God thinks, what God desires for us. Our hearts are to reflect, in some way, God's heart, which means Jesus' heart. As Jesus says elsewhere in Matthew's Gospel, 'Learn from me for I am gentle and humble in heart'. It is the Holy Spirit who comes to us from God and the risen Lord who can mould our hearts into images of the Lord's heart. In the light of today's gospel reading, we pray that this work of the Spirit will be brought to completion in us.

27 August, Thursday, Twenty-First Week in Ordinary Time
Matthew 24:42–51

Both today's first reading and the gospel reading have a focus on the day of the Lord's coming at the end of time. Jesus stresses that his coming again at the end of time cannot be calculated. The same is true, by implication, of his coming at the end of our own personal time, the end of our lives. We don't know the day or the hour, and, so we need to be alert to the Lord's coming every day of our lives. As Jesus says in the gospel reading, 'Stay awake'. He clearly did not mean that literally. We all have to sleep on a regular basis. We are to stay awake in the sense of being alert to the Lord's presence here and now, as we wait for his coming at the end of time and at the end of our lives. Jesus is calling for a state of spiritual wakefulness. Paul reminds us in that first reading that there is a great deal to be alert to, because the Lord who is coming is already very active among us and within us here and now. Paul tells us in that reading, 'You will not be without any of the gifts of the Spirit while you are waiting for our Lord Jesus Christ'. The Lord is constantly gracing us through the Holy Spirit during this time of watchful waiting. Paul goes on to say that the Lord will keep us steady and without blame until the day of our Lord Jesus Christ. The Lord is working in our lives to keep us faithful, to enable us to go on living in a way that will leave us ready whenever he comes. We wait for the Lord's coming by cooperating with the many ways that the Lord is working on our behalf each moment of our lives.

28 August, Friday, Twenty-First Week in Ordinary Time
Matthew 25:1–13

The parable in today's gospel reading may reflect a marriage custom in the time of Jesus whereby bridesmaids waited at the bride's house for the arrival of the bridegroom. When he arrives they go out to meet him with lighted torches and then they escort the bridegroom and his bride to the house of the bridegroom, where the marriage feast is ready and the guests are waiting. What distinguishes the five bridesmaids who are described as 'sensible' from the other five is that, when the bridegroom arrived much later than expected, they had enough oil to ensure that their torches did not extinguish. They were able to welcome the bridegroom as was expected of them and escort him and his bride to the bridegroom's house. In the Gospels, Jesus refers to himself as the bridegroom. The parable encourages us to have our torches blazing brightly when the Lord comes to us, whenever that might be. Earlier in Matthew's Gospel Jesus had said to his disciples, 'You are the light of the world … let your light shine before others so that they may see your good works.' The parable could be calling on us to keep the light of our good works shining. We are not to allow that light to go out; we need to keep it burning for the long haul. We are to keep the flame of faith, which shows itself in good works, alive in our hearts to the very end. When the bridegroom, the Lord, comes at the end of time or at the end of our own earthly time, he will hope to see the flame of our loving faith burning brightly. The Lord who comes to us at the end is the Lord who is present to us now. If we are to welcome him with torches burning brightly at the end, we need to open ourselves to the oil of his presence now. We will stay the course only with the Lord's help. We need to keep opening ourselves to the resource only he can give us if the light of our faith is to burn brightly at the time of his final coming.

29 August, Saturday, The Passion of Saint John the Baptist
Mark 6:17–29

We have a lovely mosaic in our parish church of John the Baptist baptising Jesus. Not long afterwards, both of them would be put to death by the power of Rome. Jesus was crucified at the orders of Pontius Pilate, the Roman governor in Judea, and John the Baptist was beheaded on the orders of Herod Antipas, who ruled Galilee on behalf of Rome. Jesus more than likely saw his own destiny revealed in what happened to John. John was executed because he had challenged Herod for acting against the Jewish law by marrying the wife of his brother Philip. John was a courageous witness to God's will for our lives. In the story we have just heard, he stands out as a beacon of light against the darkness of the other characters, that unholy trinity of Herod, Herodias his wife, and her daughter. Between them they managed to eliminate what the gospel reading refers to as a 'good and holy man', just as Jesus, the ultimate 'good and holy man', would be eliminated by another coalition of darkness. It seems to be in the nature of light that it often finds itself shining in darkness. The light of the Lord's presence shines in our own darkness, in the dark and difficult experiences of life. Jesus spoke of John as a 'burning and shining lamp'. John the Baptist is a great inspiration to us to allow the light of our faith, the light of the Gospel, to shine, even when it is not popular or convenient to do so. Our calling is to allow the light we have received in baptism to shine brightly, in season and out of season. In his first encyclical, *Light of Faith*, Pope Francis declared, 'There is an urgent need to see once again that faith is a light, for once the flame of faith dies out, all other lights begin to dim. A light this powerful cannot come from ourselves but from a more primordial source: in a word, it must come from God.'

31 August, Monday, Twenty-Second Week in Ordinary Time
Luke 4:16–30

When the minister of the word steps up at Mass to read the word of God, the reading has already been chosen for him or her. It is laid out in what we call the lectionary. When Jesus stepped up to read from the word of God in his local synagogue, according to today's gospel reading, he had greater freedom to choose his reading. The scroll of the prophet Isaiah was given to him, but Jesus was free to choose any passage he liked from that scroll. He very deliberately went looking for a particular passage, unrolling the scroll until he found it. This particular passage, which he proclaimed aloud to the people in the synagogue, must have meant a great deal to him. Indeed, the words of Isaiah that he looked for and found summed up his own under-standing of his mission. Like Isaiah, Jesus understood that the Spirit of God, the Holy Spirit, was pushing him towards certain kinds of people, in particular, what the passage from Isaiah refers to as the poor, the captives, the blind and the downtrodden. All of these needed to hear good news, the good news that they were loved by God and that God wanted to enhance the quality of their lives. This is also the mission of the Church. Pope Francis once spoke of the Church as a field hospital for the wounded. 'The thing the Church needs most today is the ability to heal wounds and to warm the hearts of the faith-ful; it needs nearness, proximity. I see the Church as a field hospital after battle.' We are all among the wounded and we all need that field hospital from time to time. Pope Francis is also asking all of us to be-come that kind of church, taking up Jesus' work of healing by sharing in the sufferings of others.

1 September, Tuesday, Twenty-Second Week in Ordinary Time
Luke 4:31–37

In the gospel reading Jesus encounters someone whose spirit is very disturbed, who shouts at Jesus at the top of his voice. Jesus does not respond in kind to this aggressive tone. Rather than being disturbed by the man's disturbance, he brings calm to it. The Spirit of God at work in Jesus was more powerful than this disturbed and aggressive spirit that was at work in the man who was present in the synagogue. Sometimes a disturbed and aggressive spirit can take hold of us, and we too need the Lord's calming presence. We need the Holy Spirit to overcome our disturbed human spirit. In today's first reading, Saint Paul declares that 'instead of the spirit of the world, we have received the Spirit that comes from God'. The same Spirit that shaped the life and ministry of Jesus has been poured into our hearts. The Holy Spirit resides deep within us. There are times when we are driven by other spirits that are in conflict with the Holy Spirit. As a result, we speak and act in ways that are not of the Spirit of God. Our calling is to allow the Holy Spirit to become the dominant spirit in our lives. When that happens, we come to reflect something of the authoritative, life-giving presence of the Lord that is so evident in today's gospel reading.

2 September, Wednesday, Twenty-Second Week in Ordinary Time
Luke 4:38–44

In today's gospel reading we find that twofold rhythm in the life of Jesus. After a long day attending to the sick and the broken in and around the house of Simon Peter, he left the house very early the next morning and sought out a lonely place where he could be alone in prayer with God his Father. It is evident that people really appreciated his healing ministry. Large numbers brought their sick friends to the house of Simon where Jesus was. However, they didn't seem to appreciate his going away to a lonely place to pray. The crowds went looking for him and when they found him they tried to prevent him leaving them. They wanted access to him all the time; they didn't want to let him go, not even to pray. Jesus must have been aware that his prayerful communion with God was the source of his ministry to the sick and needy, and, in that sense, his prayer was even more important than his work. In our own culture and in our own lives prayer can easily fall down the list of priorities. We tend to be more easily satisfied with the visible results of whatever efforts we make or whatever work we do. Prayer can seem a waste of time in comparison. The people of Capernaum seemed to be of that view with regard to Jesus. A priest friend of mine, who died some years ago and from whom I learned a lot, said to me once that prayer was the pouring out of time before God. From a merely human point of view it may seem a waste of time but, in reality, it is the giving of time to God, a giving of ourselves to God. In that giving, we receive more than we give. It is perhaps above all with regard to prayer that the saying of Jesus rings true: 'Give, and it will be given to you. A good measure, pressed down, shaken together, running over, will be put into your lap.'

3 September, Thursday, Twenty-Second Week in Ordinary Time

Luke 5:1–11

In today's first reading, Paul declares that 'the wisdom of this world is foolishness to God'. It is another way of saying what the prophet Isaiah had said many centuries before, that God's ways are not our ways and God's thoughts are not our thoughts. In the gospel reading, Peter seems to be acting and speaking according to the wisdom of the world. He and his companions had experienced a fruitless night's fishing. The wisdom of the world, and the wisdom of fishermen, suggested that there was no point in heading out to try and catch fish, now that it was day. Yet, that is what Jesus asks Peter to do, and, in fairness to Peter, even though it seemed foolish, he responded to

Jesus' word. When Peter and his companions netted a huge number of fish, Peter realised that he was in the presence of someone through whom God was working in a very powerful way. Being in the presence of someone so good brought home to Peter his own sinful state. The wisdom of the world, and the wisdom of the Jewish law, would have suggested that a holy man like Jesus should keep his distance from a sinner like Peter. However, once again, Jesus was working out of a different kind of wisdom. He did not leave Peter; rather, he spoke a reassuring word to him and then commissioned him to share in his work of drawing people into the nets of God's love. The wisdom of the world can incline us to see things in a negative way, the emptiness of the sea, the emptiness of our lives, but the wisdom of God always sees life throbbing beneath the surface. That is the wisdom out of which we are invited to live.

4 September, Friday, Twenty-Second Week in Ordinary Time
Luke 5:33–39

It is clear from today's first reading that some people in the church of Corinth are passing judgement on Paul's ministry; they are judging it negatively. In response, Paul writes, 'Not that it makes the slightest difference to me whether you, or indeed any human tribunal, find me worthy or not'. Paul is aware that the only one who can really judge his ministry is the Lord, and the Lord will pass judgement in his own time. In the gospel reading, the Pharisees are passing judgement on the life and ministry of Jesus and his disciples. They judge negatively the fact that Jesus and his disciples do not fast in the way that the disciples of the Pharisees and the disciples of John the Baptist fast. Like Paul in the first reading, Jesus is not prepared to accept this negative judgement of others. He declares that he is doing something new. He has ushered in a celebratory time which is new; it is like the celebrations that take place at a wedding, with Jesus himself being the bridegroom and all who respond to him in faith being his bride, his beloved. People don't normally fast at wedding feasts. Using another image, closely related to that of the wedding feast, Jesus says that he is bringing new wine, and the old wineskins, the traditional way of doing things, won't be able to cope with the vibrancy of this wine. In both readings, those who were passing judgement had a very partial view of what was happening. It is always tempting to rush to judgement without attending fully to the reality we are judging so as to really understand it. The words of Jesus in the gospel reading about the newness of his ministry suggest that the Holy Spirit is often several steps ahead of us. If we hold on to the past too tightly, we can judge negatively the new direction the Holy Spirit may be prompting us to take. Our old wineskins need constant renewing to hold the new wine of the Lord's Spirit.

5 September, Saturday, Twenty-Second Week in Ordinary Time

Luke 6:1–5

In the Gospels a lot of the criticism directed against Jesus by the religious authorities relates to food. He was often criticised for eating with the wrong kind of people, those considered sinners according to the Jewish law. In today's gospel reading, it is Jesus' disciples who are at the receiving end of criticism for the way they eat. The religious leaders criticise them for eating in a way that was in breach of the Sabbath law. In picking ears of corn and rubbing them in their hands, they were considered to be engaged in the work of reaping, and such 'work' was forbidden on the Sabbath. Just as Jesus defended himself against the criticism of his eating style, so on this occasion he defends his disciples. He does so with reference to an incident in the Jewish Scriptures which shows that the normal regulations can be overruled when the basic human need of hunger has to be met. In a similar way, Jesus claimed, the hunger of his disciples, their need for food, took precedence over a rather narrow interpretation of the Sabbath law.

For Jesus, the human person, not human law, even religious law, was always at the centre. The basic needs of others took priority over all else, whether it was their physical need for food, or their spiritual need for God's love and mercy. Jesus teaches us that attentiveness to the other, responsiveness to the call of the other, is what really matters. Human regulations of whatever kind must be at the service of the well-being of others and should promote human flourishing.

7 September, Monday, Twenty-Third Week in Ordinary Time
Luke 6:6–11

It is clear from today's gospel reading that the Pharisees and Jesus are concerned about very different things. The Pharisees' primary concern was that the Jewish law relating to the Sabbath should be kept. No work was to be done on the Sabbath, regardless of the nature of that work. Even healing a disabled man could not be done on the Sabbath because it was work. Jesus had a very different concern. His primary concern was to do good, to enhance the lives of others. As far as Jesus was concerned, doing good was never untimely. Doing others some good should always take priority over the requirements of any law, no matter how revered that law. When Jesus asks his opponents the question, 'Is it against the law on the Sabbath to do good, or to do evil?', the answer he would have expected was, 'It is against the law to do evil on the Sabbath'. By implication, it could never be against God's law to do good on the Sabbath. Jesus spent his life doing good, doing God's life-enhancing work. He took every opportunity that came his way to do good for others, regardless of the day of the week or the time of the day. We are all called to do some good for others. We might feel that we are doing very little good for others, but even the little good we do for others matters a great deal to the Lord. There must have been many disabled people whom Jesus never encountered, yet he did what he could for those who did cross his path. There is a great deal of good we cannot do, for various reasons, but there is some good we can all do, and if we all do the good we are capable of, we will be creating a space for the coming of God's kingdom among us.

8 September, Tuesday, The Nativity of the Blessed Virgin Mary
Matthew 1:1–16, 18–23

The feast of the Nativity of the Blessed Virgin Mary is one of several feasts of Mary in the Church's liturgical calendar. We consider the birth of Mary a blessed day for all of us because as a young woman she would go on to say 'yes' to God's call to become the mother of God's Son, Jesus. With the birth of Mary, the story of Jesus has already begun. The gospel reading declares that Mary conceived her child, Jesus, through the Holy Spirit. The Holy Spirit was at work in Mary's life not only at the moment of Jesus' conception, but throughout her earthly life. She was a woman of the Spirit, even before the Holy Spirit came down upon her and Jesus' first disciples at Pentecost. We are all called to be men and women of the Spirit, as Mary was. Our baptismal calling is to allow the Holy Spirit to shape our lives, all we do and say, just as the Holy Spirit shaped the life of Mary. According to Saint Paul in today's second reading, God's purpose for our lives is that we become 'true images of his Son, so that his Son might be the eldest of many brothers and sisters'. Just as Mary brought Jesus into the world, we are called to bring Jesus into the world by becoming true images of Jesus, God's Son. Just as Mary brought Jesus into the world through the power of the Holy Spirit, we can only become images of God's Son, bringing him into our world, through the power of the same Holy Spirit. We need the Holy Spirit to keep overshadowing us if we are to grow into the image of God's Son, so that we can continue Mary's work of bringing Jesus into our world today.

9 September, Wednesday, Twenty-Third Week in Ordinary Time
Luke 6:20–26

There is a very strange paradox at the heart of today's gospel reading. Jesus begins by declaring happy those who are afflicted in any way, the poor, the hungry, those who are weeping. That seems to fly in the face of the normal human way of looking at things. When we are afflicted in any of these ways, we generally consider ourselves to be very unfortunate. When we look back on such an experience we say to ourselves, 'That was a bad day. That was an awful week. Hopefully, things will improve'. Yet from Jesus' perspective our affliction, our vulnerability, creates a space for God to act and to reverse our situation. The ultimate expression of this is the death and resurrection of Jesus. When Jesus was crucified, when he was at his most afflicted and most vulnerable, God raised him to new life. Our greatest struggles have the potential to open us up to the God of life, and can create a space for God to act in a life-giving way in our lives. Paul knew this from his own experience; he spoke of God's power being made perfect in weakness. Jesus is not canonising poverty or misery – elsewhere in Luke's Gospel he insists that the rich provide for the poor. However, in today's gospel he insists that God will certainly provide for us in our poverty, in our affliction, in our weakness and vulnerability, if we are open to his presence.

10 September, Thursday, Twenty-Third Week in Ordinary Time
Luke 6:27–38

Today's gospel reading is one of the most challenging pieces of Jesus' teaching in the Gospels, with its call to love our enemies, to do good to those who hate us, to bless those who curse us, to pray for those who treat us badly. This was no more the normal way of relating to people in the time of Jesus than it is today. Jesus goes on to refer to what would have been the norm then, as it is today, namely, loving those who love us, doing good to those who do good to us. As Jesus says, even sinners do as much as that. That was and is the norm in human relationships, because it is the natural way to relate and it comes easily to us. Jesus calls us to a way of life that is not easy and that doesn't always come naturally to us. There is nothing instinctive about loving our enemies or doing good to those who hate us or praying for those who treat us badly. That way of relating seems to go against every instinct of our nature. Yet Jesus does not ask us to do the impossible. He must have understood that this way of relating was possible for his followers, and, even more, that it is in harmony with what is deepest and best in us. Jesus' teaching reflects the biblical understanding of the human person as made in God's image. Who is this God in whose image we are made? In that gospel reading, Jesus refers to God as kind to the ungrateful and the wicked. Jesus is calling on us as images of God to relate to others in the way that God relates to humanity. Jesus was the perfect image of God; his way of relating to people was the perfect reflection of how God relates to us. In that sense, Jesus calls on us to relate to others as he does. We can only do that with his help, in the power of the Spirit whom the Lord is always offering us. The way of life Jesus portrays in the gospel reading is 'life in the Spirit'. Such a way of life is life at its most fully human, because it is a life that reflects the life of God most fully.

11 September, Friday, Twenty-Third Week in Ordinary Time
Luke 6:39–42

Some of the images Jesus uses in the Gospels can be somewhat exaggerated for effect. He once made reference, for example, to a camel passing through the eye of a needle. Another example of that kind of image is found in today's gospel reading with the reference to someone with a plank in his eye. There is humour in the image of someone with a plank in his eye struggling to take the splinter out of the eye of someone else. Behind the humour there is a serious message. Before looking to the faults of others we need to look to our own faults. To attempt to criticise and correct others without being aware of our own failings is the equivalent of the blind trying to lead the blind. We need to work on ourselves before working on others, Jesus is saying. Working on ourselves is a lifetime's work, and there is probably enough there to be going on with, without turning our attention to others. We are all called to engage in the ongoing work of personal conversion, which involves a turning more fully towards the Lord and all he stands for. In turning towards the Lord, we will find ourselves turning away from what is not of him. The gospel reading suggests that this is our primary work; working on others comes later, if it comes at all. It has been said, probably rightly, that we can only change ourselves; we cannot change others. If we change ourselves, however, others can be empowered to change for the better too.

12 September, Saturday, Twenty-Third Week in Ordinary Time
Luke 6:43–49

What is visible is not always what is most important. The two houses in the parable that Jesus speaks in today's gospel looked the same. However, in reality they were fundamentally different, because their foundations were different. One was built on sand and the other on rock. What was most important about the two houses, their foundations, was not visible. Jesus is speaking in that parable about the importance of getting the foundations of our lives right, what's below the surface. Just as the houses in the parable had to be able to deal with rivers in flood, we know from our own experience that we often have to deal with very challenging situations. We can be hit with all kinds of difficulties, whether relating to our health, our relationships or our work. Our ability to deal with those difficulties will depend on what our lives are built upon. In the gospel reading Jesus presents himself as the only foundation worth building upon. Listening to his words and acting on them, following in his way, ensures that our lives are built on rock, and that we will be able to withstand the storms of life when they come along. If we build our lives on the Lord, the Lord will enable us to hold together when the great tests come along, whatever form they might take. The Lord wants to be the foundation of our lives. But if that is to happen, he needs us actively to take him as the foundation of our lives. If we are to know the security that only he can give us, we need to entrust ourselves to his word, and allow ourselves to be shaped by that word, saying with Mary, 'Let it be to me according to your word'.

14 September, Monday, The Exaltation of the Holy Cross
John 3:13–17

The discovery of the relics of the true cross by Saint Helena, the mother of Constantine, is dated to 14 September 320. The annual commemoration of that event has been celebrated since, in praise of the redemption won for us by Christ. No one in the time of Jesus would ever have put together the two words 'triumph' and 'cross'. Far from being a triumph, death by crucifixion was considered to be the most degrading and terrifying form of execution. It was a way for the Roman authorities to show its triumph over all those who dared to threaten Roman order and peace. Yet, as Christians, we have no difficulty in looking upon the cross of Jesus as a triumph. Rome did not have the last word when it came to Jesus, because God raised Jesus from the dead and he made him the cornerstone of a new community, which went on to include a future Roman emperor, Constantine. Through the eyes of the resurrection we can see the cross of Jesus as the triumph of love over hatred, of Jesus' love over the hatred of his enemies, of God's love over the hateful rejection of his Son. This is how John in his gospel understood the cross of Jesus. It was the glorious revelation of God's love for the world, in the language of today's gospel reading. Jesus himself says that a man has no greater love than to lay down his life for his friends. We venerate the cross because it is a powerful manifestation of a love that is greater than any human love. That is why the earliest Christians tended to depict the crucified Jesus as a glorious Christ with arms outstretched, reigning in love from the cross. Today we celebrate a triumph in which we all share. We are all embraced by the love of God that shines through Christ crucified. The cross has become good news for us. Saint Paul in his letter to the Romans expressed that good news very simply and very powerfully: 'God proves his love for us in that while we still were sinners, Christ died for us'.

15 September, Tuesday, Our Lady of Sorrows
Luke 2:33–35

Although today is the feast of Our Lady of Sorrows, it is not a sorrowful feast. Mary's sorrow was the consequence of her motherly love for her Son, Jesus. Those we love invariably bring us suffering and sorrow. If we give our heart to someone, sooner or later it will be broken. The only way to keep our heart from being broken is to keep it locked away, not giving it to anyone or anything. However, that would be to live a very impoverished life. Our fundamental call as human beings is to love. Our basic call as followers of the Lord is to love others as he has loved us. The more we love, the more we expose ourselves to sorrow and pain. Jesus was loving in a way that was unique because he fully revealed God's love. He loved more completely than any other human being ever did or could. That is why his suffering was greater than that of any human being, not so much his physical suffering as his suffering of heart, the suffering that comes from the rejection and betrayal of love. Mary was the human being who was closest to Jesus. Her love for Jesus had a special quality, the quality of a mother's love. Because of her unique love for Jesus, she shared in Jesus' suffering in a unique way. It is her love for Jesus that is at the heart of today's feast. The depth of her sorrow and suffering reflects the depth of her love for the Lord. We can learn from her to stand in love at the foot of other people's crosses. She also inspires us to remain faithful to Jesus her Son out of love, even if that means we have to travel the way of the cross. Today's feast also reminds us that we can turn to Mary for help and strength when our love for others, and, in particular, our love for the Lord, brings us sorrow and suffering.

16 September, Wednesday, Twenty-Fourth Week in Ordinary Time
Luke 7:31–35
The Gospels suggest that Jesus was very observant of day-to-day life around him. His powers of observation come through especially in the parables he spoke. The image of the sower sowing seed, of the wealthy man with two very different sons, of the traveller who fell among robbers, are all drawn from his own experience of day-to-day life. Jesus was not only observant of life, but he recognised that all of life speaks to us of God's relationship with us and of ours with God. Today's gospel reading suggests that Jesus was very observant of children, and of children's play in particular. Even the play of children in the marketplace spoke to Jesus about how people respond to God's call and presence. Jesus saw the children who play at being pipers for other children to dance and who play at singing dirges for other children to cry as images of his own ministry and of the ministry of John the Baptist. Jesus identifies readily with the children's acting out the role of the piper who invites people to dance. It is interesting to think of Jesus as a piper and of his ministry as a tune, and of ourselves as invited to dance to the tune that Jesus plays. Jesus' life plays the music of God and we are invited to move to that music.

Jesus is God's musician, and our calling is to listen to God's music, whichis played through the life, death and resurrection of Jesus, and to allow that music to move and shape us.

17 September, Thursday, Twenty-Fourth Week in Ordinary Time
Luke 7:36–50

Paul makes a very strong statement in today's first reading: 'By God's grace, this is what I am', namely an apostle. He was very aware that his transformation from a persecutor of the Church to the primary apostle to the Gentiles was not his own doing. It was the risen Lord's gracious initiative towards him which made this transformation possible. All his work as an apostle was his grateful response to the Lord's gracious love towards him. In the gospel reading, the woman who breaks in upon a meal at which Jesus was a guest was also aware that the transformation that had taken place in her life was not her own doing. It was the result of Jesus' gracious love towards her, unconditionally communicating God's forgiveness to her. Her extravagant gesture of washing the Lord's feet with her tears and drying them with her hair was her grateful response to the Lord's gracious love towards her. Both Paul and the woman acted out of gratitude to the Lord for what they recognised was an undeserved gift. Both of these people show us the shape of our own lives as followers of Jesus. We too have been greatly graced by the Lord. He lived, died and rose again for us; he has poured the Holy Spirit into our hearts and continues to do so. He offers himself to us as Bread of Life in the Eucharist. He does all this out of love for us, without asking us to earn or deserve these gifts, this gift of himself. Our lives are to be one great act of thanksgiving to the Lord who has abundantly graced us. Like Paul and the woman, we give ourselves to the Lord in love because we want to show appreciation for all the ways he has graced us.

18 September, Friday, Twenty-Fourth Week in Ordinary Time

Luke 8:1–3

In today's short gospel reading Luke tells us that among those who accompanied Jesus on his journeys was a group of women. They appear to have been women of some means, because they provided for Jesus and the twelve out of their own resources. In that culture, it would have been unusual to see women following a male religious leader in such a public way. The normal setting for women would have been the domestic space. It would not have been usual for a woman to be meeting in public with a man who was not a relative. Jesus was in the process of forming a new kind of community in which the gender and social differences of the time were no longer important. Saint Paul expressed that vision of Jesus very clearly when he said in his letter to the Galatians, 'There is no longer Jew or Greek, there is no longer slave or free, there is no longer male and female; for all of you are one in Christ Jesus.' If Jesus' vision and practice inspired Paul, it needs to keep on inspiring us in the Church today. We have to do all we can to ensure that our parish community is as inclusive and embracing as the community Jesus gathered about himself. Jesus created a space for men and women to serve each other and to serve him. We need to keep on working to create that same kind of space in which everyone's gifts are recognised and everyone has an opportunity to use them. In different ways we are each called to serve the Lord out of our own unique experiences and resources.

19 September, Saturday, Twenty-Fourth Week in Ordinary Time

Luke 8:4–15

The parable of the sower and its interpretation is a realistic portrayal of the obstacles Jesus encountered in his preaching of God's word. Those same obstacles are alive and well today in all of our lives as the risen Lord continues to proclaim God's word. Like the seed that fell on the path, which the birds immediately consume, the Lord's word often makes little impact on us. As we might say today, it goes in one ear and out the other. Like the seed that fell on rock and that grew initially but then died away because it had no root, we can hear the Lord's word and receive it but we don't really make it our own. We don't make a real home for it in our hearts. Our response to the Lord's word is a very surface one and easily falls away when living the word starts to make demands on us and to cost us something. Like the seed that fell among thorns and initially took root but was then choked by the thorns, the word can take deep root in our hearts, but over time we allow the pleasures and anxieties of life to choke the word. Life takes us over in various ways and the Lord and his word get squeezed out. This realistic analysis of the obstacles to hearing and living the Lord's word could leave us a bit discouraged. However, this is not the purpose of this parable. The sower is aware that a lot of the seed he sows will never mature, but he continues to sow because he is confident that some of that seed will fall on good soil and bear a wonderful harvest. The sower did not get discouraged. The Lord who sows the seed of his word today does not get discouraged either. He keeps sowing in the knowledge that there is good soil out there somewhere. He knows that such good soil is to be found in all of our lives. He will not give up on us; he keeps sowing. We should not give up on ourselves either. The Lord's labour in the field of our lives will bear fruit, whenever we open ourselves anew to his good work within us and among us.

21 September, Monday, Saint Matthew, Apostle and Evangelist
Matthew 9:9–13

Jesus seems to have had a great capacity to see good in people who would usually have been written off by others, especially by those who took their religious faith seriously. Matthew is an example of such a person. He was a tax collector, somebody who worked for the Romans and who was presumed to be taking more money in taxes from the ordinary people than was necessary. As long as the tax collector gave the Romans what they were expecting, he could keep for himself anything collected over and above that figure. When it came to tax collectors there was a presumption of dishonesty. Those who were careful to keep the demands of the Jewish law would certainly have considered them sinners who had placed themselves beyond the scope of God's love. However, Jesus looked at people like Matthew with very different eyes, more as a doctor would look on people who are ill and in need of healing. Jesus brought people like Matthew, those labelled sinners, within the scope of God's love, by eating with them, proclaiming the reign of God's love to them, inviting and empowering them to live as God's beloved sons and daughters. He even called some of them, like Matthew, to form part of his inner circle, the twelve. The story of Matthew reminds us that the Lord does not keep his distance from us just because we are not all we could be. Rather, the Lord sees the good in us that we often fail to see in ourselves. He is constantly coming towards us, inviting us into the embrace of God's love. The healing power of God's love can then empower us to live the kind of life that Paul outlines in our first reading, bearing with one another charitably, 'in complete selflessness, gentleness and patience'.

22 September, Tuesday, Twenty-Fifth Week in Ordinary Time
Luke 8:19–21

Today's gospel reading follows almost immediately after the parable of the sower and its interpretation. In that parable, the seed that falls on good soil is identified with those who 'hear the word [of God], hold it fast in an honest and good heart, and bear fruit with patient endurance'. We are not only to hear the word, but to persevere in living the word, so that it bears rich fruit throughout our lives. In today's gospel reading, Jesus declares that those who hear the word in this persevering way are his mother and brothers (and sisters). 'My mother and brothers are those who hear the word of God and put it into practice.' In Luke's Gospel, Mary, the physical mother of Jesus, who features in today's gospel reading, is portrayed in this exemplary way, as the good soil on which the seed of God's word fell. She, more than any other disciples in this gospel, heard the word of God, held it fast in an honest and good heart, and bore fruit with patient endurance. In the first chapter of Luke, she surrenders herself to God's word. 'Let it be with me according to your word.' She persevered in living that word, as is evidenced by her presence again in the first chapter of Luke's second volume, the Acts of the Apostles. She is there at the first Pentecost, in the upper room, with the eleven disciples, some other women, and the brothers of Jesus. We can look to Mary to help us to hold fast the Lord's word in an honest and good heart, and to bear fruit with patient endurance. We ask her to pray for us, sinners, now, as well as at the hour of our death.

23 September, Wednesday, Twenty-Fifth Week in Ordinary Time
Luke 9:1–6

It is striking that in today's gospel reading, Jesus sends out the twelve in a way that we would regard as very unprepared. They are to take nothing for the journey, neither staff, nor haversack, nor bread, nor money, nor a spare tunic. Many of us who have to set out on a journey tend to be overprepared. What was Jesus getting at? Jesus seems to be sending out the twelve in a rather vulnerable state, so that they would be forced to rely less on themselves and more on the hospitality of others. He was asking them to rely on God to provide for them in and through the hospitality of those to whom they would preach the Gospel. In today's culture there is a great emphasis on being self-sufficient. We tend to overprovide for ourselves. When that happens we can be less disposed to receiving from others, receiving from God giving to us through others. Jesus was teaching his disciples that, whereas they have a great deal to give others, the Gospel of the kingdom of God, they also have a great deal to receive from others. Whereas Jesus was giving them a share in his own power and authority, yet they remained vulnerable and in need of what others could offer them. In the journey of faith, we all have to learn both to give from what the Lord has given us and to receive from what the Lord has given others. We can only do so much to prepare ourselves, because much of what we need comes to us from others. Saint Paul spoke of the Church as the body of Christ in which each member had much to give to others and much to receive from others. We are all interdependent on the shared journey of faith. The Lord has much to give others through us and much to give us through others.

24 September, Thursday, Twenty-Fifth Week in Ordinary Time
Luke 9:7–9
The author of the Book of Ecclesiastes, from which our first reading is taken, seems to have a rather jaundiced view of life. He looks out upon the natural world and, rather than being inspired by its wonder, he says of it, in the words of our reading, 'all things are wearisome'. All he sees in nature, and in life generally, is tiresome repetition. 'There is nothing new under the sun.' In the gospel reading, Herod Antipas, the son of Herod the Great, seems to look upon the life-giving ministry of Jesus and his disciples with somewhat jaundiced eyes. The reading says that Herod was puzzled by Jesus and was anxious to see him. That could suggest that there was a certain openness in Herod to Jesus. However, a few chapters later in this gospel, the Pharisees come to Jesus and warn him, 'Get away from here, for Herod wants to kill you', and, of course, Herod had already killed John the

Baptist. Both readings invite us to reflect on how we see the world, how we see other people, how we see ourselves. Like the author of Ecclesiastes, are we prone to seeing wearisome monotony where, in reality, there is wonderful diversity; like Herod, are we prone to seeing a threat when, in reality, this is a moment of opportunity through which the Lord is calling out to us. How we see the world shapes who we are, how we behave, how we relate to others. We need to keep refining the eyes of our minds and hearts, so that we see the world with the Lord's eyes, eyes that are attuned to the signs of life and creativity all around us.

25 September, Friday, Twenty-Fifth Week in Ordinary Time
Luke 9:18–22

Today's first reading from the Book of Ecclesiastes is often read at funeral Masses. People are drawn to that list of times in a human life. It has a very poetic quality and it seems to cover so much of human living. I counted the number of times mentioned in that reading and there are twenty-eight in all. Yet, there is one time that is significant for us as Christians that is missing from that long list, and that is the time to pray. There is no mention of the human activity of prayer in that catalogue of human activities. The time to pray was of critical importance to Jesus. At the beginning of today's gospel reading, there is a reference to Jesus praying alone in the presence of his disciples. The reference to Jesus praying alone while in the presence of others might strike us as strange. Was he or was he not alone? It seems that although Jesus was in the presence of his disciples, he was in a very deep and prayerful communion with God. He was alone with God while surrounded by others. Sometimes we can be alone with God even though we are in the presence of others. The evangelist Luke in that gospel reading seems to suggest that the two questions that Jesus put to his disciples came out of his prayer: 'Who do the crowds say

I am?' 'Who do you say that I am?' Jesus' prayer flowed into everything he said and did. His prayerful communion with God shaped how he related to others. Our prayerful communion with God will shape all of our lives too. The time to pray will feed into and influence all the various times that are mentioned in that first reading. Our prayerful communion with God will have a powerful impact for good on the quality of our communion with others. That is why, for us, as for Jesus, the time to pray is a time of great importance. If we were to list the times of our lives as disciples of the Lord, the time to pray would have to be given a prominent place.

26 September, Saturday, Twenty-Fifth Week in Ordinary Time
Luke 9:43–45

We sometimes struggle to understand one another. Someone close to us says or does something that leaves us perplexed; we don't know what they mean by it. Or perhaps someone fails to say or do something, and that can leave us equally perplexed. Silence, inactivity, can sometimes be harder to interpret. If we sometimes struggle to understand one another, it is no surprise to read in the Gospels that the disciples struggled to understand Jesus. In today's gospel reading, when Jesus spoke of himself as someone who would be handed over into the power of men, the disciples did not understand what he said. They had just witnessed the Transfiguration, followed by his healing of an epileptic boy; everyone was full of admiration for him. What is all this talk about him being handed over into the power of men? The disciples would have to live with their confusion for a while longer. Only time would allow them to understand what Jesus meant; only after his death and resurrection did they come to understand such sayings. We all need time to understand one another. What perplexes us now about someone may well become clearer over time. Understanding, especially understanding of others, is never instantaneous. We have to be patient and to be prepared to wait. That is all the more true of our relationship with the Lord. We are constantly growing in our understanding of what he has said and done, and of the extraordinary person that he was and is today.

28 September, Monday, Twenty-Sixth Week in Ordinary Time
Luke 9:46–50

I have often been struck by the saying of Jesus at the end of today's gospel reading:'Anyone who is not against you is for you.' It is a good principle to live by. We can get discouraged today by the numbers who are not coming to church. Yet, in my experience, most of those who would not publicly associate themselves with the community of faith are not against us. They are not hostile. They often welcome the presence of the Church at certain moments of their lives, especially in times of sickness and death. You often hear parents say of family members that whereas they do not come to Mass they are good people. They often give their time and energy in the service of others. I am sure that the Lord looks upon them and gives thanks to his heavenly Father for them. In the gospel reading, Jesus is teaching his disciples not to have too narrow a view of who belongs to his movement in the world and who does not. Jesus is reminding them that the Holy Spirit is at work outside the circle of those who publicly claim to be disciples of Jesus. The same Holy Spirit is at work today beyond the boundaries of the Church. Our calling is to be the best disciples of Jesus that we can be. We are to make the gospel attractive by our generous and joyful way of life. That entails rejoicing in the signs of God's Spirit wherever it is to be found. In the words of one of our hymns, 'where charity and love abound, there is God'.

29 September, Tuesday, Saints Michael, Gabriel and Raphael

John 1:47–51

There are three archangels mentioned by name in Scripture, Michael, Gabriel and Raphael. Michael protects the people of God. According to the Book of Revelation, he was God's agent in defeating Satan in heaven and casting him down to earth. Raphael, acting as God's agent, heals the blindness of Tobias in the book of Tobit. Gabriel proclaims God's message to Zechariah and to Mary at the beginning of Luke's Gospel. There are spiritual beings who act on God's behalf in relation to God's people, protecting, healing and proclaiming God's word. In the gospel reading, Jesus speaks of the angels of God ascending and descending on the Son of Man. This is a reference to the dream of Jacob in the Book of Genesis. Jacob dreamt that he saw the angels of God ascending and descending on a ladder connecting heaven and earth. He came to realise that the place where he was sleeping was being touched by heaven and he went on to call that place Bethel, which literally means 'house of God'. The archangels brought a touch of heaven to earth in the Scriptures. However, in the gospel reading Jesus is suggesting by his image of the angels of God ascending and descending upon him that he is uniquely the meeting place of heaven and earth. He, above all, is the one where heaven touches earth, where God encounters humanity. These are the 'greater things' that Jesus invites Nicodemus and all of us to recognise. The risen Lord is with us today as the one who brings something of heaven to earth. He calls us and empowers us to go forth in his name as his messengers, bringing something of the life of heaven to this earth. We not only pray, 'Thy kingdom come on earth as it is in heaven', but we try to make that prayer something of a reality through our lives.

30 September, Wednesday, Twenty-Sixth Week in Ordinary Time
Luke 9:57–62

In all of the Gospels, the journey of Jesus is also understood as the journey of his disciples. As Jesus had to steel himself to take the path God wanted him to take, those who seek to be his disciples also need something of his steel. This was the message that Jesus was conveying to the three prospective disciples in the gospel reading. In his exchange with these three people, Jesus uses harsh, even shocking, images. He wants to convey that being his disciple is not an easy option. It requires that element of steeliness that Jesus himself had. When Jesus calls the second of the three people to follow him, the man asks to be let go to bury his father first. This seems a very reasonable request. Yet we probably need to imagine a situation where the father is still alive and well, and the son is asking to continue living at home until his father dies, whenever that will be; it could be years into the future. Jesus' reply to this man is rather enigmatic. 'Leave the dead to bury their dead.' Jesus is clearly emphasising to this prospective disciple the urgency of responding to his call. 'Your duty is to go ... .' Jesus is saying to him that now is the time to say 'yes' to his call and not some time in the distant future. The Lord's call to each of us always has an element of urgency about it. Our response to his call can lack a sense of urgency at times. We can have a good sense of what the Lord is asking of us, but we can be strongly tempted to put off our response. The call of Jesus to 'go and spread the news of the kingdom of God' is always urgent. Each day, today, we are called to spread the good news of the kingdom of God by making the Lord's love present in a tangible way to those we meet.

1 October, Thursday, Twenty-Sixth Week in Ordinary Time
Luke 10:1–12

You may have come across a plaque with the saying, 'Bidden or not bidden, God is present'. Swiss Psychiatrist Carl Jung had these words inscribed above the entrance to his home and the quote is often attributed to him. Jung found it in the Latin writings of Desiderius Erasmus, a sixteenth-century Dutch Catholic priest, social critic, teacher and theologian. The saying declares that God's presence to us is not determined by our openness to God's presence or our lack of openness to it. I was reminded of that saying in today's gospel reading. Jesus sends out the seventy-two disciples on mission. He is aware that they will be well received in some towns but made most unwelcome in others. However, irrespective of how they are received, their message is to be the same: 'The kingdom of God is very near to you.' Even to the town that does not make them welcome they are to say, 'Yet, be sure of this: the kingdom of God is very near'. We don't have to make God present. God is always present to us. God's presence is assured. The presence of God's kingdom, God's realm of liberating love, is a given. The crucial question is how responsive we are to God's presence, to the presence of the risen Lord, God-with-us. The first reading suggests that Job, even in the midst of his darkest hour of suffering, came to the awareness that God had not abandoned him. 'These eyes will gaze on him and find him not aloof.' The Lord is never aloof from us, even when we are often aloof from him. We do not have to go seeking the Lord after we have been aloof from him, because he is always seeking us; he is always there, fully present to us.

2 October, Friday, The Guardian Angels
Matthew 18:1–5, 10

A few years ago on this feast of the guardian angels, Pope Francis gave a homily at his morning Mass. In it he said that 'according to

Church tradition we all have an angel with us, who guards us'. The pope concluded with a series of questions: 'How is my relationship with my guardian angel? Do I listen to him? Do I bid him good day in the morning? Do I tell him: "Guard me while I sleep?" Do I speak with him? Do I ask his advice? Is he beside me?' It is probably true to say that most of us would answer 'no' to those questions. I have the distinct impression that Pope Francis could answer 'yes' to them. In the first reading, God promises his people Israel an angel to guard them and to bring them to the place he had prepared for them. This is one of the roles of the guardian angels in our lives. They accompany us on our journey of faith, guarding us from evil and leading us towards our final destination. If this is their role in our lives, we need to develop our relationship with them. In the gospel reading, Jesus makes reference to angels, declaring that the angels of children are continually in the presence of God the Father in heaven. The disciples are concerned about what Pope Francis would call 'careerism'. 'Who is the greatest in the kingdom of heaven?' To cut across this unhealthy preoccupation, Jesus takes a child and sets the child in front of them, declaring, 'The one who makes himself as little as this little child is the greatest in the kingdom of heaven'. What does Jesus see as great in little children? It is their natural tendency to be open and receptive to others, their instinctive awareness of their dependence on others. It is what Jesus refers to elsewhere in the Gospels as meekness. Pope Francis declares in that homily that this is the attitude we need towards God, and towards the messengers God sends us, the angels. The pope declares that we must 'ask the Lord for the grace of this meekness, to listen to the voice of this companion who is a sign of God's love for us'. Taken together, our two readings today suggest that this companion is with us on the journey of life and is also in the presence of God the Father in heaven interceding for us.

3 October, Saturday, Twenty-Sixth Week in Ordinary Time
Luke 10:17–24

Every so often in the Gospels we are given a little insight into the prayer of Jesus. It is as if we are being allowed to eavesdrop on the most intimate relationship in Jesus' life, his relationship with God, his Father. Today's gospel reading gives us an insight into Jesus' prayer, a joyful prayer of praise inspired by the Holy Spirit. 'Filled with joy by the Holy Spirit, he said, "I bless you Father, Lord of heaven and earth".' The prayer of praise is the most selfless form of prayer there is. It is a movement towards God without any reference to ourselves. The prayer of petition is also a movement towards God but with a view to God moving towards us in our need. Jesus himself was no stranger to the prayer of petition; such was his prayer in the Garden of Gethsemane. On this occasion, however, Jesus praises God for who God is and for what God is doing. What is God doing, according to this prayer of Jesus? He is revealing something really important to those whom Jesus calls 'mere children'. God the Father is revealing to children the intimate relationship that exists between Jesus and himself, a relationship of love which leads to mutual knowledge. 'No one knows who the Son is except the Father, and who the Father is except the Son.' Who are these children who are receiving this revelation? The reference is probably to those who have the openness of the child to God's message spoken through Jesus, in other words, the disciples. It is to the disciples that Jesus goes on to say, 'Happy the eyes that see what you see'. The disciples who are receptive to what God is showing them are contrasted with 'the learned and the clever', those who are so sure of what they know that they are closed to what God is trying to reveal to them about the relationship between himself and Jesus. 'Happy the eyes …'. There is a beatitude here that can potentially embrace us all, provided we have something of that childlike openness to what God wants to reveal to us through his Son and the Spirit.

5 October, Monday, Twenty-Seventh Week in Ordinary Time
Luke 10:25–37

Today's gospel reading begins with a question addressed to Jesus by a lawyer, an expert in the Jewish law, 'What must I do to inherit eternal life?' It was a very practical question, 'What must I do?' The gospel reading ends with Jesus saying to the lawyer, 'Go and do likewise.' 'Go and do what the Samaritan in the story did'. It is as if Jesus was saying, 'You asked me what you are to do, and I am showing what you are to do by the parable I have just told'. A very practical question was given a very practical answer. What was it that the Samaritan did in the story Jesus told? The first thing he did, and the most important thing, was to allow himself to be moved emotionally when he saw the half-dead traveller by the roadside. Two other people had already seen that sorry sight of the half-dead traveller and were unmoved. They saw the man, but they didn't really see him. It was a surface seeing. The Samaritan's seeing was an attentive seeing; he didn't just see, he noticed, which is why he was moved emotionally by what he saw. As the gospel reading says, when the Samaritan saw the half-dead man, he was moved with compassion. Because he was moved emotionally, he immediately started to move physically, engaging in a whole series of actions on behalf of his fellow traveller, bandaging the man's wounds, pouring oil and wine on them, placing the man on his horse, carrying him to an inn and paying for him to be looked after, with the promise to pay more on his return journey if necessary. Every action the Samaritan performed was a step towards the poor unfortunate man's healing, yet it all began with the Samaritan's way of seeing this person in need. He saw him with the eyes of Jesus, compassionate eyes. It is often said of Jesus in the gospel story that he saw and had compassion. The story Jesus told invites us to ask ourselves, 'How do I see others? How attentive is my seeing? Do I allow myself to be moved by what I see? It is significant that in the story the person who saw with the eyes of Jesus was an outsider, a Samaritan, some-one considered by Jews at the time as not belonging to God's people. He wasn't religious by Jewish standards. Jesus may be reminding us that even people not considered religious in the conventional sense can make his compassionate ministry present to those who need it most.

6 October, Tuesday, Twenty-Seventh Week in Ordinary Time
Luke 10:38–42
In today's gospel reading Jesus is offered hospitality by two women. Martha seems to be the more senior of the two women and Mary the more marginal. It is said that Martha welcomed Jesus to her house. Martha's way of showing hospitality was to roll up her sleeves and prepare an elaborate meal in a rather anxious frame of mind. Her anxious activity made her rather angry with her sister, whom she per-ceived not to be carrying her weight sufficiently. She comes across as somewhat angry with Jesus, too, for not giving Mary a telling off. 'Lord, do you not care … ? Tell her to help me.' However, Mary was showing Jesus a different kind of hospitality. She was sitting at his feet, listening to what Jesus had to say. It was traditional for students to sit at the feet of the rabbi or teacher; Mary was taking up the posi-tion of a disciple. In the Gospels Jesus often defends people against the criticism that others make of them. On this occasion he defends Mary against Martha's criticism. Jesus validates the kind of hospital-ity that Mary is showing him, the hospitality of listening. Indeed, on this occasion it seems that this was the kind of hospitality that Jesus actually desired. 'Mary has chosen the better part.' The parable of the good Samaritan, which precedes this passage, shows that there is a time and place for anxious activity on behalf of others. There is also a time for listening. The gospel reading suggests that true hos-pitality attends to what the guest really wants, not to what we think the guest wants. In terms of our relationship with Jesus, there is a

time to be active on his behalf and a time to listen to his word. Both are important in their time.

7 October, Wednesday, Our Lady of the Rosary

Luke 1:26–38

The Rosary has been a very important prayer in the life of the Church for many centuries. It is a prayer that invites us to reflect on the birth, life, death, resurrection and ascension of Jesus and on the coming of the Holy Spirit at Pentecost, as well as on Mary in glory. Today's two readings present us with two of the mysteries we reflect on in the Rosary. The gospel reading is the first Joyful Mystery, the annunciation to Mary. The first reading is the beginning of the story of Pentecost; the disciples are in continuous prayer, together with Mary the mother of Jesus and other members of Jesus' family as they wait for the coming of the Spirit. In the gospel reading, Mary is told by Gabriel that the Holy Spirit would come upon her and so the child to be born of her will be holy and will be called Son of God. It could be said that Gabriel announces Mary's personal Pentecost. The Holy Spirit was needed at this moment of crucial new beginning. The first reading reflects another moment of new beginning, the beginning of the Church. Again the Holy Spirit is needed at this second moment of new beginning, and, once again, this second moment involves Mary. Having had her own personal Pentecost, she is present at the Pentecost of the whole community of believers. There are always moments of new beginning in our own lives. Regardless of where we are on our life's journey, the Lord is always calling us to make some new beginning. The same Holy Spirit is given to us as our resource at each of our own moments of new beginning, as he was given to Mary and the early Church. As we set out on whatever new beginning we are making, no matter how small, we can confidently pray, 'Come Holy Spirit, fill my heart'.

8 October, Thursday, Twenty-Seventh Week in Ordinary Time

Luke 11:5–13

In the gospel reading this morning, Jesus encourages us to keep on asking God, to keep on seeking from God, to keep on knocking on God's door, in the assurance that God will not ultimately disappoint us. Jesus also directs us towards what we need to be asking God for, what we need to be seeking from God and knocking on God's door to obtain, and that is the Holy Spirit. 'If you, who are evil, know how to give your children what is good, how much more will the heavenly Father give the Holy Spirit to those who ask him?' Just a few verses before our gospel reading, Luke had described Jesus as 'filled with joy by the Holy Spirit'. The same Holy Spirit that filled the life of Jesus will be given to us if we keep asking God for it. At the beginning of Luke's second volume, the Acts of the Apostles, the Holy Spirit comes down upon the first followers of Jesus, in response to their prayer. The words of Jesus in today's gospel reading suggest that each of us can have our own Pentecost experience if we ask for it and seek it. Indeed, we need such a Pentecost experience, not just once but throughout our lives. That is why Jesus calls on us to keep on asking for the gift of the Holy Spirit. This is a prayer that God will certainly answer because we need the Holy Spirit if God's purpose for our lives is to come to pass. It is the Spirit who unites us to Jesus and to God the Father and, thereby, empowers us to live as God desires us to live and to love others as God loves us.

9 October, Friday, Twenty-Seventh Week in Ordinary Time

Luke 11:15–26

It is extraordinary to think that, according to today's gospel reading, some people thought Jesus' power to heal and make whole was not from God but from the devil. They were saying that far from being of God, Jesus was of the devil. How could someone who revealed the goodness of God be associated with the prince of devils? The tendency to demonise has reared its head throughout human history. One group demonises another. An individual is demonised without foundation. Once someone or some group is demonised, it gives those doing the demonising a licence to do terrible things to them. Declaring Jesus to be in league with Satan is the most extreme example of such irrational demonising. In response to this perception of him, Jesus declares that it is the finger of God that is revealed in all he does and that it is the kingdom of God that is breaking out through him. The gospel reading encourages us to look for the signs of the finger of God in the lives of those we might be tempted to demonise in whatever way. The parable of the weeds and the wheat reminds us that there is a mixture of the good and the not so good in each of one of us. Jesus is totally good; Satan is totally evil. The rest of us are somewhere in between. We are called to celebrate the good that is in our lives and in the lives of others. Jesus also calls on us to be more attentive to the plank in our own eyes than to the speck of dust in the eye of another.

10 October, Saturday, Twenty-Seventh Week in Ordinary Time
Luke 11:27–28

This must be one of the shortest gospels in the Lectionary. Jesus and a woman from the crowd exchange beatitudes. The woman declares blessed the mother of Jesus, the womb that bore him and the breasts he sucked. Jesus, in reply, declares more blessed those who hear the word of God and keep it. Jesus' mother is included among those who hear the word of God and keep it. Indeed, Luke's Gospel, from which this short gospel reading is taken, portrays Mary as the one who supremely heard the word of God and kept it. Towards the beginning of the gospel she declares to the angel Gabriel, 'Here I am, the servant of the Lord; let it be to me according to your word', with 'your word' referring not just to the word of Gabriel but to the word of God which

Gabriel proclaims. Mary's whole life was according to God's word. She pondered that word and it shaped her life. Luke tells us that when the shepherds made known to Mary what had been told to them about Mary's child, she treasured all their words and pondered them in her heart. While Jesus' beatitude embraces Mary in a special way, it has the potential to include us all. We are all called like Mary to live our lives according to God's word, to treasure that word and ponder it in our hearts, so that it shapes our lives. In his letter to the members of the church in Colossae, Paul exhorts them, 'Let the word of Christ dwell in you richly'. We are called to be people of the word, people whose lives proclaim God's word, as did the life of Mary.

12 October, Monday, Twenty-Eighth Week in Ordinary Time
Luke 11:29–32

In the gospel reading, Jesus draws on the Jewish Scriptures to show how people from beyond Israel, pagans, were sometimes more responsive to God's messengers than God's own people were. The Queen of the South, who was a pagan, came to Jerusalem to hear the wisdom of Solomon. The people of the pagan city of Nineveh repented in response to the preaching of the prophet Jonah. Jesus declares that something greater than Solomon and greater than Jonah is here, and, yet, many of his contemporaries do not take him seriously. They come to him looking for some sign from him to prove his credentials. Jesus is indeed greater than Solomon and Jonah, greater than all the wise people and prophets of Israel, and he is here among us, today. He is not just 'here' to his contemporaries but 'here' to believers of every generation. The gospel reading challenges us never to take the wonder of our faith for granted. God became flesh in Jesus, not in Solomon or any of the prophets, and Jesus, God with us, has given us his flesh to eat and his blood to drink. Someone greater than Solomon and Jonah is 'here', especially at every Eucharist. Unlike the Queen of the South in the gospel reading, we don't have to come from the ends of the earth to find him, because he has come from heaven to find us and to be with us where we are. The only response we can make to such a privilege is one of thanksgiving, and the place where we give thanks above all is in the Eucharist. Saint Paul would remind us that such thanksgiving must flow over into our lives so that the life we live becomes an act of thanksgiving to God's gracious love for us in Christ.

13 October, Tuesday, Twenty-Eighth Week in Ordinary Time
Luke 11:37–41

We are familiar with the expression 'missing the wood for the trees'. We find an example of that in today's gospel reading. A Pharisee who had invited Jesus to a meal was taken aback when Jesus did not observe the usual Jewish rituals of washing before eating. Jesus then accused the Pharisees as a group of being preoccupied with non-essentials, such as external cleanliness, while not paying enough attention to essentials, what God would consider to be true cleanliness, such as the giving of alms to the poor. When it comes to our faith, we need to keep returning to the essentials. You could say that the Second Vatican Council was a collective effort on the part of the whole Church to get back to essentials. Saint Paul had a great nose for the essentials when it came to the Christian calling. In Galatia, he was up against some Jewish Christians who were insisting on the necessity of the Jewish rite of circumcision for converts from paganism. This for Paul was a clear case of focusing on non-essentials. In today's first reading Paul states clearly what he considers to be the essentials. 'What matters is faith that makes its power felt through love', or, 'faith working through love'. We are called to faith, an entrusting of ourselves to Christ, who gave himself for us in love on the cross. Our faith is to find expression in a life of love, in a life that allows the love of Christ to flow through us and touch the lives of others. Paul would say that everything else is secondary.

14 October, Wednesday, Twenty-Eighth Week in Ordinary Time
Luke 11:42–46

In today's gospel reading Jesus is very critical of the Pharisees because they take the seats of honour in the synagogues. Looking for honours was very deeply rooted in the culture to which Jesus belonged. Most of the generous giving that went on was with a view to getting honour. If someone built a public bath, for example, their name was clearly inscribed on it for all to see. Perhaps things haven't changed all that much in that regard. Jesus had a very different attitude to honour. He certainly did not seek it for himself and he did not encourage his disciples to seek honour for themselves, even though they were prone to doing so. On one occasion they argued among themselves as to which of them was the greatest, and James and John asked Jesus for seats of honour on his left and right in his kingdom. Rather than getting honour from others, Jesus put the emphasis on giving honour or showing honour to others. The primary one to whom honour was to be shown was God. We are to live in such a way that we bring honour to God and not to ourselves. Even our good works for others are to bring honour to God and not to ourselves. At the beginning of the Sermon on the Mount in Matthew's Gospel Jesus tells his disciples, 'Let your light shine before others, so that they may see your good works and give glory to your Father in heaven.' Jesus assures us that in living in a way that brings honour and glory to God, we will receive honour from God, which is the only honour worth having.

15 October, Thursday, Twenty-Eighth Week in Ordinary Time
Luke 11:47–54

In today's gospel reading Jesus criticises the lawyers, the experts in Jewish religious law, for taking away the key of knowledge. Their study should have given them access to God's truth and to the person of Jesus who was the full revelation of God's truth. However, not only are they in the process of rejecting Jesus, they are also influencing others to do the same. In the words of the gospel reading, 'They have not gone in themselves and have prevented others going in who wanted to'. Jesus was always very critical of those who were an obstacle to other people coming to faith in him, who prevented others from coming to discover him as God's truth for themselves. If, like the lawyers, we do not go in ourselves, if we are not trying to come to Jesus ourselves, then we will not be able to lead others to Jesus and may well find ourselves preventing others from coming to him. The reverse is also true. As we grow in our relationship with Jesus, we make it easier for others to do the same. We have an influence on each other's faith, in one direction or another. If we are trying to grow in our faith, we won't necessarily lead others to the Lord. However, if our faith is growing ever weaker, we certainly won't lead others to the Lord. Our primary responsibility is to go in ourselves, in the language of the gospel reading. Having done so, we can be sure that the Lord will find a way to work through us to touch the lives of others.

16 October, Friday, Twenty-Eighth Week in Ordinary Time
Luke 12:1–7

Jesus shows an awareness throughout the Gospels that his followers would have to face opposition, hostility and, sometimes, even death. He was implying, as goes the master, so the pupil. Yet, while being realistic about the opposition his followers would face, Jesus does not want them to be paralysed by this prospect. He calls on his followers repeatedly not to be afraid. In today's gospel reading, addressing his disciples as his friends, he says to them, 'Do not be afraid of those who kill the body.' Jesus wants us to be courageous in our witnessing to him. He assures us that we can be courageous in the living of our discipleship because we are not alone. God will always be there to provide for us. As Jesus says in our gospel reading, if God is concerned for one sparrow, he is surely concerned for the followers of his Son, each one of whom is worth more than hundreds of sparrows. When it comes to our life of faith, fear can be very disabling. It can be tempting to keep a low profile, to keep our head beneath the parapet. However, Jesus looks for something more from us and he assures us that if we witness to our faith in him with courage and conviction, we won't suddenly find ourselves alone in no-man's land. We will experience God's tender love and care, just as Jesus experienced God's faithful presence in the hour of his passion and death. We will know the strength of God's Spirit, the Holy Spirit. As Paul reminds us in today's first reading, 'you too have been stamped with the seal of the Holy Spirit of the Promise'.

17 October, Saturday, Twenty-Eighth Week in Ordinary Time
Luke 12:9–12

In his letters Paul often tells us how he prays. It is clear from what he says about his prayer that the prayer of thanksgiving was a central feature of his prayer life. At the beginning of his letters he often tells the members of the church to whom he is writing that he prays in thanksgiving for them. We find an example of that in today's first reading, which is taken from the beginning of his letter to the church in Ephesus. He tells the community that he thanks God for them because he has heard about their faith in the Lord Jesus and the love that they show towards all the saints. The 'saints' is Paul's way of referring to the baptised. Paul gives thanks for their faith in the Lord and their love for others. Faith and love often come together in this way in Paul's letters. In his letter to the Galatians he speaks of faith expressing itself in love. He is reminding us that our relationship with the Lord, our faith, and our relationship with others, our love, are inseparable. Authentic faith will always show itself in love. Our faith in the Lord opens us up to receive the Lord's gift of the Holy Spirit, and the fruit of the Spirit is love. The Holy Spirit is the link between faith and love. In the gospel reading, Jesus promises his disciples the gift of the Holy Spirit, when the time comes. That time for them was Pentecost. For us that time was our baptism, but not only our baptism. We live in a perpetual Pentecost; the time of the Church is always a Pentecost time. The Lord always stands ready to pour out the gift of the Holy Spirit afresh into our hearts. Each day, we are invited to receive in faith this gift of the Spirit and to allow this gift to bear the fruit of love in our lives.

19 October, Monday, Twenty-Ninth Week in Ordinary Time
Luke 12:13–21
In today's gospel reading, Jesus tells a story of a man whose whole focus in life is to accumulate more and more. He is already rich at the beginning of the story. None the less, it seems that what he possessed wasn't enough for him. After an exceptionally good harvest, he decides to go on a building spree. He knocks down perfectly good barns and builds bigger and better ones to store his extra grain and make his future even more secure than it already was. It is a story of someone who is thoroughly focused on himself; his speech is peppered with the words 'I' and 'my'. In commenting on his own story, Jesus declares that even though this man looked very rich, at a more fundamental level he was very poor, because he was not rich in the sight of God. In immersing himself in his own possessions, he had lost sight of God completely. He never spoke to God; he was not aware of God,

yet God was aware of him, and, at the end of the story, God spoke to him. God never loses touch with us, but we can lose touch with God. When that happens, our life is impoverished, even if we are well endowed with this world's goods. In a sense, the gospel reading calls on us to put first things first, to put God before all else. Being rich in the sight of God is more important than being rich in our own eyes or in the eyes of others. We are rich in the sight of God when we live our lives in the Spirit of God's Son, who, more than any human being, was rich in the sight of God.

20 October, Tuesday, Twenty-Ninth Week in Ordinary Time
Luke 12:35–38

The phrase 'waiting for the knock on the door' is often used in a negative sense. It suggests the arrival of an unwelcome visitor with disturbing consequences for those who live in the house. This is not how the image is used in today's gospel reading. The one who knocks on the door is someone who wants to serve those who are awake when he knocks and who are ready to open the door to him. Even though he is master of the household, he will relate to his servants as most people in that culture would expect the servants to relate to him. He will put on an apron, sit them down at table and prepare a meal for them. In this little parable, Jesus is giving us an image of how he wants to relate to us. In the first reading, Paul reminds us that we are all members of God's household. In that household, God's Son, who is master or Lord of the household, wishes to be our servant, in keeping with his saying in the Gospel of Luke, 'I am among you as one who serves', and in keeping with his action in John's Gospel when he washed the feet of his disciples. Yet, if he is to serve us as he desires, he needs us to be open to his presence, his daily coming. In the words of the gospel reading, we are to have our lamps lit, awake to his coming, at all times. The gospel reading assures us that if we live in that state of openness and responsiveness to the Lord's daily coming, then the Lord will serve us in ways that will surprise us.

21 October, Wednesday, Twenty-Ninth Week in Ordinary Time
Luke 12:39–48

In today's first reading, Paul speaks out of a sense of having been greatly graced by God. Although 'less than the least of all the saints' (the baptised), he has been entrusted with a 'special grace'. The grace Paul speaks about is the Gospel, which unveils the mystery of Christ. Paul is overawed by 'the depths that I see in the mystery of Christ'. He is very aware that this grace that has been entrusted to him carries with it a responsibility. He is now a servant of this Gospel with which he has been graced, responsible for proclaiming it to those who have never heard it. In the language of the gospel reading, Paul sees himself as a 'steward', who has been given much by his master and who now needs to show that he is worthy of what has been entrusted to him. We have all been graced in various ways by the Lord. We have been baptised into Christ; we have been given a share in his Spirit; we have been entrusted with the Gospel; we are members of Christ's body, the Church; we receive his coming as bread of life in the Eucharist; we are touched by his merciful presence in the Sacrament of Reconciliation. Like trustworthy stewards, we have been entrusted with a great deal by the Lord. Today's gospel reading calls on us to be 'faithful and wise' stewards. We need to keep treasuring the many graces we have received from God and live out of what has been entrusted to us. We have been graced by the Lord so that we can grace others with what we have received.

22 October, Thursday, Twenty-Ninth Week in Ordinary Time
Luke 12:49–53

In the course of his letters, Paul often speaks about his prayer. He tells us the content of his prayer, what he gives thanks to God for, what he petitions God for, the people that he prays for. We have a wonderful example of Paul's prayer in today's first reading, which is one of my favourite passages from Paul's letters. Paul's prayer in this passage is both a prayer of petition and a prayer of praise. In both of these prayers, Paul refers to the power of God or the power of the Spirit. He petitions God to give the members of the church in Ephesus the power through the Spirit for their hidden selves to grow strong, so that Christ may live in their hearts. He goes on to give praise to God, whose power working in us can do infinitely more than all we can ask or imagine. Paul declares that through the power of God, the power of the Spirit, at work in our hearts, Christ comes to live in us and, when that happens, our hidden selves, our true selves, grow strong. There is a very beautiful, Trinitarian, vision of the Christian life contained in that prayer. God the Father sends the Holy Spirit into our lives so that Christ, his Son, can live in us and, thereby, our true selves, our Christ-selves, grow strong. It is through his Son, in particular his Son's death, resurrection and ascension, that God the Father sends the Holy Spirit into our lives. In the gospel reading, Jesus makes reference to his role of sending us the Holy Spirit from the Father. 'I have come to bring fire to the earth,' he says, the fire of the Spirit, the fire of God's love. Each day, we are called to open our hearts afresh to this gift of the Holy Spirit who comes to us from the Father through the Son, so that God's Son may be formed in us and we become our true selves, in the words of that first reading, 'filled with the utter fullness of God'.

23 October, Friday, Twenty-Ninth Week in Ordinary Time

Luke 12:54–59

In the gospel reading, Jesus declares how easily people interpret the face of the earth and the sky in order to predict the weather. Wind from the west brings rain; a wind from the south brings heat. Even though we have a very different climate in Ireland from that of the Galilee of Jesus' day, it remains true for us also that a wind from the west tends to bring rain and a wind from the south tends to bring warmth, if not heat. However, Jesus goes on to say that his contemporaries are not so good at interpreting the times in which they live. They are failing to recognise that God is visiting them and calling out to them in and through his own ministry. Something hugely significant was astir among them and they were failing to respond to it. The community of disciples today, the Church, is constantly engaged in that work of interpreting the times. We always need to ask ourselves, 'What is the Lord saying to us in and through these times in which we live today?' We can look out on our world, our society, our culture, and get very discouraged. Yet the Lord stands among us just as he stood among his contemporaries and he continues to work among us and to call out to us. This is the world, this is the culture and these are the times within which the Lord is calling us to be his disciples, his witnesses. He doesn't want us to flee from the world or culture but to interpret what it is to be his followers in the midst of our world, with all its challenges to faith. The call of Paul in the first reading remains valid today. In the midst of the times in which we find ourselves, we are being called to lead a life worthy of our vocation, bearing with one another charitably in complete selflessness, gentleness and patience, doing all we can to preserve the unity of the Spirit.

24 October, Saturday, Twenty-Ninth Week in Ordinary Time
Luke 13:1–9

At the beginning of today's gospel reading, there is mention of two tragedies. One was brought about by the abuse of power; Pilate's troops had killed Galilean worshippers while they were offering sacrifice in the Temple. The second tragedy was an unfortunate accident; a tower fell down in Siloam and killed fourteen people. Both kinds of tragedies happen today. People continue to be killed because of the brutal abuse of power and people lose their lives through unexpected accidents. Jesus warns his contemporaries against thinking that those who lost their lives in these two tragedies were somehow greater sinners than others. He dismisses any simplistic connection between suffering and sin. Instead, he uses these two incidents to get his listeners to reflect on the vulnerability and fragility of human life. Our physical lives can be taken from us without any prior warning. For this reason, we need to value the present moment and see it as an opportunity to turn more fully towards the Lord and away from our own selfish desires, or in the language of Jesus in the gospel reading, as an opportunity to repent. Sometimes tragic events that impact us have a way of making us take stock of our lives. The Lord can be calling out to us through such events. In the parable of the fig tree which follows Jesus' reflection on these tragic events, we are introduced to a farmer who sees hope for a fig tree whose plight appears hopeless. The farmer stands up to the owner of the vineyard where the tree is planted and makes a case for the tree having a future, in spite of its failure to bear fruit for three years. There is an image here of Jesus' own way of relating to us. The Lord who calls out to us through all of life's happenings, including the tragic ones, sees us with eyes of hope. His reluctance to give up on us encourages us to keep making the most of the present moment, to keep opening our lives more fully to his call to us and his desire for us.

26 October, Monday, Thirtieth Week in Ordinary Time
Luke 13:10–17

In some of the gospel stories, people who are in need approach Jesus. In other stories, Jesus approaches them without any initiative on their part towards him. In these stories Jesus is often moved by what he sees to take the initiative. Today's gospel reading is a good example of this kind of story. Jesus sees a woman who had been bent double by an enfeeblement for eighteen years. Upon seeing her, he calls her over and, laying his hands on her, declares to her that her infirmity has been healed. In response, she glorifies God. There is a pattern here of how the Lord relates to each one of us. He sees us before we see him. He calls out to us before we call upon him. What matters for us is that we notice the Lord seeing us and are attentive to the Lord calling us. If we respond to the Lord's seeing and calling, as the woman did, we too will experience the Lord's healing and life-giving presence, and, like the woman, we will be moved to give glory to God for it. We often become so absorbed in our own issues that we miss this moment of grace when the Lord looks upon us and calls out to us. The synagogue official in the gospel reading was troubled by the issue of Jesus working on the Sabbath and of needy people encouraging Jesus to work on the Sabbath. He missed the moment of grace for the woman, which was also a moment of grace for him. His indignation, his anger, blinded him to the significance of the moment. It can be easy for any of us to get so emotionally engaged by what is relatively unimportant that we miss the Lord's seeing us and calling us. We need to keep developing the art of noticing and responding.

27 October, Tuesday, Thirtieth Week in Ordinary Time
Luke 13:18–21

The two parables of Jesus we have just heard suggest that the kingdom of God can come to pass in and through what is small, insignificant and almost invisible. The mustard seed is tiny, and when sown in a garden becomes invisible, yet it goes on to become a tree that provides shelter for the birds of the air. A woman uses a tiny amount of yeast and when placed in three measures of flour it remains invisible, yet it helps to make enough bread to feed a large number of people. Jesus was often alert to what would have been considered small and insignificant, invisible to most people. The poor widow who puts two copper coins into the Temple treasury comes to mind. Here was a tiny gesture that would have gone unnoticed by many, yet Jesus saw in her a sign of his own self-giving love for all. He recognised the presence of the kingdom of God in her seemingly insignificant gesture. On another occasion, he spoke of the significance of giving a cup of cold water to someone. We all have opportunities every day to do little things in a loving way. Something of God's kingdom can grace our world through our own small and often hidden acts of love. Such acts will often be invisible to others and will never make the news, yet they help to make one of the petitions in the Lord's Prayer become more of a reality: 'your kingdom come on earth, as it is in heaven'.

28 October, Wednesday, Saints Simon and Jude, Apostles
Luke 6:12–19

Today we celebrate the feast of Saints Simon and Jude, two members of the twelve that Jesus selected from among the larger group of disciples. The choosing of the twelve was a key decision for Jesus. It is only Luke who tells us, as we read in today's gospel reading, that, before he chose the twelve, Jesus spent the whole night in prayer to God. This was a decision he prayed about; his choice of the twelve came out of his prayer. Indeed, Luke emphasises that Jesus prayed before all of these key moments in his life: just after his baptism; just before he set his face to go to Jerusalem; in the Garden of Gethsemane as he faced into his passion and death; on the cross just before his death. We will often find ourselves praying at important moments in our own lives too. At such moments, we recognise our need for guidance and strength from above. Our prayer at such moments does not necessarily mean that everything will work out perfectly for us. Although Jesus spent the whole night in prayer before he chose twelve from among the disciples, one of the twelve, Peter, went on to deny him, another, Judas, went on to betray him, and the others all deserted him. Yet we can be sure that our prayerful surrender to the Lord at such times will always create space for him to work, even when circumstances do not work out as we had hoped.

29 October, Thursday, Thirtieth Week in Ordinary Time
Luke 13:31–35

Jesus seems to have been a keen observer of nature and of the animal world. He would have seen a hen in the farmyard gathering her brood of chicks under her wings. That sight spoke to him of his own ministry. He was also in the business of gathering people. He wanted to form a new kind of community, consisting of people who would not normally gather together, Jew, Samaritan and Gentile, rich and poor, law abiding and sinner, male and female. In today's gospel reading he laments the fact that the people of Jerusalem, for the most part, were not open to being gathered by him. He longed to gather them together as a hen gathers her brood under her wings, but they refused; they were not willing. Jesus had a great desire to be in communion with others, but if that desire was to come to pass, it needed to find some openness in others. Even Jesus could be powerless before the mystery of human freedom. He could call and invite and plead, but he could not coerce. Even as his desire for others was being met with murderous resistance, even as he hung from the cross, he continued to call and invite and plead; he continued his work of gathering. When he rose from the dead, that work of calling and inviting and gathering continued and continues to this day. The Lord does not and cannot cease his work of gathering people around himself. He continues to await our response; he continues to lament when it is not forthcoming and to rejoice when it is. In the first reading, Saint Paul tells us that there are spiritual forces at work trying to prevent us from responding to the Lord's work of gathering us to himself. To resist such forces, Paul says, human strength is not enough. We need God's strength, God's armour, which is why, in the words of that reading, we need to pray in the Spirit on every possible occasion.

30 October, Friday, Thirtieth Week in Ordinary Time
Luke 14:1–6

In the gospel reading, Jesus is the guest at a meal hosted by a leading Pharisee. It is clear that his host and the other guests had more than hospitality on their mind. The gospel reading says that 'they were watching him closely'. In other words, they were hostile to him. The man with dropsy at the meal was probably planted there by the host and other guests; they wanted to see if Jesus would break the Jewish law by healing the man on the Sabbath. Indeed, Jesus was prepared to risk incurring the hostility of the most powerful people of his time for the sake of this unnamed man. Jesus showed a love that did not count the cost. He gave life to others, even if it meant suffering and death for himself. The gospel reading says that Jesus 'took the man, cured him, and sent him away'. Each of those three actions reveals Jesus' totally unselfish love for the man. In sending him away, Jesus was showing that he had no desire to possess the man or to profit personally from his healing of him. The love the Lord showed to this man is the love the Lord has for us all, and the love he calls on us to have for each other. Sometimes, like the Lord, we are called to show such love even in the face of hostility and rejection.

31 October, Saturday, Thirtieth Week in Ordinary Time

Luke 14:1, 7–11

Jesus often saw the ordinary activities of people as an opportunity to teach people something about the ways of God. In today's gospel reading, he is at a banquet hosted by a leading Pharisee. He notices how keen his fellow guests are to grab the most honourable seats at the banquet, which are those closest to the host. In response to what he sees, Jesus speaks a parable about how sometimes at banquets those who seek places of honour often find themselves having to take a more lowly seat, whereas those who are happy to take a lowly seat often find themselves asked to take a more honourable seat. What has this to say about the ways of God by which we are to live? Jesus was the person who lived fully according to God's ways. He never sought to be honoured by others. He wasn't motivated by the desire to gain the approval and admiration of others. On the contrary, in one of his letters Saint Paul says that Jesus emptied himself, taking the form of a servant, and humbled himself, becoming obedient unto death on a cross, the least honourable form of death in that culture. The Gospels suggest that Jesus often had to challenge the practice of honour-seeking among his own disciples. James and John asking for the best seats in Jesus' kingdom, one at his right and the other at his left, comes to mind. In response to this attitude, which was typical of the culture, Jesus said, 'Whoever wishes to be great among you must be your servant, and whoever wishes to be first among you must be slave of all', after his own example. Jesus suggests that these are the people God will honour. The only honour worth having is honour from God, and God will honour those who empty themselves in the service of others, after the example of Jesus.

2 November, Monday, Commemoration of all the Faithful Departed

Matthew 11:25–30

Today is the day when we give expression to what we refer to in the creed as 'the communion of saints'. We believe that there is a deep spiritual communion between those of us who are still on our pilgrim way and those who have come to the end of their pilgrim journey. As the funeral liturgy of the Church states, 'All the ties of love and affection that knit us together in this life do not unravel with death'. Saint Paul puts it more simply in his first letter to the Corinthians: 'Love never ends'. One of the ways we expressed our communion with our loved ones before they died was by praying for them. If we are people of faith, we will pray for those who are significant for us. Just as our love for our loved ones does not cease when they die, neither does our praying for them cease, which is an expression of our enduring love for them. Today is a special day of prayerful remembrance for our loved ones who have died. A traditional prayer we often pray for those who have died is 'Eternal rest grant unto them, O Lord, and let perpetual light shine upon them'. We can sometimes think of rest as something passive, the absence of activity. We could also think of rest in a way suggested by that lovely psalm that is often prayed at a funeral, 'The Lord is my Shepherd'. Towards the end of that psalm we read, 'near restful waters he leads me to revive my drooping spirits'. Rest is associated with a revival of our spirits. Eternal rest is an eternal revival of our deepest self. One of the early saints of the Church, Saint Ephrem, wrote, 'in the kingdom our departed ones achieve their full stature'. When we are praying that God would give our departed loved ones eternal rest, this is what we are praying for. The invitation of Jesus in today's gospel reading, 'Come to me', and his promise, 'I will give you rest', suggests that already in this earthly life we can begin to enter into this reviving rest which allows us to reach our full stature.

3 November, Tuesday, Thirty-First Week in Ordinary Time
Luke 14:15–24

The parable in today's gospel reading envisages a situation where people had already accepted an invitation to a feast and had said they were coming. Then the second invitation went out just as the meal was ready, and it was at that point that they started to make excuses. Having initially said 'yes', they said 'no' at very short notice. Having said 'yes' to the invitation, they failed to follow through on it. Therein lies the challenge for all of us. We are to follow through on the 'yes' we make to the Lord's call, to live out that 'yes' in the day-to-day affairs of our lives. The parable suggests that the Lord is determined that his feast would be a crowded affair. When the people originally invited went on to say 'no', others were invited. There were to be no empty seats at this host's table. The Lord's determination cannot be questioned. He wants as many as possible to come to the banquet of life. What is at issue is our determination to respond. We might pray in response to today's gospel reading that our response to the Lord's invitation would be as persistent as his invitation, that our determination to be in communion with him would match his determination to be in communion with us.

4 November, Wednesday, Thirty-First Week in Ordinary Time
Luke 14:25–33

The opening words of today's gospel reading seem very harsh to us today. We are dealing here with a Semitic idiom expressing preference. If you prefer one thing, or even one person, over another, you are said to love the one and hate the other. Jesus is not calling on his disciples to hate their families, but to love him more than they love even their families. He is to be the primary love or the primary loyalty in our lives. Elsewhere in the Gospel Jesus quotes what he terms the first commandment, to love God with all one's soul, strength and mind. However, because Jesus is God-with-us, to love God in this total way is to love Jesus in this total way. As followers of Jesus we are called to give him our primary allegiance; our relationship with him is to influence all our other relationships. Jesus calls for great loyalty and devotion. That is why he calls on potential disciples to think it through, just as a builder has to think through whether he will be able to finish building the tower if he starts on it or a king has to think through whether to go to war with inferior forces. The Lord wants us to be wholehearted rather than halfhearted in our following of him. He wants a 'yes' from us that is in some way a reflection of his 'yes' to us.

5 November, Thursday, Thirty-First Week in Ordinary Time
Luke 15:1–10
The joy of the Gospel has been a very strong theme of the preaching and writing of Pope Francis. His letter on the call to holiness in to-day's world was entitled *Rejoice and Be Glad*. The note of joy is very strong in today's gospel reading. When the shepherd finds his lost sheep, he 'joyfully' takes it on his shoulders and when he gets home he calls together his friends and neighbours, saying to them, 'Rejoice with me!' When the woman who lost her coin finds it, she too calls her friends and neighbours together and says to them, 'Rejoice with me!' The shepherd and the woman are both images of Jesus. He is seeking out the lost, as they did, and gathering them together into a new community. As he does so, he says to all, 'Rejoice with me', 'Rejoice at God's good work'. However, there were those who, far from rejoicing with Jesus, took offence at what he was doing. 'This man welcomes sinners and eats with them.' On another occasion, Jesus compares such people to children who refuse to dance when other children play the pipes. Their sullen response to what God was doing through Jesus was in sharp contrast to the rejoicing in heaven. Jesus wanted some of

that heavenly joy to be reflected among those who witnessed what he was doing. God's good work continues today through the risen Lord and the Holy Spirit, even in the midst of these difficult times for the Church. There is something here to rejoice in. The Lord continues to say to us, 'Rejoice with me'. We all possess what Paul calls in the first reading 'the supreme advantage of knowing Christ Jesus my Lord'. We know that Christ Jesus our Lord is at work within us and among us and that is reason enough for joy.

6 November, Friday, All the Saints of Ireland
Luke 6:20–26

The saints are those who responded fully to the Lord's call to become his disciples. Today's gospel reading says that Jesus fixed his eyes on his disciples before speaking to them. He addresses them as poor, hungry, weeping, hated and abused. Most of the Irish saints whom we remember today could have been addressed in a similar way. In many ways, the life of Jesus' first disciples became more of a struggle for them after they left their former way of life to follow Jesus. Getting involved in Jesus' way of doing things brought new demands, and had left them poorer, needier, more vulnerable and less acceptable to many. Yet Jesus declares to his struggling disciples that they are blessed, because in becoming his disciples and in remaining faithful to him, they would experience the abundance of God's generosity. 'You shall be satisfied … you shall laugh … your reward will be great in heaven.' When our own following of the Lord makes demands on us and leaves us more vulnerable, the Lord declares us blessed too. Our efforts to walk in the way of the Lord, to become saints, will often mean taking the path less travelled. Some people looking at our lives might see us as losing out. Our remaining faithful to the Lord's way can appear to leave us less fortunate from a human point of view. Today's gospel reading declares, however, that, in reality, we are truly fortunate. Jesus assures us that whatever we have to put aside in order to be faithful to him will seem very little in comparison to what we will receive from him. He promises his struggling disciples, 'yours is the kingdom of God'. He makes the same promise to disciples in every generation, to all who are striving to be saints, to be loving in the way Jesus is loving. This promise of the kingdom of God does not simply pertain to the next life; it begins to be fulfilled for us in this life. If we give our lives over to the Lord, as the saints did, we will begin to know the blessings of the kingdom of God in this present life, and we will experience them to the full in eternal life.

7 November, Saturday, Thirty-First Week in Ordinary Time
Luke 16:9–15

In today's first reading, Paul writes from prison to one of the churches he established, the church in the city of Philippi in northern Greece. This was a church with whom he had a very warm relationship. They had helped him in all kinds of practical ways since he first began to preach the Gospel in northern Greece. In today's first reading, Paul says to this church, 'No other church helped me with gifts of money. You were the only ones; and twice since my stay in Thessalonika you have sent me what I needed.' As a result of this church's generosity to him, Paul goes on to say, 'Now for the time being I have everything that I need and more'. It seems that this very early Christian community in Philippi was being faithful to the message of Jesus in today's gospel reading from Luke. There Jesus calls on us to use money in the service of others so that at the end of our lives they will welcome us into the tents of eternity. Jesus suggests that the resources of this world are given to us on trust, to be used for others. If we are faithful to that trust of earthly riches, 'little things', then we will be entrusted with genuine riches, the riches of eternal life, 'great things'. At the end of today's first reading, Paul assures the Philippians that their generosity towards him will create a space for God to 'fulfil all your needs in Christ Jesus, as lavishly as only God can'. Paul is assuring us that when we are generous with what has been entrusted to us, we open ourselves up to experiencing God's lavish generosity towards us. In the words of Jesus earlier in Luke's Gospel, 'Give and it will be given to you'.

9 November, Monday, The Dedication of the Lateran Basilica
John 2:13–22

We don't often celebrate the feast of the dedication of a church. However, the Basilica of Saint John Lateran is a special church. It is the cathedral church of the diocese of Rome. As the diocesan cathedral, it is the church of the bishop of Rome, who, of course, is the pope. It is the church of the pope in his role as bishop of Rome. For this reason, this particular church has been given a rather long title, 'Mother and Head of all the churches of the city and of the world'. Why is this church sometimes called the Lateran Basilica or the Basilica of Saint John Lateran? The 'Laterani' were an old Roman family who probably once owned the land on which the Emperor Constantine, the first Christian emperor, built this basilica in the early decades of the fourth century. Of the three readings for this feast, only the first reading focuses on an actual building, the Temple in the city of Jerusalem, understood as the place of God's living presence in the world. When Paul was writing to the church in Corinth in today's second reading, there were no Christian buildings in existence. Paul's focus in that reading is not on a building but on the community of faith, the Church. He says to the local church in Corinth, 'You are God's building ... you are God's Temple'. Later in that same letter, he asks each member of the church, 'Do you not know that your body is a temple of the Holy Spirit within you?' In the gospel reading, even though Jesus is present in the Temple in Jerusalem, he places the focus not on the building but on himself. Speaking of himself, he says, 'Destroy this sanctuary [this temple] and in three days I will raise it up'. Jesus is saying that he is the place where God is truly present in the world, not some building, no matter how sacred. Paul says that the Christian community, the body of Christ, is the place where God is truly present in the world, as is each individual member of the Church. If Jesus was the supreme expression of God's presence in the world, we, as Church, as the community of believers, are to be the living expression of God's loving presence in our world today. The Lord, now risen, continues to be God's presence in the world today through each one of us in all our diversity.

10 November, Tuesday, Thirty-Second Week in Ordinary Time
Luke 17:7–10

In today's first reading, Saint Paul makes a distinction between worldly ambitions and the ambition to do good. Paul equates 'worldly ambitions' with 'everything that does not lead to God', which we are to give up. It can be good to ask ourselves the question, 'Where is this leading me?' 'Is it leading me to God?' We try to discern as we go through life what is leading me to God and what is leading me away from God, what is damaging my relationship with God and what is deepening my relationship with God. In the gospel reading, Jesus identifies one attitude that can be damaging to our relationship with God. It is the attitude of entitlement before God. It is the attitude that says to God, 'I have served you well. I have lived a good life. Now it is your turn to serve me. You need to show your gratitude to me'. In contrast to such an attitude, Jesus puts before us the attitude of those who, after they have done all that God asks, simply say to God, 'I am merely your servant; I have done no more than my duty'. In other words, 'You owe me nothing'. Our ambition to do good, our good life, our service of the Lord, does not entitle us to anything from

God. Before we did anything, God has already been generous with us. As Paul says at the beginning of the first reading, 'God's grace has been revealed' in the life, death and resurrection of God's Son. We have all been greatly graced by God, through Jesus. All the good we do, our service of God, is no more than our grateful response to God's prior generous love towards us.

11 November, Wednesday, Thirty-Second Week in Ordinary Time
Luke 17:11–19

I have often been struck by the phrase in the gospel reading, 'one of them turned back, praising God'. Of the ten lepers that were healed by Jesus, only one 'turned back' to Jesus, a Samaritan. That 'turning back' was the outward expression of something very important that was happening within him, a turning away from a focus on himself, including his healing, towards God, the source of his healing, whom he recognised as powerfully at work through Jesus. There is a sense in which we all need to stop ourselves in our tracks like the Samaritan, and turn back to acknowledge the ways that God has blessed us, and give thanks and praise to God for all we have received. So much of what is good in our lives has been given to us. The most significant people in our lives have been given to us; they came to us as gifts. We discover in ourselves certain abilities. We may have worked to develop them, but they were given to us initially. The faith that brings us together at the Eucharist has been given to us. The community of believers where we meet the Lord in a special way has been given to us. We are a graced people and the most appropriate response to being graced is praise and thanksgiving. Very often our prayer is one of petition; we easily identify with the prayer of the lepers, 'Jesus! Master! Take pity on us'. We regularly pray some version of that prayer, as we come before the Lord in our need. It was the Samaritan alone who moved beyond the prayer of petition, who 'turned back, praising

God'. It was only the Samaritan who threw himself at the feet of Jesus and thanked him. We too need to keep turning back to give praise and thanks to the Lord, because we are continually being graced by him, even in those times when life is a real struggle.

12 November, Thursday, Thirty-Second Week in Ordinary Time
Luke 17:20–25

The question asked of Jesus by the Pharisees in today's gospel reading, 'When is the kingdom of God to come?' implies that the kingdom of God has not yet come. However, at the core of Jesus' preaching was the proclamation of the good news that the kingdom of God is at hand. The reign of God's powerful love was already at work in all that Jesus was doing and saying, in his healing the sick, in his gathering of the new community, which included the outcasts, in his forgiving sinners, in his powerful words, which consoled some and disturbed others. That is why, in response to the question of the Pharisees, Jesus says, 'The kingdom of God is among you'. The risen Lord would say the same to us today. 'The kingdom of God is among you.' Wherever the Spirit of Jesus is alive and active, the kingdom of God is there. It is there when those who had been made to feel unwanted are given a sense of home, when the sick and the suffering experience a compassionate and healing presence, when those who seek the Lord, without perhaps always realising it, are helped to find him, when those burdened by a sense of past failures are helped to experience God's unconditional love and forgiveness. In the first reading, the kingdom of God would be present if the church that meets in Philemon's house did what Paul asks, receiving back the runaway slave Onesimus as a brother in Christ, as if he were Paul himself. There are so many ways we can help to make a reality the words of Jesus in today's gospel reading, 'The kingdom of God is among you'.

13 November, Friday, Thirty-Second Week in Ordinary Time
Luke 17:26–37

The first reading from the second letter of Saint John expresses our baptismal calling in a very succinct way, 'to live a life of love'. The author assures us that all the Lord's commandments can be reduced to this one commandment to love. It is above all Jesus who shows us what it means to love, by his life, death and resurrection. He also gives us the power to love as he loved and continues to love by pouring the Holy Spirit into our hearts. To love in this sense is to give of ourselves in the service of the Lord and his people. In the words of today's gospel reading, it is to be prepared to lose our lives for others, rather than putting our efforts into preserving our lives at all costs. That gospel reading also speaks about the coming of the Son of Man and the suddenness of that coming. The reference is primarily to the coming of the Son of Man at the end of time, but we can apply what is said to Jesus' coming at the end of our own earthly lives. If we live a life of love each day of our lives, then we will be found ready and waiting whenever the Son of Man comes to us. At the end of our lives and at the end of time, it is the quality of our love that will matter most in the Lord's eyes. Saint John of the Cross wrote, 'in the evening of life, we will be judged on love alone'. Have we shown to others something of the love that God has shown to us by the sending of his Son, something of the love that Jesus has displayed in his life, death and resurrection?

14 November, Saturday, Thirty-Second Week in Ordinary Time
Luke 18:1–8

As believers living in today's world, it can be tempting to lose heart at times. We can sense that faith in God and in Jesus, being part of the faith community we call Church, is not greatly valued by today's commentators. We can also lose heart as believers for more personal reasons. We encounter some great suffering and we wonder where God is in it all. We feel some injustice has been done to us and we conclude that God has not stood by us. According to today's gospel reading, Jesus spoke the parable of the judge and the widow to encourage his disciples not to lose heart but to keep on praying, to pray continuously, even in times of great darkness. By means of this parable Jesus is encouraging us to have a persistent faith. The widow is an example of such persistent faith. When an injustice was done to her, she did not lose heart. She kept hammering away at the judge who alone could grant her justice until he caved in to her demands, fearful perhaps that she would resort to violence if he didn't respond to her. Jesus is encouraging us to have something of the gutsy determination of the widow. Our persistent prayer is not to an unjust judge who couldn't care less about God or his fellow human beings. We pray to a God who is passionately concerned about us. All the more reason why we should have a persistent faith that finds expression in continual prayer. Having spoken the parable, Jesus asks the question, 'When the Son of Man comes will he find any faith on earth?' When he comes at the end of time, will he find people with the kind of persistent faith displayed by the widow, or will his disciples have lost heart by then, worn down by the trials of life? It is a question that puts it up to us, in the words of the letter to the Hebrews, 'to run with perseverance the race that is set before us, looking to Jesus the pioneer and perfecter of our faith'.

16 November, Monday, Thirty-Third Week in Ordinary Time

Luke 18:35–43

The figure of the blind man in today's gospel reading is one of those gospel characters who can cast light on our own faith journey. Although he couldn't see, there was clearly no problem with his hearing or his speaking. When he heard a crowd going past, he asked what it was all about. The question, 'What is it all about?' is one of those fundamental questions of meaning that remains with us throughout the course of our faith journey. It is a question we live with and struggle with, rather than one that lends itself to an easy answer. The answer people gave to the blind man's question was that Jesus of Nazareth was passing by. The Lord continues to pass us by today. Even if we don't see him clearly and don't have a strong sense of his presence, he is continually passing us by. We don't have to do anything to make Jesus pass us by, to make him present. He is present to us, and it only falls to us to respond to his presence, and, in that regard, the blind man can be our teacher. He called out to Jesus in prayer, even though the people around Jesus insisted in no uncertain terms that he be quiet. Sometimes, we too need to show our faith in the Lord, in the face of pressure to keep quiet, to keep our faith to ourselves. Just as the man was not put off by the crowd's insistence that he be quiet, neither was Jesus put off. He insisted that the man's desire for a real communion with him be respected. As Saint Paul reminds us, nothing need come between us and the love of God made visible in Jesus. The personal question Jesus asks the man is addressed to us all, 'What do you want me to do for you?' We each have to answer that question for ourselves, but, again, the blind man has something to teach us about how to answer it. Aware of his blindness, he asked Jesus to let him see again, and, then, with his restored sight he followed Jesus on the way. We are always in need of healing for our own spiritual blindness, so that we can follow in the way of Jesus more fully.

17 November, Tuesday, Thirty-Third Week in Ordinary Time
Luke 19:1–10

In the reading from the Book of Revelation today, the risen Jesus addresses the church in Laodicea as rich, in terms of the goods of this world. Yet, in reality, he says, the church is 'pitiably poor'. This church could be seen as a mirror image of Zacchaeus in the gospel reading. As a senior tax collector, he is a wealthy man, yet, in a deeper sense, he is pitiably poor. Whereas the church in Laodicea needed to be told it was pitiably poor, Zacchaeus was aware of his own spiritual poverty, his own restlessness. It was this awareness that led him to take the unconventional step of climbing a sycamore tree to catch a glimpse of Jesus who was passing by. Saint Augustine said that our hearts are restless until they rest in God. This inner restlessness, if we allow ourselves to feel it, can lead us to seek out the Lord, in the way Zacchaeus sought him out. When we seek out the Lord, we invariably discover that the Lord is seeking us more than we are seeking him. Zacchaeus just wanted to catch a glimpse of Jesus. However, when Jesus saw Zacchaeus, he showed that he wanted a much deeper communion with Zacchaeus: 'I must stay at your house today.' We are reminded again of the words of the risen Lord to the church in Laodicea in the first reading, 'I am standing at the door, knocking. If one of you hears me calling and opens the door, I will come in and share their meal, side by side with them.' As Jesus says to Zacchaeus, 'the Son of Man came to seek out and save the lost'. The Lord is always seeking us out in his love. If we allow ourselves to be found by the Lord, he will empower us to follow him more generously and joyfully, just as he empowered Zacchaeus to live more fully as a son of Abraham.

18 November, Wednesday, Thirty-Third Week in Ordinary Time
Luke 19:11–28

Immediately after speaking the parable in today's gospel reading, Luke has Jesus enter the city of Jerusalem on a colt, to the cries of 'Blessed is the king who comes in the name of the Lord'. Jesus' imminent entry into the city of Jerusalem led some of his followers to believe that the kingdom of God, whose presence Jesus had announced, would soon come in all its fullness. Jesus speaks this parable to counter the expectation that the full arrival of God's kingdom was imminent. The parable suggests, rather, that there would be a long interval between Jesus' enthronement as king at his resurrection and his return at the end of time in power and glory. This long interval is a time of opportunity for creative service of others, a time to use the gifts and resources we have been given in doing the Lord's work. One of the servants to whom the master in the parable entrusted resources did nothing with what he had been given, because of fear. Fear left him paralysed, held him back. It is striking the number of times Jesus says in the Gospels, 'Do not be afraid'. Jesus was very aware how fear can prevent people from responding to his call. The opposite of faith in the Gospels is not so much unbelief but fear. When we rise above our fears in response to the Lord's call, we make it easier for others to do the same. We encourage each other – we give each other courage – by being courageous ourselves.

19 November, Thursday, Thirty-Third Week in Ordinary Time
Luke 19:41–44

One of the most distressing experiences in life is to be rejected by someone we love and care about. This is the kind of sadness that engulfs Jesus at the beginning of today's gospel reading as he sheds tears over the city of Jerusalem. This city and its people always had a special place in God's purpose. According to the Jewish Scriptures, it was the place where God had chosen to dwell. Jesus knew that the message of God's kingdom, God's reign of love, that he had preached throughout Galilee, also had to be preached in Jerusalem, the city that was closest to God's heart and, therefore, to Jesus' heart. Yet, unlike Galilee, where Jesus' message and ministry were often well received, Jerusalem proved to be impervious to his message. It would live up to its darker reputation as a city that kills God's prophets. The powerful people of the city were soon to reject Jesus in the most violent way.

God was visiting the city in love through Jesus and this love was rejected. An opportunity for the city to experience the peace that comes from receiving God's loving visit was lost, and the gospel reading suggests that this broke Jesus' heart. Jesus is helpless before people's refusal to receive his love, God's love. Jesus' desire to be in a loving relationship with us is never in doubt, but his desire needs to find an echo in our hearts if it is to come to pass. He respects our freedom to reject his love and the peace it brings, but it continues to break his heart. Yet he does not give up on us, just as he did not give up on Jerusalem. As risen Lord, the first place he instructed his followers to preach the Gospel in was the city of Jerusalem, 'beginning in Jerusalem'. The Lord continues to wait for our response, indeed he works for our response by sending the Holy Spirit in our lives to prompt us and move us.

20 November, Friday, Thirty-Third Week in Ordinary Time
Luke 19:45–48

In the Jewish Scriptures the prophet Malachi had written, 'The Lord whom you seek will suddenly enter his Temple'. The scene in today's gospel reading where Jesus enters the Temple is the fulfilment of that prophecy. Earlier in Luke's Gospel, the twelve-year-old Jesus had spoken of the Temple as 'my Father's house'. At the beginning of today's gospel reading, Jesus quotes God's word as found in Isaiah: 'My house will be a house of prayer'. The Temple, God's house, was to be a place of prayer. Jesus, God's Son, acts authoritatively in God his Father's house, because far from being a house of prayer it had become a 'robbers' den'. Buying and selling, the making of money, had become a higher priority than prayer. Those responsible for the activities of the Temple saw it as a resource that could serve their own purposes, rather than a place that was to serve God's purpose. It has been said that Jesus comforts the afflicted and afflicts the comfortable. Those whose management of the Temple had left them comfortable were now experiencing the disturbing side of Jesus' words and actions and, in response, Luke says that 'they tried to do away with him'. Yet the people as a whole, Luke tells us, 'hung on his words'. We are invited to stand with the ordinary people in hanging on the Lord's words. The Lord's words bring light and life, love and mercy, into our lives, healing our wounds and restoring our spirit. However, there are times when we will also experience his words as disturbing our comfort zones. At such times, too, we need to hang on his words, because, even then, the Lord's words remain words of spirit and life for us.

21 November, Saturday, Presentation of the Blessed Virgin Mary
Matthew 12:46–50

Today's memorial commemorates the presentation of the child Mary in the Temple of Jerusalem by her parents. We seldom think of Mary as a child. All the images of her with which we are familiar are either as an adult or in heavenly glory. Yet, when we are first introduced to Mary in the Gospels at the moment of her annunciation, we should probably think of her as a very young woman, no more than a teenager. She must have grown up in a very faith-filled home, otherwise she would not have emerged as a woman of such strong and generous faith at the time of the annunciation. Today's feast celebrates the fact that as a very young child Mary's parents presented her to the Lord in the Temple, gave her over to the Lord's purpose for her life. It was as if her parents were saying, 'Lord, here is our child. We know that she belongs to you more than she belongs to us'. Mary's parents were recognising that her relationship with the Lord was even more significant that her relationship with them. Today's feast reminds us that the most important relationship in our lives is our relationship with the Lord. Every day we try to present ourselves to the Lord, offering ourselves to him. Every day we pray that God's purpose for our lives would come to pass and that God's will would be done in our lives. In the gospel reading Jesus declares that those who do the will of his Father, in whose lives God's will is done, are his brothers and sisters and mother. It was above all Mary who did the will of Jesus' heavenly Father. In the prayer that Jesus gave us to pray, the Lord's Prayer, we pray, 'Father in heaven, your kingdom come, your will be done on earth as it is in heaven'. Heaven is that state where God's kingdom has fully come, where God's will is fully done. To the extent that we do the will of our heavenly Father here and now, something of heaven comes to earth. When we allow God's purpose for our lives to shape us, as Mary did, then we create an opening for God's kingdom to come among us.

23 November, Monday, Thirty-Fourth Week in Ordinary Time
Luke 21:1–4

The widow who gives all she had to live on to the Temple treasury could be understood as an image of Jesus who gave all he had, his life, to God and to God's people. Although she gave very little in monetary terms, two small coins, her giving was more generous than the larger contributions of others, because she gave her all, as Jesus would give his all. She reminds us that generosity is not always easy to measure. Those who appear to be giving little may, in reality, be more generous than those who appear to be giving a lot. At the end of the day, it is really only the Lord who can measure generosity, because he alone knows what we are capable of giving. The Lord's assessment of generosity will often be very different from our assessment of it. Whereas we tend to look at what is visible, the Lord looks deeper; he looks at the heart. The widow would not have made much of a visible impression on those who saw her, but she made a big impression on Jesus and he deliberately drew other people's attention to her. The gospel reading reminds us that it is in those times when we feel very impoverished, when we sense that we have nothing to give, that we can be at our most generous. The little we give in those difficult circumstances can in fact display greater generosity than the more we might give in more favourable circumstances.

24 November, Tuesday, Thirty-Fourth Week in Ordinary Time
Luke 21:5–11

This is the last week of the Church's liturgical year. As we come to the end of the liturgical year, today's gospel reading speaks about endings. In particular, Jesus announces the end of the Temple in Jerusalem. 'Everything will be destroyed,' he says. The Temple was one of the seven wonders of the world at the time. It had taken nearly sixty years to build and it was still not quite complete at the time of Jesus. It must have seemed incredible that it could be destroyed. Yet, this is what happened in the year 70, forty years after the death and resurrection of Jesus, when the Roman army under the command of the future emperor, Titus, razed the Temple and the city of Jerusalem to the ground. In the Roman Forum today, there is still to be seen on the Arch of Titus a depiction of Titus' victory procession in Rome with the seven-branched candlestick of the Temple being carried aloft. There is so much that looks permanent that is not destined to last. That is as true of today as it was of Jesus' day. The Book of Revelation, from which we are reading these days, portrays God alone as the one who is destined to last. He is the one 'who is and who was and who is to come'. The author would say the same of Jesus, God's Son. When all else fails, the Lord God endures. In one of his letters, Saint Paul speaks of another reality that lasts: 'Love never ends'. Saint John, in one of his letters, declares that 'God is Love'. God's love is the same yesterday, today and tomorrow, and therein lies our assurance in the midst of so much else that passes away.

25 November, Wednesday, Thirty-Fourth Week in Ordinary Time

Luke 21:12–19

It was Mother Teresa who said that, in calling us to share in his work, the Lord does not ask us to be successful but to be faithful. In today's gospel reading, Jesus paints a bleak picture of what lies ahead for his disciples, as they set out to bear witness to him. The story he tells of what is to come is anything but a success story. He speaks of persecution, imprisonment, betrayal, hatred. What the Lord looks for in all of these negative experiences is mentioned in the last line of the gospel reading — endurance or perseverance. The Lord wants us to be faithful in the midst of apparent failure. It is tempting to lose faith when our relationship with the Lord and our efforts to serve him seem to bring us more grief than joy. We can identify easily with the seed that fell on rocky soil, those who endure only for a while; then, when trouble or persecution arises on account of the word, immediately they fall away. It is the Lord who makes possible our endurance to the end, rather than just for a while. Jesus promises his disciples and us in today's gospel reading, 'I myself will give you eloquence and wisdom'. In times of struggle and failure we are invited to rely on the resources the Lord gives us, so that we may endure to the end, and not just for a while.

26 November, Thursday, Thirty-Fourth Week in Ordinary Time

Luke 21:20–28

Both of today's readings speak of the fall of great cities. Jesus prophesies the fall of Jerusalem to the Roman armies with the terrible suffering that will bring for its inhabitants. 'Jerusalem will be trampled down by the pagans.' The first reading from the Book of Revelation speaks of, indeed celebrates, the fall of Babylon. 'Babylon the Great has fallen.' Babylon is code for Rome. At the beginning of the sixth century before Christ, the Babylonian Empire had destroyed the city of Jerusalem and the Temple, resulting in the Babylonian Exile for the Jewish people. By the time the Book of Revelation had been written, just towards the end of the first century AD, Jerusalem and its Temple had again been destroyed, twenty-five years earlier, by the empire of Rome, the new Babylon. The churches for whom this book was written had also experienced the destructive power of Rome. The reading speaks about God's servants that Rome has killed. Is there any light in all this darkness, any hope in all this destruction? It is a question that could be asked in many a war-torn situation today. Both readings, however, end on a note of hope. In the gospel reading Jesus assures his disciples that all this destruction is the prelude to his coming as Son of Man with power and glory. His power and glory are not the power and glory associated with worldly empires like Babylon and Rome. Far from being destructive, the Lord's power is life-giving and liberating from evil. 'Your liberation is near at hand.' Even in the darkest of situations, the Lord's coming with the liberating power of his love is always assured. His coming will be experienced by those who, in the words of the gospel reading, stand erect, holding their heads high. This is not an arrogant posture. Rather, it is a posture of trust in the Lord, whose light and love no darkness or hatred can overcome, and who holds out to his faithful servants an invitation to his great wedding feast, in the words of the first reading.

27 November, Friday, Thirty-Fourth Week in Ordinary Time
Luke 21:29–33

In today's gospel reading, Jesus speaks about heaven and earth passing away. We know from our own experience that a great deal passes away. Many of us will be able to think of very significant relationships that have passed away, relationships that we considered central to our existence. In this month of November we may have been thinking about and praying for such people. There is much that we want to hold on to that we know we will have to let go of. The time will come when we will have to let of our health, and even of life itself. Having said that heaven and earth will pass away, Jesus immediately says, 'My words will never pass away'. When we have to let go of so much, the Lord's words remain. We can continue to draw life and light and strength from the word of the Lord, no matter how much we have to let go of. The Lord's word endures because the Lord himself endures. The Book of Revelation, from which we are reading these days, speaks of him as the one who was, who is, and who is to come. We could say of the Lord's words, that they were, they are and they are to come. As we come to the end of the Church's liturgical year, we thank the Lord for the gift of his words, which will never come to an end. We rejoice that here is a gift that never passes away.

28 November, Saturday, Thirty-Fourth Week in Ordinary Time
Luke 21:34–36
In the gospel reading Jesus warns against becoming so immersed in the attractions and cares of life that we fail to see beyond them. We need to step back and find a space in which we can become aware of the Lord and his presence to us. In the language of the gospel reading, we are to watch, to become watchful, attentive to the Lord within and beyond all of life. Such watchfulness and attentiveness is at the heart of prayer. That is what prayer is, which is why Jesus says, 'Stay awake, praying at all times'. That exhortation to pray at all times may sound strange to our ears. How can we pray at all times when we have so much to do, so many responsibilities to meet? Paul says something similar at the end of his first letter to the Thessalonians when he calls on the church to 'pray without ceasing'. Jesus and Paul were calling for a prayerful stance towards life, a prayerful attentiveness to the Lord at all times, before all situations, in the midst of all our tasks. To help us do this, we could take a very short prayer drawn from the

Scriptures, the simple Advent prayer, which was our response to the Responsorial Psalm, 'Marantha, Come Lord Jesus'. We could pray that prayer anywhere we happen to be, at any time. In the words of the gospel reading, such a prayerful posture towards life will give us the strength from God that we need to survive whatever is ahead of us.